Black-bellied Whistling Ducks, East Texas

National Geographic Guide to

# Birdwatching
# Sites

## Eastern U.S.

By Mel White

*Above:* Northern Saw-whet Owl
*Right:* View from Cadillac Mountain,
Acadia National Park, Maine
*Preceding pages:* Great Egrets,
Everglades National Park, Florida

# Contents

# Your Guide to the Guide

Curiosity may have killed the cat, but it's given many a casual feeder-watcher a whole new life as an avid birder. "What's that yellow-and-black bird with the big bill eating my sunflower seeds?" you wonder. Or, "What kind of bird is that little brown thing I saw climbing a tree like a miniature woodpecker?"

So there's a trip to the bookstore, and a first field guide. The mystery bird gets a name, and for some that's enough; the guide goes on the shelf, neglected until the next winged stranger arrives in the backyard. Others, though, will find more questions in those colorful pages of previously unheard-of species. Who knew there were so many kinds of sparrows? You mean loons spend the winter in Alabama? Where can I see some of these pretty little birds called warblers?

Then comes a phone call to a birdwatching friend, and an early-morning walk in a nearby park. At the end of the day, you've seen 50 or 60 species—more than you would have thought possible when your identifications went no further than hawk, gull, or finch. "This is nothing," your friend says. "If we put some effort into it, we could find a hundred species in a day around here, easy."

A few experiences like this and you begin to realize that there are lots of birds to be seen if you go to the right places. And now you'd better be careful. Next thing you know, you'll be planning your vacations around spring migration at Florida's Dry Tortugas, summer in the Appalachians, fall at Cape May, New Jersey, or winter at Niagara Falls.

**How This Guide Works** In this book you'll find more than 275 of the right places to go birdwatching in the eastern United States, from the Rio Grande Valley of Texas to Minnesota, and from the Florida Keys to Maine. In consultation with local birders,

we've chosen some of the top sites in each state: city and state parks, national wildlife refuges, nature preserves, lakes and marshes, and in some cases something as unstructured as a particularly productive stretch of beach or road.

The text presents a short description of each area and a list of a few of the most typical or notable species found there. It's the nature of books like this that only the highlights can be covered: Many regionally common birds—say, Red-bellied Woodpecker in the South, Black-capped Chickadee in the North, or Laughing Gull along the coast—

Prairie Warbler, Jamaica Bay, Long Island

will go unremarked, while rarities and locally scarce species receive disproportionate coverage. After all, it's the chance to find an unusual species, or one you've never seen before (a "life bird"), that entices birders to visit new places.

If you're new to this business of traveling to see birds, remember that birds travel, too. Note as you read that some sites are rewarding year-round, while others are at their best only in nesting season or winter, or in the migration periods of spring and fall.

States are grouped into chapters by region, with sites throughout the state arranged in a logical flow. Site numbers are keyed to the map at the beginning of each chapter, to aid you in finding your way from one site to the next (sites near one another occasionally share the same number). Throughout the book sidebars feature species of regional interest, as well as ideas for the traveling birder.

At the end of each chapter we've included practical information about the sites that can help you plan your trip. First you'll find telephone numbers of rare bird alerts, or hot lines. These are recorded messages, updated frequently, that list unusual species seen in a state or locality, often with directions to sites or numbers to call for more information. When you arrive in McAllen, Texas, for instance, to begin your birding tour of the lower Rio Grande Valley, you should call the hot line there to learn about any rarities in the area. In fact, many birders start calling the hot line for their destination several days before a visit to aid in trip planning. (It goes without saying that you should call your home rare bird alert regularly to keep up with what's being seen locally.) This section also includes mailing addresses and telephone numbers of the sites or their administrative offices, so you can call or write ahead for additional information. Symbols indicate facilities available at each site, although be advised that these can be seasonal or limited.

At the end of the guide, we've included a bibliography of some of the many excellent state and local bird-finding guides now available. As you become more experienced and serious about birding, these guides can take you to more sites in your own region and in the places you visit. Many parts of the United States are covered by these books, and their number is growing each year.

## A Few Other Ideas

New birders should first of all join their local Audubon chapter or birding club. On field trips, and with advice from experienced birders, you'll begin to learn the species in your area and the best places to find them. The study of migration patterns, habitats, and abundance provides endless opportunity for discovery no matter where you live, and amateurs can contribute to ornithological knowledge with conscientious observation and record-keeping. You'll soon discover the fun and challenge of spring "big days" and Christmas bird counts, wherein birding becomes a bit more structured and even competitive (even if only with yourself).

The leading national organization for birdwatchers is the American Birding Association, or ABA (800-850-2473), with headquarters in Colorado Springs, Colorado. The ABA publishes a semimonthly magazine, *Birding,* and a monthly newsletter, *Winging It,* with articles on many aspects of birding, from identification to destinations. Many ABA members are involved in the sporting side of birding,

Watching egrets
and other waders,
Everglades National
Park, Florida

in which the object is to see as many species as possible in
a defined geographic area, or in a given period of time. This
is certainly not a requirement, though, and many other
members watch birds just for fun.

One of the benefits of ABA is its membership guide, published annually, which lists thousands of birders all over the
country who are willing to provide advice to travelers, and
in many cases even to guide visitors to good birding sites
in their home regions. If you join ABA, don't be shy about
asking for help either by telephone or letter. Birders are by
and large a friendly bunch who enjoy talking about their
favorite places, and one inquiry to the right person could
save you hours of driving or hiking in search of that elusive species you're determined to find.

The Internet increasingly offers another source of information. All around the country, bird clubs and ornithological societies are setting up web sites, many of which offer
guides to birding spots, lists of local contacts, and schedules
of upcoming field trips. One place to start your search is the

National Audubon Society's website (*www.audubon.org*); check here for local chapters in the area you'll be visiting. Chapter sites will often have links to other regional birding web sites, which will have links to other sites...and so forth. Or you can use a search engine, inquiring about something as specific as "Seney National Wildlife Refuge" (many parks and refuges now have maps and bird lists online) or as general as "birding+Georgia."

If you're a beginner, or even if you're not, consider attending one of the many birding festivals held annually around the country. Most feature programs and field trips led by experts, often concentrating on regional specialties. As more local tourism groups wake up to the economic impact of traveling birders, more of these festivals are springing up, especially in popular birding destinations. A few of the most popular festivals in the East: the Delmarva Birding Weekend, in April in eastern Maryland; the Kirtland's Warbler Festival, in May in central Michigan; the Detroit Lakes Festival of Birds, in May in western Minnesota;

the Cape May Autumn Weekend/Bird Show, in October or early November in New Jersey; the Rio Grande Valley Birding Festival, in November in southern Texas; the Hummer/Bird Celebration, in September in Rockport, Texas; and the Eastern Shore Birding Festival, in October in Cape Charles in eastern Virginia. Call the National Fish and Wildlife Foundation (*202-857-0166*) for a directory listing many more festivals.

**Beyond Your List**

Birding is fun and rewarding even if you approach it only on the level of a sport or hobby, like golf or coin-collecting. It's exciting to spot the elusive Swainson's Warbler along a Louisiana bayou after you've spent countless hours searching for it. It's satisfying to look over the list of birds you've seen and remember your first trip to the Outer Banks of North Carolina, or that fantastic May morning at Crane Creek in Ohio when the sky seemed to rain birds.

After they've been at it awhile, though, most birders become conservationists. Learning where to look for birds, understanding a bit about ecosystems and habitat requirements, leads to some inescapable conclusions. Piping Plovers need undisturbed beaches and lakeshores; if these places are taken over by sunbathers and off-road vehicles, there won't be any more Piping Plovers. Red-cockaded Woodpeckers need mature pine woods; if all the pines are clear-cut before they reach maturity, this species will disappear.

Increasingly, birders are realizing that their interest in, even love for, birds doesn't exempt them from responsibility. Playing a tape of a bird's song or call is often an effective way to bring it in close, and sometimes avoids habitat damage caused by trying to get near a bird. But for some vulnerable species, or in heavily birded places, the tape recorder should be left in the car. Wanting, even really wanting, to see a Black Rail doesn't give you an excuse to go thrashing about in a marsh to flush one out, especially where the species is nesting. Parks and refuges

Black Rail

occasionally close areas where a sensitive species—Bald Eagle or Peregrine Falcon, for example—is nesting; ethical birders obey such regulations, realizing that the birds' welfare comes before the desire to put a checkmark on a list.

It's no wonder that birding ranks among the country's **Get Started**
fastest-growing outdoor pursuits. All it takes to get started is a pair of binoculars, a field guide, and a notebook; you can watch birds alone or, if you prefer, you can share the adventure with friends and family; you're observing some of the earth's most colorful and interesting creatures; you'll be traveling, in many cases, to beautifully scenic wild places that you might otherwise never have discovered; and the challenges will last a lifetime, for no one will ever see all the different kinds of birds there are.

# MAP KEY and ABBREVIATIONS

National Monument............................ NAT. MON.
National Park.......................................... N.P.
National Preserve
National Recreation Area....................... N.R.A.
National Seashore

National Forest........................... NAT. FOR., N.F.
State Forest............................................. S.F.

National Wildlife Refuge........................ N.W.R.

State Park................................................ S.P.

### ADDITIONAL ABBREVIATIONS

Conservation Area................................................. C.A.
Environmental Demonstration Area........ ENV. DEM. AREA
Fish and Wildlife Area........................................... F.W.A.
Memorial............................................................... MEM.
National................................................................. NAT.
National Battlefield Park....................................... N.B.P.
National Historical Park......................................... N.H.P.
National Lakeshore............................................... N.L.
National Seashore................................................. N.S.
Natural Area.......................................................... N.A.
Preserve............................................................... PRES.
Recreation Area.................................................... R.A.
Scenic Area........................................................... S.A.
State  Conservation Park...................................... S.C.P.
State Game Area................................................... S.G.A.
State Natural Area................................................. S.N.A.
State Nature Preserve........................................... S.N.P.
State Recreation Area........................................... S.R.A.
State Wildlife Area................................................. S.W.A.
Wildlife Area.......................................................... W.A.
Wildlife Management Area...................................... W.M.A.

Interstate Highway
10

U.S. Federal Highway
90

State Road
35

County, Local, or Other Road
74

Trans-Canada Highway
20

Other Canadian Highway
55

Ferry
· · · · · · · · · · · · · · · · · ·

State Boundary

National Boundary

National Forest Boundary

1 Featured Area
▪ Point of Interest
⊛ National Capital
⊛ State or Provincial Capital
| Dam
+ Peak

13

# New England

All the New England states save Vermont have a seacoast, and it's along this meeting of land and water—rocky, sandy, or marshy; bluff-lined or flat—that many of the region's top birding sites are located.

One reason, of course, is seabirds. With the uniformity of their ocean habitat, and including in their number some of the world's most accomplished fliers, these birds are notorious wanderers. Birders who brave the chilly winter wind of Rhode Island's Sachuest Point or Halibut Point in Massachusetts or who take to the sea on a whale-watch boat, always hope for a true rarity to put an exclamation point on the day. Even species a bit more frequently seen make the coast an exciting place. Few birders become so jaded that their hearts don't speed up at the powerful flight of a jaeger or the beauty of a Harlequin Duck.

The coast is a great place to look for land birds, as well. The ocean acts as a barrier to their movement, so vagrants from the West often end their roaming on the coastline,

*Preceding pages and above:* Atlantic Puffins
*Right:* Nature cruise boats, Mount Desert Island, Maine

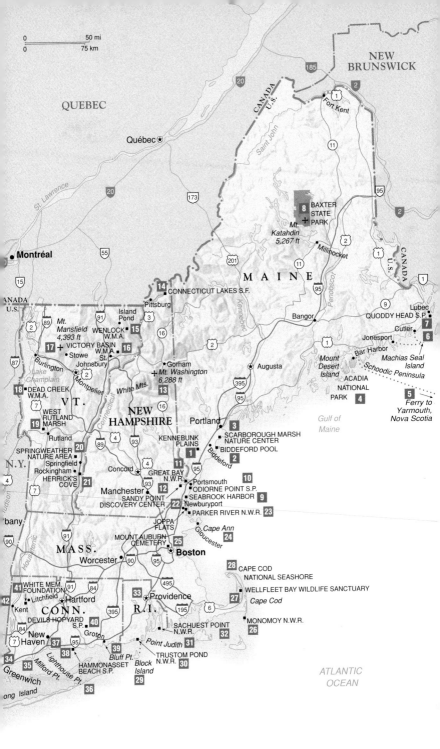

0    50 mi
0    75 km

**NEW BRUNSWICK**

**QUEBEC**

185

2

Fort Kent

1

11

95

CANADA
U.S.

Québec ✪

Saint John

St. Lawrence

20

173

8  BAXTER STATE PARK

Mt. Katahdin
5,267 ft

Millinocket

95

2

● Montréal

55

201

11

**M A I N E**

825

CANADA
U.S.

15

Penobscot

1

CANADA
U.S.

1

14  CONNECTICUT LAKES S.F.

Pittsburg

Bangor

9  Lubec

QUODDY HEAD S.P.  7

89

91

Island Pond

3

WENLOCK
W.M.A.  15

16

Cutler

Jonesport  6

2

Mt.
Mansfield
4,393 ft

17  VICTORY BASIN
W.M.A.  16

St.
Johnsbury

Stowe

2

Kennebec

1

Bar Harbor

Machias Seal
Island

Schoodic Peninsula

Burlington

● Stowe

Montpelier

Gorham

Mt. Washington
6,288 ft  13

White Mts.

Augusta ✪

Mount
Desert
Island

ACADIA
NATIONAL
PARK  4

Lake
Champlain

87

18  DEAD CREEK
W.M.A.

7

**V T.**

White Mts.

395

*Gulf of
Maine*

**5**

*Ferry to
Yarmouth,
Nova Scotia*

19  WEST
RUTLAND
MARSH

Rutland

**NEW
HAMPSHIRE**

16

Portland

95

SPRINGWEATHER
NATURE AREA  20

Springfield

Rockingham

89

4

93

KENNEBUNK
PLAINS  1

3  SCARBOROUGH MARSH
NATURE CENTER

BIDDEFORD POOL

Biddeford

**N.Y.**

HERRICK'S
COVE  21

7

Concord

4

GREAT BAY
N.W.R.  11

Portsmouth

2  10  ODIORNE POINT S.P.

9  SEABROOK HARBOR

Manchester

12  SANDY POINT
DISCOVERY CENTER

Newburyport

22  PARKER RIVER N.W.R.  23

4

90

bany

**MASS.**

JOPPA
FLATS

*Cape Ann*

24

Hudson

MOUNT AUBURN
CEMETERY  25

Gloucester

Worcester

Housatonic

90

95

✪ **Boston**

28  CAPE COD
NATIONAL SEASHORE

495

● WELLFLEET BAY WILDLIFE SANCTUARY

41  WHITE MEM.
FOUNDATION

91

84

33  ✪ Providence

27  *Cape Cod*

42

Kent

Litchfield

**CONN.**

✪ Hartford

**R.I.**

195

6

MONOMOY N.W.R.  26

DEVILS HOPYARD
S.P.  40

395

SACHUEST POINT
N.W.R.

32

New
Haven

Groton

37

84

95

39

Point Judith  31

TRUSTOM POND
N.W.R.  30

34

38

HAMMONASSET
BEACH S.P.

Bluff Pt.

Block
Island

Lighthouse Pt.

Milford Pt.

Greenwich

*Long Island*

36

*Block Island*  29

*ATLANTIC
OCEAN*

or on an island such as Block, off Rhode Island, or South Monomoy, in Massachusetts. In fall, north winds blow southbound migrants down against the coast, concentrating flocks into higher than normal numbers.

There are famous and popular birding sites in New England, such as Acadia National Park in Maine and Parker River National Wildlife Refuge in Massachusetts, and others like Vermont's Victory Basin Wildlife Manage-

**Special Birds of New England**

*Boreal Chickadee*

| | | | |
|---|---|---|---|
| | Harlequin Duck | Iceland Gull | Black-backed |
| | Surf Scoter | Glaucous Gull | Woodpecker |
| Cory's Shearwater | White-winged | Black-legged | Yellow-bellied |
| Greater Shearwater | Scoter | Kittiwake | Flycatcher |
| Sooty Shearwater | Black Scoter | Roseate Tern | Gray Jay |
| Wilson's Storm- | Oldsquaw | Arctic Tern | Boreal Chickadee |
| Petrel | Spruce Grouse | Common Murre | Bicknell's Thrush |
| Leach's Storm- | Piping Plover | Thick-billed Murre | Saltmarsh Sharp- |
| Petrel | Purple Sandpiper | Razorbill | tailed Sparrow |
| Northern Gannet | Ruff | Black Guillemot | Nelson's Sharp- |
| Great Cormorant | Red-necked | Atlantic Puffin | tailed Sparrow |
| Glossy Ibis | Phalarope | Snowy Owl | Snow Bunting |
| Mute Swan | Red Phalarope | Northern | Rusty Blackbird |
| Brant | Pomarine Jaeger | Saw-whet Owl | Red Crossbill |
| King Eider | Parasitic Jaeger | Three-toed | White-winged |
| Common Eider | Black-headed Gull | Woodpecker | Crossbill |

ment Area where a birder might spend a summer morning alone with the Gray Jays and Magnolia Warblers.

Newcomers will find some fine locations in this region to discover the continually fascinating world of birds. The National Audubon Society's Audubon Center in Green-wich, Connecticut, and Maine Audubon's Scarborough Marsh Nature Center are two such places, offering programs on birds and other aspects of natural history. The venerable Massachusetts Audubon Society operates a number of sanc-tuaries and nature centers. Preserving 1,000 acres of Cape Cod's rapidly developing landscape, the Wellfleet Bay Wildlife Sanctuary offers birding trips around the cape.

Beginning in Maine, this chapter proceeds southward to end in Connecticut. ■

# MAINE

**1** Though Maine's rugged, beautiful seacoast is the deserved focus of much birding and other natural-history interest, it's the open-country species that make a visit to the **Kennebunk Plains** worthwhile. Take Me. 99 west from Kennebunk toward Sanford, and look for a parking area on the north side of the road 2.7 miles after crossing I-95. Walk the old roads through this grassland preserve in nesting season and look for Wild Turkey; Upland Sandpiper; Least Flycatcher; Horned Lark; Eastern Bluebird; Brown Thrasher; Prairie Warbler; Field, Vesper, Savannah, and Grasshopper Sparrows; Indigo Bunting; and Bobolink. Clay-colored Sparrow has been found here on occasion.

**2** One of Maine's most famous birding spots, **Biddeford Pool** is reached by taking Me. 9/208 south from Biddeford 5 miles and turning east on Me. 208. Look for parking on the south side of the road in about 1.5 miles, and ask permission to use the path to the pool at the deli across the street. Birding is best here a few hours before or after high tide, when waders (spring through fall) and migrant shorebirds are feeding on mudflats near shore. Hudsonian Godwit is fairly regular in small numbers in late summer, and near-constant birding attention has turned up a long list of rarities. Gulls are always present, and in summer or migration you may find Roseate, Common, Arctic (rare), or Black Terns.

Continue into the town of Biddeford Pool and follow Lester B. Orcutt Boulevard east. As you approach the coast, look north for the entrance to **East Point Sanctuary.** The shrubby vegetation here provides good land birding in migration, and from the shoreline a scan of the ocean from fall through spring may turn up all sorts of seabirds. With

- Seabirds on whale-watch cruises
- Northern specialties in Baxter State Park

Information section p. 53

Somes Pond, Acadia National Park, Mount Desert Island

luck you might find a Dovekie, Thick-billed Murre, or Razorbill in winter. Look for wintering Purple Sandpiper on the rocks.

**3** Take US 1 north from Biddeford, and in 6 miles turn south on Me. 9 (Pine Point Road). In 0.8 mile, stop at the Maine Audubon Society's **Scarborough Marsh Nature Center,** adjacent to the state's largest salt marsh. Open late spring through Labor Day, the center offers nature programs and canoe tours, and rents canoes for those who want to explore the marsh on their own. You can also access the marsh by continuing south on Pine Point Road 0.2 mile to a trail leading out to the **Dunstan River.** (Be aware that this is a popular duck-hunting area in fall.) Herons, ibises, and egrets feed here from spring through fall, and you might find an American Bittern in migration. Salt-marsh and Nelson's Sharp-tailed Sparrows both nest here and can be seen on canoe trips or from the trail. Geese, ducks, and shorebirds use the marsh for resting and feeding in migration. After birding the marsh, continue south on Pine Point Road. Just past the turn where Me. 9 heads west, go east on King Street to the public boat-launch area, another spot to find waders, shorebirds, gulls, and terns. This is a particularly good place to see Roseate Tern in summer, and is also good for Whimbrel and Hudsonian Godwit in late summer.

**4** Good birding is even more appealing when its setting is one of the most beautiful areas on the northeastern coast. **Acadia National Park** attracts millions of visitors each year with its surf-splashed rocky headlands, rugged hills, and placid ponds. Birders enjoy all those attractions while searching for seabirds and a good assortment of nesting land birds. Mostly located on **Mount Desert Island** (other park areas are found on **Isle au Haut, Baker Island,** and the **Schoodic Peninsula**), Acadia is easily explored along paved roads and on hiking trails, including 57 miles of carriage roads—broad, level paths crisscrossing much of the park.

A bird list is available at the visitor center on Me. 3, north of Bar Harbor. Your next step might then be a drive up **Cadillac Mountain** for an overview of this dramatic landscape. In fall, Cadillac can be a productive hawk-watch site. From here you can look down on the islands off Bar Harbor, 1,530 feet below, where Osprey and Bald Eagle nest; Common Raven gives its croaking call as it passes by. Not far to the west, trails around **Jordan Pond** make a good introduction to some of the park's nesting birds, including Ruffed Grouse, Black-capped Chickadee, Red-breasted Nuthatch, Brown Creeper, Winter Wren, Golden-crowned Kinglet, Hermit Thrush, Black-throated Blue and Black-and-white Warblers, Ovenbird, and Dark-eyed Junco; in spring, you'll hear the laughing call of

### Atlantic Puffin

The Atlantic Puffin, with its clownishly colorful bill, is more widespread in Maine waters now than it was a quarter century ago. Thanks to reintroduction efforts that began in the 1970s, puffins have returned to nest on islands from which they had been wiped out by persecution and predation. For many years, puffin chicks were transplanted from colonies in Canada to Maine islands, where they were raised by biologists. As adults, they eventually returned to their foster homes and began breeding on their own. Though they are occasionally seen from land or on seabird cruises, puffins spend most of their nonbreeding lives far out at sea. Their bill, bright orange, yellow, and blue, loses its intense coloration in winter. These appealing birds are not shy and easily seen on tours to **Machias Seal Island,** on the U.S.-Canada border (see p. 23).

Common Loon from the pond. As you drive the park's Loop Road near Bar Harbor, stop at **Acadia Wild Gardens** for an introduction to some of the plants found on the island. Walk nearby trails for Yellow-bellied Sapsucker; Eastern Wood-Pewee; Alder and Least Flycatchers; Chestnut-sided, Black-throated Green, and Canada Warblers; and American Redstart. Continuing on the one-way Park Loop Road, stop to scan the cliffs of **Champlain Mountain,** where Peregrine Falcon nests. A few miles beyond, where the drive borders the Atlantic around **Otter Point,** watch for Common Eider, Black Guillemot, and other seabirds.

Some of the park's best birding is found on the southwest part of Mount Desert, between the Seawall Campground and the famously picturesque Bass Harbor Head lighthouse. Walk the **Wonderland Trail** (1.4 miles round-trip) and the **Ship Harbor Nature Trail** (1.3-mile loop) and look for breeding Yellow-bellied and Alder Flycatchers, Blue-headed Vireo, Ruby-crowned Kinglet, Swainson's Thrush, and warblers including Nashville, Black-throated Green, Palm, Wilson's, Northern Parula, and American Redstart. Spruce Grouse might be found here, too, but is rare and elusive.

In the warmer months, several companies offer whale-watching tours from Bar Harbor out into the Atlantic. Some also specialize in seabird-watching, with experienced onboard naturalists (*cruise information available in Bar Harbor; Chamber of Commerce 207-288-3393*). Though dependent on the season, and the luck of the day, some of the birds that might be seen on an offshore cruise are Common Loon; Greater, Sooty, and Manx Shearwaters; Wilson's Storm-Petrel; Northern Gannet; Double-crested and Great Cormorants; Common Eider; Osprey; Bald Eagle; Red-necked and Red Phalaropes; Razorbill; and Atlantic Puffin.

Arctic Tern feeding chick

**5** For years, the *Bluenose* ferry between Bar Harbor and Yarmouth, Nova Scotia, was a favorite birding trip, offering the chance to see oceanic species from the vantage point

of a large, stable ship. The crossing took around six hours each way, and birders scanned the waves for the species listed above, as well as uncommon to rare birds such as Northern Fulmar, Cory's Shearwater, Leach's Storm-Petrel, Great and South Polar Skuas, Pomarine and Parasitic Jaegers, Black-legged Kittiwake, and Common and Thick-billed Murres. In 1998, the *Bluenose* was replaced with a new ship called **The Cat** *(207-288-3395 or 888-249-7245)*, which makes the crossing in 2.5 hours at speeds approaching 50 miles an hour. While this pelagic birding isn't as leisurely as it once was, it's still a convenient way to get out into the Gulf of Maine and search for birds seldom if ever seen from shore.

Tour leader on the boardwalk, Machias Seal Island

**6** One of the icons of Maine tourism, the Atlantic Puffin nests on a few islands off the state's coast, and in larger colonies in Canada. A boat trip to **Machias Seal Island** has long been a reliable way to see nesting puffins; two companies specializing in this summertime journey are Norton's Tours in Jonesport *(207-497-5933)* and the Bold Coast Charter Company in Cutler *(207-259-4484)*. When weather allows, visitors can land on the island and see not only puffins but Common Eider, Common and Arctic Terns, Razorbill, and Black Guillemot. Common Murre is also often seen in summer, though it doesn't nest on the island, and at least a few pelagics are usually found on the trip out and back.

**7** From Me. 189 just west of Lubec, at the eastern extremity of Maine's coastline, turn south on Boot Cove Road toward **Quoddy Head State Park.** In 1.8 miles, look for a dirt road on the east leading down to the bay. Check the vegetation bordering the salt marsh here for nesting Nelson's Sharp-tailed Sparrow. In spring and in late summer and fall, migrant shorebirds may be feeding and resting.

**White-winged Crossbill**

The White-winged Crossbill and its relative the Red Crossbill are famous—perhaps notorious is a better word—for the irregularity and unpredictability of their movements. Some years they're seen all over the North Woods, using their specially adapted crossed bills to feed on seeds of pine, fir, spruce, and hemlock. Other years there are none to be found, and a visiting birder looking for one of these finches leaves frustrated, having searched in vain.

Return to Boot Cove Road, drive south 0.6 mile, and turn east to Quoddy Head State Park, a good spot for seabirds and interesting land birds as well. At the famous **West Quoddy Head Light,** scan the water and offshore rocks for a seasonally changing list of birds including Red-throated and Common Loons; Common Eider; Surf, White-winged, and Black Scoters; Oldsquaw; Black-legged Kittiwake; Common and Arctic Terns; Razorbill; and Black Guillemot. When winds are blowing toward shore, a migrant Northern Gannet might be found or a Greater or Sooty Shearwater.

Trails in the state park lead though spruce-fir forest and boggy wetlands where nesting birds include Spruce Grouse and Black-backed Woodpecker (both scarce); Olive-sided and Yellow-bellied Flycatchers; Gray Jay; Boreal Chickadee; Golden-crowned and Ruby-crowned Kinglets; Tennessee, Yellow, Magnolia, Black-throated Green, Blackburnian, Blackpoll, and Black-and-white Warblers; Northern Parula; and Lincoln's and White-throated Sparrows. Red and White-winged Crossbills are irregular in their appearance but may be around anytime of year.

**8** Maine's famed **Baxter State Park** awaits the adventurous traveler in the north-central part of the state: 204,000 acres of fine birding for those prepared for its remoteness, wildness, and bugginess (bring insect repellent).

The park's high point is 5,267-foot **Mount Katahdin,** where Bicknell's Thrush sings on the sparsely wooded slopes at 3,000 feet and above. Below is deciduous and spruce-fir forest where breeding birds include Common Loon, American Bittern, Ring-necked Duck, Hooded Merganser, Northern Goshawk, Ruffed and Spruce Grouse, Three-toed and Black-backed Woodpeckers (both prefer burned or disease-killed areas), Gray Jay, Boreal Chickadee, more than 20 species of warblers, Rusty Blackbird, Purple Finch, Pine Siskin, and Evening Grosbeak.

The area around **Roaring Brook Campground** offers a good selection of birds in varied habitats along the trails to **Sandy Stream Pond.** Three different trails lead from this point into the highlands for upper-elevation birds including Bicknell's Thrush. But much can be seen simply driving the park's main **Tote Road;** stopping to investigate different habitats, from woodland to second growth to bogs and marsh, will contribute to a longer and more diverse bird list.

Mount Katahdin, Baxter State Park, northern Maine

# NEW HAMPSHIRE

● Seabirds along
   the Atlantic coast
● Bicknell's Thrush
   on Mount
   Washington

---

Information
section p. 53

Some of New Hampshire's best birding is found along its 18-mile-long seacoast, squeezed in between Maine and Massachusetts. Several parks and other access points allow observation, linked together by N.H. 1A.

**9** From the intersection of N.H. 1A and N.H. 286, just north of the Massachusetts state line, drive less than a mile north on N.H. 1A to the parking lot at **Seabrook Harbor** *(from the N, lot is 0.4 mile S of bridge over harbor inlet)*. Migrant shorebirds can be abundant here on mudflats exposed by low tide. Check gull flocks for unusual species among the common Ring-billed, Herring, and Great Black-backed, including in winter the "white-winged" gulls, Iceland and Glaucous. Loons and waterfowl appear here in migration and winter, and check from spring through fall for waders including Great Blue Heron, Snowy Egret, Glossy Ibis, and an occasional Black-crowned Night-Heron. The threatened Piping Plover, long absent as a breeder from Seabrook Beach across N.H. 1A, has recently begun to nest successfully again here, so watch for this small shorebird, too.

On the north side of the bridge on N.H. 1A, turn west to Hampton State Pier for another viewpoint of the harbor. Just across the highway, **Hampton Beach State Park** is crowded with sunbathers in summer, but offers a chance to scan the Atlantic for Northern Gannet in spring and fall, and for Red-throated and Common Loons, Horned and Red-necked Grebes, Great Cormorant, and sea ducks in migration and winter. Check the rock jetties here for wintering Purple Sandpiper.

Continuing north on N.H. 1A, stop at **Rye Harbor Marina** *(turn E on Harbor Rd.)* to look for waders, waterfowl, and gulls. From here, drive north just over 3 miles and watch

for a parking spot on the right offering a view of **Pulpit** Rye Harbor
**Rocks,** just offshore, where you may see sea ducks and have
another chance at a Purple Sandpiper.

**10** Just north of Pulpit Rocks lies **Odiorne Point State Park,** where the **Seacoast Science Center** teaches
about the coastal environment through aquariums and other
exhibits. Here, too, scan the sea for waterbirds including the
typical winter sea ducks of the region: Common Eider; Surf,
White-winged, and Black Scoters; Oldsquaw; Common
Goldeneye; and Red-breasted Merganser. Careful searching
might turn up a rarity such as King Eider or Harlequin Duck.
Nature trails lead through woodland that can be very productive during spring and fall songbird migration.

**11** **Great Bay National Wildlife Refuge,** for more than 30 years an Air Force base, has turned its woodlands,
fields, shrubby thickets, and salt marsh over to wildlife. The
refuge borders Great Bay, a huge estuary connecting the
Piscataqua River and the Atlantic. Take the Pease International Tradeport exit from US 4; enter the tradeport, and

White Mountains,
near Chocorua

turn right on Arboretum Drive to the entrance. Wintering Bald Eagles are a specialty here, and the 2-mile **Ferry Way Trail** leads to the bay shore where these magnificent raptors can usually be seen. Osprey nests on the bay, so watch for this fish hawk flying over the water and diving for prey. Also look for a variety of migrant and winter waterfowl, from the huge Mute Swan to the little Bufflehead, and for wading birds from spring through fall. Another refuge trail, just a half-mile long, goes to **Upper Peverly Pond,** where in nesting season you'll find Great Blue and Green Herons and Wood Duck. The refuge is also a good place to find Wild Turkey.

**12** Next visit **Sandy Point Discovery Center** (just W of Greenland, 5.5 miles W off I-95 on N.H. 33 to Depot Rd. Open June–Oct.), where a boardwalk leads through woodland to a salt marsh on the edge of Great Bay. Osprey nests in this area, and migration can bring good viewing of shorebirds and waterfowl. Great Bay harbors the state's largest winter concentration of American Black Duck, and flocks of this species are usually seen from any viewpoint.

**13** The White Mountains of central New Hampshire comprise a region of legendary ruggedness and beauty. Their high point is **Mount Washington,** at 6,288 feet the tallest peak in the northeastern United States. Since ornithologists split Bicknell's Thrush as a separate species from Gray-cheeked Thrush (see sidebar p. 33), birders have taken a new interest in Mount Washington—a toll road to its summit provides a straightforward way to find this species. This steep and winding route, which opened as a carriage road in 1861 (improvements have been made since then), leaves N.H. 16 about 7 miles south of Gorham. As you drive up, look for species such as Ruffed Grouse; Olive-sided Flycatcher; Brown Creeper; Winter Wren; Swainson's and Hermit Thrushes; Northern Parula; and Magnolia, Black-throated Blue, Blackburnian, Bay-breasted, and Blackpoll Warblers. About 3 miles from the entrance, begin listening for the song of Bicknell's Thrush. Overlooks and trailheads along the road allow you to search for this localized highland species.

Just to the west as the raven flies (though a long round-about by car) are two fine spots to look for species of the area. From US 302 near Bretton Woods, follow either Base Road or Mount Clinton Road to the route leading to the cog railway that climbs Mount Washington from the west. Don't take this road, but continue north on Jefferson Notch Road 3.2 miles to **Jefferson Notch,** elevation 3,009 feet. The **Caps Ridge Trail** here affords good access to high-elevation species, and Black-backed Woodpecker and Bicknell's Thrush have both been found near the trailhead. Walk part of the trail and you may find Olive-sided and Yellow-bellied Flycatchers; Gray Jay; Boreal Chickadee; Golden-crowned Kinglet; Magnolia, Blackburnian, Bay-breasted, and Blackpoll Warblers; and Pine Siskin.

Return to US 302 by way of Base Road and drive west 2.2 miles; turn south on **Zealand Road,** which ascends the Zealand River Valley. You can stop along the road to bird or walk intersecting trails, looking for many of the same species listed for Jefferson Notch. You may meet a moose here, or, if you're very lucky, you could stumble upon a Spruce Grouse.

**14** The elusive Spruce Grouse is also one of the attractions of the **Connecticut Lakes region** of extreme northern New Hampshire, along with other boreal species such as Gray Jay, Boreal Chickadee, a colorful assortment of warblers, and Rusty Blackbird. Birding in this area essentially

involves driving US 3 from Pittsburg north 26 miles to the Canadian border, along the way passing lakes where Common Loons give their haunting calls in summer. The upper part of this route passes through **Connecticut Lakes State Forest,** a strip of land bordering the highway. Otherwise, birders explore the region by driving private roads belonging to timber companies, whose large trucks have the right-of-way on sometimes narrow gravel roads.

Female Spruce Grouse, an elusive North Woods bird

About 6 miles north of Pittsburg, you'll reach the dam at First Connecticut Lake. Drive 4.5 miles farther, turn right on Magalloway Road, and in 1.1 miles turn left onto **Smith Brook Road.** Follow this for a few miles, birding along the way. For another good birding route, continue north on US 3 to the dam at Second Connecticut Lake. Turn right in 3 miles and, after the road crosses a stream, right at a T intersection and continue on **East Inlet Road.**

Along either of these roads, or even at pull-offs along US 3, the birds you may find include Ruffed and Spruce Grouse; Northern Saw-whet Owl; Black-backed Woodpecker; Olive-sided, Yellow-bellied, and Alder Flycatchers; Blue-headed and Philadelphia Vireos; Gray Jay; Common Raven; Boreal Chickadee; Winter Wren; Golden-crowned and Ruby-crowned Kinglets; Swainson's and Hermit Thrushes; Nashville, Magnolia, Yellow-rumped, Black-throated Green, Blackburnian, Bay-breasted, Blackpoll, Mourning, and Wilson's Warblers; Northern Parula; Northern Waterthrush; Rusty Blackbird; and Purple Finch. It's a list that says North Country, and it makes a trip to the international border an inviting one indeed.

# VERMONT

Up in the part of the state that Vermonters call the **Northeast Kingdom,** birders delight in exploring the flat spruce-fir woods for northern species at home in this boreal environment. The star may be the Spruce Grouse, a bird that's often ridiculously easy to approach once it's found (hence the folk name "fool hen"), but one that often eludes the most determined searchers time after time. Just when all hope has been lost, a birder may chance upon one by pure luck right along a road or trail in boggy woods.

**15** A good place to look for Spruce Grouse and many other notable species is **Wenlock Wildlife Management Area** (*Vt. 105, 8 miles SE of Island Pond*). Watch for signs designating the area and check old roads running south from the highway. Where Vt. 105 crosses a railroad track 8 miles from Island Pond, go 1.5 miles farther and turn south on South America Road. A quarter mile later a trail leads west to **Moose Bog,** one of the area's top birding sites. Look here and in nearby woods for Ruffed Grouse (more common than Spruce); Northern Saw-whet Owl; Black-backed Woodpecker; Olive-sided, Yellow-bellied, and Alder Flycatchers; Blue-headed and Philadelphia Vireos; Gray Jay; Boreal Chickadee; Red-breasted Nuthatch; Winter Wren; Golden-crowned and Ruby-crowned Kinglets; Tennessee, Nashville, Chestnut-sided, Magnolia, Cape May, Black-throated Blue, Yellow-rumped, Black-throated Green, Blackburnian, Mourning, and Canada Warblers; Northern Parula; Northern Waterthrush; Lincoln's and White-throated Sparrows; Rusty Blackbird; and the erratic but sometimes common White-winged Crossbill.

Not even the luckiest or most skillful birder will find all these species, of course. To add to your own list, travel some

- Northern birds in the Northeast Kingdom
- Geese and wetland species at Dead Creek Wildlife Management Area

Information section p. 54

of the nearby roads running north from Vt. 105, such as **Lewis Pond Road,** back at the rail crossing, or **Black Branch Road,** about 1.5 miles east of South America Road.

**16** Another spot to find many of these same boreal species is **Victory Basin Wildlife Management Area** *(E from St. Johnsbury on US 2 to North Concord, then N on Town Hwy. 1 toward Victory and Gallup Mills).* Bird along the road, and watch for parking areas and trails in the wildlife area, which stretches for nearly 9 miles along the road north of Victory. Spruce Grouse isn't found here, although the Department of Fish and Wildlife has tentative plans to reintroduce this species in the future.

**17** About 18 miles northeast of Burlington, **Mount Mansfield** is known to all as Vermont's highest peak at 4,393 feet in elevation. Birders know it as one of the best places to find Bicknell's Thrush, a species confined as a breeder in the United States to higher northeastern mountains. The stunted spruce-fir forest on this peak has a good population of the thrush, easily accessed by a toll road that turns west off Vt. 108 about 6 miles northwest of Stowe. Bicknell's is best found in June and July, when it sings most often. In late September, it migrates to the Greater Antilles.

On the way up the toll road, you may find the Bicknell's relatives, Swainson's, Hermit, and Wood Thrushes, along with Yellow-bellied Sapsucker; Yellow-bellied and Least Flycatchers; Winter Wren; Golden-crowned Kinglet; Yellow-rumped, Black-throated Green, and Blackpoll Warblers; and Purple Finch. Near the top, look for Common Raven, White-throated Sparrow, and Dark-eyed Junco, and keep an eye out for Peregrine Falcon, which nests at nearby **Smuggler's Notch State Park.** You'll begin hearing Bicknell's Thrush sing from a point a little less than 4 miles above the entrance gate and on up to the Summit Station at the top.

**18** One of Vermont's most famous birding locations, **Dead Creek Wildlife Management Area,** lies southwest of Vergennes and just east of Lake Champlain. Although the area itself is productive, local birders have

several favorite routes through the surrounding country-side, which can host migrant waterfowl and shorebirds in many places, and where nesting species include Northern Harrier; Upland Sandpiper; Horned Lark; Vesper, Savannah, and Grasshopper Sparrows; and Bobolink. In winter, birds such as Rough-legged Hawk, Gyrfalcon (very rare), Snowy Owl, Northern Shrike, Lapland Longspur, Snow Bunting, and Common Redpoll could show up anywhere in area fields.

From Vergennes, drive south on Vt. 22A across Otter Creek, turning west on Panton Road. Continue west where Basin Harbor Road turns off north in 1.4 miles; about 1.2 miles later, go south on Sand Road toward the wildlife area's **Stone Bridge Dam Access,** reached by turning right at a T intersection. Depending on water level, wetlands here can have excellent migrant shorebirds, as well as wading birds (including American and Least Bitterns and Black-crowned Night-Heron), ducks, Virginia Rail, Sora, and Common Moorhen.

Return to Vt. 22A, go south to **Addison,** and take Vt. 17 west. In spring and fall, thousands of Snow and Canada Geese (and possibly a few Ross's in fall) may be present in fields along the road, and in migration a scan from the viewing shelter or the access area farther west will turn up waders, ducks, and shorebirds. Just after crossing Dead Creek, turn south and explore along the side road for waders, rails, and other wetland birds in the marsh.

Continue on Vt. 17 west to **Chimney Point State Historic Site.** Follow the entrance road through the site, under the Champlain Bridge, and down to the boat launch on Lake Champlain, another excellent spot for winter loons, grebes, ducks, Bald Eagles, and gulls. From here, take Vt. 125 east toward Middlebury. This stretch of rolling cropland and pasture is good for Rough-legged Hawk and other winter raptors (including rare Northern Hawk Owl) and Northern Shrike.

### Bicknell's Thrush

Once classified as a race of the Gray-cheeked Thrush, Bicknell's Thrush now ranks as a full species. Found in breeding season only in the north-eastern United States and eastern Canada, Bicknell's Thrush nests in this country in spruce-fir woods above 3,000 feet. Easily accessible places where it can be found in nesting season include New York's **Whiteface Mountain, Mount Mansfield** (see p. 32) in Vermont, and **Mount Washington** (see p. 29) in New Hampshire.

Fall flock of migrant Snow Geese, Dead Creek Wildlife Management Area, near Lake Champlain

**19** Marsh birds are the attraction at the **West Rutland marsh.** From the intersection of Vt. 4A and Vt. 133 in West Rutland, drive 2 blocks northwest on Vt. 4A, then north on Marble Street 2.6 miles before turning west on Pleasant Street to cross the marsh. To complete the loop, turn south on Whipple Hollow Road, drive 1.4 miles to Water Street, and turn east to cross the marsh again back to Marble Street. While making this circuit, look for nesting American and Least Bitterns, Virginia Rail, Sora, Common Moorhen, Alder and Willow Flycatchers, Blue-headed and Warbling Vireos, several species of swallows including Purple Martin, Marsh Wren, Yellow and Chestnut-sided Warblers, Swamp Sparrow, and Bobolink.

**20** Northwest of Springfield, **Springweather Nature Area** encompasses a fine trail system in its 70 acres of mixed forest alongside North Springfield Reservoir. To reach it from the intersection of Vt. 11 and Vt. 106 in Springfield, drive northwest on Vt. 106 about 1.8 miles and turn north on Reservoir Road. From fall through spring, turn left in 0.6 mile to admire the views and scan the reservoir from the dam for waterbirds. Then return to Reservoir

Road and drive north 0.8 mile to the nature area entrance on the left. The fields, woodland, and wetlands here create a diversity that makes for good birding at all seasons, but especially in spring and fall migration. A bluff overlooking the reservoir and lakeside trails allows more scanning for waterfowl and other birds, possibly including migrant Osprey or Bald Eagle and a variety of ducks.

**21** Migration is the peak time at **Herrick's Cove,** southeast of Rockingham on the Connecticut River. From its junction with Vt. 103, drive north on US 5 across the Williams River and quickly turn east. Widely known as one of the state's best sites for spring and fall migrant land birds, this small area can be filled with flycatchers, vireos, thrushes, warblers, and sparrows on a good day. Be sure to check the river and cove for waterfowl, which may include Canada Goose; Wood, American Black, and Ring-necked Ducks; American Wigeon; Mallard; Lesser Scaup; Bufflehead; Common Goldeneye; Hooded and Common Mergansers; and occasionally something more unusual like Oldsquaw. Osprey and Bald Eagle also make appearances in migration, flying over the river or perched in nearby trees.

# MASSACHUSETTS

- Excellent seabird sites
- Spring migration at Mount Auburn Cemetery in Cambridge

Information section p. 54

**22** On the way to or from the famed Parker River National Wildlife Refuge on Plum Island (a trip many Massachusetts birders make several times a year), most people stop to check the harbor at **Newburyport** (*Chamber of Commerce 978-462-6680*), where the Merrimack River reaches the Atlantic Ocean just a few miles south of New Hampshire. From I-95, drive east on Mass. 113 (High Street) for 3.8 miles to Rolfe's Lane. Turn left and drive 0.6 mile to Water Street. Turn east and look for the Massachusetts Audubon Society sign. At this writing, a nature center is planned for this 6.1-acre site, complete with restored salt marsh and observation points. When complete, this will be an excellent source of birding information on the area and the starting point for many interpretive programs.

The **Joppa Flats** here, a broad expanse of mud at low tide, attract shorebirds in spring, late summer, and fall, along with wading birds, waterfowl, and gulls at various times of the year. For shorebirds, it's best to be here a few hours before or after high tide, so the birds are concentrated on the exposed mudflats near shore. The most common species are those typical of the northeast coast: Black-bellied and Semipalmated Plovers, Greater and Lesser Yellowlegs, Semipalmated and Least Sandpipers, Dunlin, and Short-billed Dowitcher. A specialty bird in the fall is the Hudsonian Godwit, which stops on the flats to feed during its southward migration. Occasionally, rarer species such as Curlew Sandpiper and Ruff are observed.

In winter, check gull flocks for the uncommon to rare species for which Newburyport is renowned, including Little, Black-headed, Iceland, and Glaucous. Marshy places along the harbor shore host migrant geese and dabbling ducks, as well as herons and egrets in the warmer months.

Farther out, look for divers such as Oldsquaw, Common Goldeneye, and Red-breasted Merganser.

Traveling east, Water Street becomes Plum Island Turnpike. Check fields near the airport for "grasspipers" such as American Golden-Plover and Upland and Buff-breasted Sandpipers. As you travel across the bridge to Plum Island, look for wintering Rough-legged Hawk, Snowy and Short-eared Owls, and Northern Shrike.

**23** On Plum Island, a south turn onto Sunset Drive leads to **Parker River National Wildlife Refuge,** one of the region's best and most popular birding sites. (Because it is so popular, the refuge limits the number of vehicles allowed to enter. In summer, arrive early if you want to increase your chances of getting in without a delay.) With beach, extensive salt marsh, freshwater impoundments, and scattered woodland and scrub, the refuge attracts a wide range of birds. Continual coverage by birders means rarities are found often: strays such as Little Egret from Europe, and

Newburyport Harbor

Fork-tailed Flycatcher from South America. The main refuge road runs south to the end of the island, passing several parking lots and trails offering birding opportunities along the way. You should sample as many as you can.

Stop at parking lot No. 1 and walk to the boat ramp across the road to check the marsh for Marsh Wren and Saltmarsh Sharp-tailed and Seaside Sparrows, and in winter for Rough-legged Hawk and Short-eared Owl. This is one of several places where you can take a boardwalk to the beach to look for migrant or wintering loons, grebes, pelagic birds and sea ducks, or wintering Snow Bunting. (Some beach areas close in nesting season to protect Piping Plover—watch for signs and do not disturb this threatened species.) About a mile south, stop at the **Salt Pannes** to look for shorebirds at high tide in spring, late summer, and fall.

### Common Eider

Of the four species of eider, the Common Eider is the only one that nests in the lower 48 states. These large sea ducks nest on islands off Maine and New Hampshire, where the female uses her famously soft down to line her nest (the bird's Latin name, *mollissima,* means "very soft.") Large flocks of Common Eiders are a common sight off the New England coast in winter.

Continuing south, the **Hellcat Interpretive Trail** offers two loops, one through dunes, the other through a man-made freshwater marsh where bitterns and rails are possible. You can also walk the dike between the North and Bill Forward Pools to look for waders and migrant waterfowl and shorebirds. A half mile south, walk the **Pines Trail** in winter and look for Long-eared and Northern Saw-whet Owls roosting in the trees (even when they're present, it's easy to overlook these inconspicuous birds). The refuge road continues south about 3 more miles. The **Stage Island Pool** near the end can be excellent for shorebirds, particularly at high tide in late summer. At parking lot No. 7, cross to the beach to check the Atlantic again for seabirds, and look for Purple Sandpiper on offshore rocks in winter.

**24** In late fall and winter, a driving circuit around **Cape Ann** (*Chamber of Commerce 978-283-1601*) can be productive for loons, grebes, ducks, gulls, and other waterbirds. It can also be a bone-chilling experience when wind exacerbates frigid temperatures. Mass. 127 and 127A travel the perimeter of this peninsula extending north from Gloucester. Following those routes and checking side roads with access to the ocean is a good idea, but two spots on the north part of the cape, beyond Rockport, are especially fine lookout points. Before heading out, you may want to stop in Gloucester at **Stage Fort Park** or **Pavilion Beach** (*both off Mass. 127*) to look over the harbor. Great numbers of gulls are attracted to the fishing fleet here, and you'll often find Iceland and Glaucous among the common species. Barrow's Goldeneye has been seen here, though it's rare, and occasionally something as odd as Thick-billed Murre will appear in this sheltered area.

In **Rockport,** take Mass. 127 north from the junction with 127A for 1.9 miles and turn east (right) on Phillips Avenue. Go 1 block to Cathedral Ledge, a prime spot to look for small rafts of Harlequin Ducks from November to May. Expect to see Red-throated and Common Loons; Horned and Red-necked Grebes; Northern Gannet; Great and Double-crested Cormorants; Common Eider; Surf, White-winged, and Black Scoters; Oldsquaw; Common Goldeneye; Red-breasted Merganser; Black Guillemot; gulls; and, down on the rocks, small flocks of Purple Sandpipers. Be on the alert for King Eider and Barrow's Goldeneye. When northeast winds blow, uncommon species such as Northern Fulmar, Black-legged Kittiwake, Thick-billed Murre, Razorbill, or Atlantic Puffin may appear.

For those willing to walk less than a half mile to an observation point, **Halibut Point State Park** offers an even better panorama of the Atlantic and its birdlife. Return to Mass. 127 north and drive a short distance to Gott Avenue. Turn right, park in the lot provided, and follow the entrance path across the street. The picturesque headland here, certainly ranking as one of the state's premier birding spots, provides excellent viewing of the pelagic species that fly past this Cape Ann extremity in fall and winter. During onshore winds in summer and fall, this spot can be good for shearwaters and jaegers, too.

**25** Celebrated as a spring "migrant trap," where songbirds pause, sometimes in great numbers, to rest and feed on their northbound flight, is the famed **Mount**

**Auburn Cemetery** in Cambridge. This venerable institution, known as the resting place for many notables (among them Winslow Homer, Henry Wadsworth Longfellow, Buckminster Fuller, and Ludlow Griscom, the pioneering expert in bird identification), is one of the top spots for spring migration in the Boston area. Located on Mount Auburn Street just west of US 3 (Fresh Pond Parkway), the cemetery has more than 10 miles of roads and paths to explore. In spring, local birders maintain a board at the entrance listing recent sightings, and there are guided bird walks led by local birding clubs most mornings. A bird list is available, as is a map of the expansive grounds. A green sanctuary in the midst of urban development, Mount Auburn can be one of the state's most exciting bird spots on a good morning in May.

**26** The eastern part of Cape Cod—the **Outer Cape,** curving north and west to Provincetown—is a fine birding destination as well as one of the region's favorite vacation spots. More than 43,000 acres of this long peninsula are protected as national seashore, while a national wildlife refuge and a Massachusetts Audubon Society sanctuary provide additional birding opportunities.

In Chatham, from the lighthouse on Shore Road, follow Morris Island Road south to a causeway leading to **Morris Island.** Park on the east side of the causeway and walk the short distance onto the island, turning east into Wikis Way and the headquarters of **Monomoy National Wildlife Refuge.** Most of Morris Island is residential, but the refuge owns land on the east and south sides where you're free to walk the beaches and observe wading birds, waterfowl, shorebirds, gulls, and terns. To reach Monomoy's North and South Islands, just offshore, requires a boat. Be sure to ask at refuge headquarters about commercial tours to **North Monomoy Island** and nearby **South Beach.** The latter can have amazing numbers of shorebirds, gulls, and terns at high tide, and in recent years has become one of the top birding spots on the cape. Better yet, call Wellfleet Bay Wildlife Sanctuary (*508-349-2615*) to ask about guided boat trips around Cape Cod and to **South Monomoy Island,** where a visit in spring or fall migration may bring sightings of excellent numbers of shorebirds, and on occasion abundant land birds in the thickets and scrub. Birders are most excited, though, by the rarities that sometimes show up on this tiny patch of land off Cape Cod's "elbow." Despite South Monomoy Island's potential, it can be difficult for a first timer; a guided trip is by far the best option here.

South Monomoy Island once hosted greater numbers of terns, but increases in populations of Herring and Great

Black-backed Gulls caused a huge drop in tern numbers. Recent measures to control gulls, however, have allowed Roseate Tern and Black Skimmer to return, as well as dramatic increases in nesting Common and Least Terns. The number of Piping Plover nests has also increased.

Mount Auburn Cemetery, Cambridge

Driving north on US 6, as you reach Eastham turn east on Doane Road to the Salt Pond Visitor Center of **Cape Cod National Seashore,** where you can pick up a map and obtain information about nature programs. Continue east on Doane Road to **Coast Guard Beach** to scan for loons, grebes, sea ducks, and shorebirds. Then return south on US 6 for 1.2 miles, turning east to Fort Hill, where you can

Marshland overlook,
Cape Cod

scan the marsh for waders and migrant waterfowl and search
scrubby areas for migrant songbirds.

 As you approach Wellfleet on US 6, watch on the
west for the entrance to **Wellfleet Bay Wildlife Sanctuary,** which protects 1,000 acres of salt marsh, pinewoods,
beach, and fields, home to an excellent diversity of species.
Shorebirding can be superb here in spring, late summer, and
fall, and spring migration can also bring good numbers of
songbirds to woods and thickets. Follow trails out to the
shore, past marshes where you may find herons and egrets
in summer and waterfowl in migration. Piping Plover and
Least Tern breed here, and guides are on hand to show these
threatened species to visitors. Sanctuary staff members are
an excellent source of advice on birding in the area. Varied natural history programs, including birding cruises, are
offered throughout the year.

**28** Near the north tip of Cape Cod and the artist colony
of Provincetown, turn north on Race Point Road

toward the Province Lands Visitor Center of the **Cape Cod National Seashore.** In spring and fall, bird along the trails in the **Beech Forest,** a fine spot for migrant songbirds. From late summer though winter, continue to the parking lot at **Race Point Beach,** which provides a convenient place from which to scan the Atlantic for loons and ducks, as well as for passing pelagic species such as shearwaters, Northern Gannet, jaegers, Thick-billed Murre, and Black Guillemot.

For those who want a better chance at pelagic species—birds such as the "tubenoses" (Northern Fulmar, shearwaters, and storm-petrels), phalaropes, skuas, jaegers, and auks that spend most of their lives at sea—whale-watching boats provide a way to get out on the ocean at a reasonable cost. Late spring through fall usually offer the best seabirding. While these cruises are aimed at finding whales, often some members of the crew are knowledgeable about birds. You can check with Chamber of Commerce offices in Province-town (508-487-3424), Boston (617-536-4100), Gloucester (978-283-1601), and Newburyport (978-462-6680) for information about whale-watching companies.

# RHODE ISLAND

Southeast Lighthouse, Block Island

**29** Most of Rhode Island's best birding spots are near the Atlantic, and one of them, **Block Island,** is surrounded by it. Lying 10 miles south of the mainland, this island is renowned for the number and variety of birds it attracts in fall migration. Mid-September to mid-October is the peak time, when birders, too, swarm the island hoping for rarities, marveling at the hunting flights of Merlin and Peregrine Falcon, and swapping stories and sightings.

Nearly any migrant eastern bird might show up on the island in fall, and the list of rarities seen includes western birds such as Say's Phoebe and Western Kingbird (a regular visitor). A section of the north end of the island, the favorite place to begin a day of birding, is now **Block Island National Wildlife Refuge,** but most of the island is private property, and birders should be discreet in their activities.

The island is small enough to be covered by bicycle, a favored alternative for some as bringing a car by ferry is expensive, and reservations must be made far in advance. Rental bikes and cars are available. A ferry ride (401-783-4613) from Galilee takes only a little more than an hour, and by air the trip is a quick hop; inns are numerous but make reservations early. The best way for a first timer to experience Block Island in fall is to join a group tour, solving the logistical problems. For information on one option, call the Audubon Society of Rhode Island (401-949-5454), which traditionally sponsors a birding weekend on the island each fall.

**30** Back on the mainland, **Trustom Pond National Wildlife Refuge** ranks at the top of the state's year-round birding destinations, with a mix of woods, fields, and wetlands. To reach the refuge, take the Moonstone Beach Road exit from US 1 about 3 miles east of Charlestown. Drive a mile south to Matunuck Schoolhouse Road and head west to the refuge entrance. From the parking area here, intersecting trails wind south through a portion of the 642-acre refuge to brackish Trustom Pond, the only undeveloped coastal salt pond in the state. Observation platforms permit scanning for Mute Swan (Tundra Swan is a rare visitor), geese, and a variety of ducks from fall through spring.

Waders including Great Blue and Green Herons, Great and Snowy Egrets, and Glossy Ibis feed on the pond from spring through fall. Look for Osprey in spring and summer. When the water level is right, Trustom Pond can attract migrant shorebirds in numbers. The threatened Piping Plover nests on the beach south of the pond, which is closed in breeding season. Once a farm, the refuge still has extensive grassland—not a common habitat in Rhode Island. Bobolink and Eastern Meadowlark sing in fields in summer, and in winter Northern Harrier, Rough-legged Hawk, and Short-eared Owl search for prey.

Trustom Pond National Wildlife Refuge, near Charlestown

**31** From fall through spring, a visit to **Point Judith** can turn up an interesting list of seabirds. Take R.I. 108 south from US 1 at Wakefield about 5 miles; just before the lighthouse at the end of the road, turn left into a small park. From here, scan the Atlantic for species such as Red-throated and Common Loons; Horned and Red-necked Grebes; Northern Gannet; Common Eider; Surf, White-winged, and Black Scoter; Oldsquaw; Common Goldeneye; and Red-breasted Merganser. Birders also hope for rarer finds, from Barrow's Goldeneye to jaegers to Black-legged Kittiwake to Razorbill.

Harlequin Duck, a winter specialty at Sachuest Point

**32** **Sachuest Point National Wildlife Refuge** occupies 242 acres of a peninsula extending south into Rhode Island Sound just east of Newport; its strategic location makes it another excellent spot for seabirds fall through spring. From the visitor center, trails along the refuge's perimeter offer views of loons, grebes, cormorants, and sea ducks. Check the rocks for Purple Sandpiper, and look over flocks of Common Eider for the rare King Eider.

Sachuest Point's star attraction, though, is Harlequin Duck, regularly seen here in winter—quite often on the east side of the refuge, near the offshore **Island Rocks.** Uncommon to rare over much of the northeast coast, the beautiful Harlequin makes braving the cold winds of the point more than worthwhile. Rough-legged Hawk and Snowy and Short-eared Owls are regular winter visitors to the refuge, and Snow Buntings frequent grassy places. As you scan the surrounding waters here, look for all the seabird species listed above for Point Judith.

**33** Providence's most famous site for spring songbird migration is a cemetery: **Swan Point Cemetery,** located off Blackstone Boulevard in the northeast part of the city, next to the Seekonk River. The most popular area with local birders is the wooded section in the northwest part of the cemetery.

# CONNECTICUT

**34** Beginners and experienced birders alike will find much to enjoy at the **Audubon Center in Greenwich,** operated by the National Audubon Society. This 522-acre sanctuary encompasses several miles of well-marked trails through woodland, old fields, and swampy places; there's even a small lake to attract waterbirds. With this diversity of habitat, the center is excellent in spring migration, when flycatchers, vireos, thrushes, and warblers can be found everywhere. Near the entrance gate, local birders staff the **Quaker Ridge** hawk-watch site in fall. Sharp-shinned, Cooper's, Broad-winged, and Red-tailed Hawks and American Kestrel are the most common raptors seen, with lesser numbers of Osprey, Bald Eagle, Northern Harrier, Red-shouldered Hawk, and other species.

Nesting birds make this a fine destination throughout the summer. They include Green Heron; Wood Duck; Ruffed Grouse; Pileated Woodpecker; White-eyed and Warbling Vireos; Carolina Wren; Eastern Bluebird; Veery; Blue-winged, Yellow, Chestnut-sided, and Worm-eating Warblers; Louisiana Waterthrush; Swamp Sparrow; and Rose-breasted Grosbeak. To reach the center, take the Round Hill Road exit from the Merritt Parkway and drive north 1.5 miles to John Street. Turn left and drive 1.5 miles to the entrance at Riversville Road.

**35** On the coast where the Housatonic River enters Long Island Sound, **Milford Point** ranks with the state's favorite birding spots. From I-95 take the exit for US 1 and turn right; after 3 lights turn left on Naugatuck Avenue. Take this until the last right before the water, Broadway, and drive 1.5 miles to the entrance of the **Connecticut Audubon Coastal Center** (*parking lot open dawn to dusk*). A handi-

- Fall hawk migration at Lighthouse Point Park
- Fine birding all year at White Memorial Foundation

Information section p. 55

capped-accessible viewing platform and an observation tower allow scanning of marshland. Look for herons and egrets from spring through fall, and for migrant and wintering waterfowl. Osprey, gulls, and terns may be flying over the marsh grasses, while Clapper Rail skulks below. Both Black-crowned and Yellow-crowned Night-Herons breed in this area.

A trail leads from the center to another viewing platform at the beach, where shorebirds can be abundant in migra-

tion. In late summer, Roseate Tern may fly with Common Terns here, and a Peregrine Falcon might show up in fall, looking for a meal of plover or sandpiper. Winter brings Red-throated Loon, Greater Scaup, possibly a scoter or Oldsquaw, and Purple Sandpiper in rocky spots. Snowy Owl is also a winter specialty of the area. Walk westward along the beach, watching for wading birds, waterfowl, shorebirds, gulls, and terns. Soon you'll reach the **Stewart B. McKinney National Wildlife Refuge,** and another observation platform. Small numbers of Piping Plover, American Oystercatcher, and Least Tern breed in this vicinity, so note signs

Observation tower, Connecticut Audubon Coastal Center, Milford Point

closing certain areas in nesting season. A great number of rarities have appeared here over the years, testimony to the strategic location of this association of bay, beach, and marsh.

**36** To reach **Lighthouse Point Park,** a noted fall hawk-watch spot, take Conn. 337 (Townsend Avenue) south from US 1 and I-95 in New Haven; in 2 miles, turn right on Lighthouse Road. From late summer to November, when weather cooperates (a cold front, followed by northwest winds that push raptors to the coast), flights of Sharp-shinned and Broad-winged Hawks and a dozen or more other species pass over the park. Experienced hawk-spotters here make this a fine place for a beginner to pick up identification pointers. Fall songbird migration is another highlight of Lighthouse Point; the woods, shrubby areas, and marshes can be full of a spectacular variety of species. Also check the beach for shorebirds, which can make a good showing from late summer through fall.

**37** North across the Quinnipiac River in New Haven, **East Rock Park** is considered by many to be the state's best spring migrant-songbird site (*enter birding areas via footbridge behind Eli Whitney Museum on Whitney Ave., or from corner of Orange and Cold Spring Sts.*). Follow trails near **Mill**

**River,** where in late April and May, flycatchers, vireos, thrushes, warblers, and other birds appear in excellent numbers. Every birder hopes to be in a migrant "fallout," when a wave of northbound birds arrives, but the complexities of weather make it hard to predict when such a day will occur. Even a slow spring day in East Rock Park, though, is likely to have plenty to occupy a morning's birding.

Snowy Owl, an irregularly occurring winter visitor from the Arctic

**38** East along Long Island Sound, **Hammonasset Beach State Park** is as popular among birders as it is with the nonbirders who throng the 2 miles of sandy beach in summer. The park is easily reached by exiting I-95 at Hammonasset Beach in Madison and driving south less than 2 miles. Migrant shorebirds and songbirds and winter waterbirds are highlights, but the varied habitats here make it one of Connecticut's top all-around birding sites: Rails hide in the marshes, warblers feed in woods, sparrows flit through grassy places, and in fall huge numbers of swallows skim wetlands.

Visit the park nature center for information, and in spring or fall head to **Willard's Island Nature Trail.** Songbirds can be abundant in this "migrant trap," and a viewing platform offers a chance to look over marshland for waders and, depending on water level, shorebirds. Clapper Rail, Willet, and Saltmarsh Sharp-tailed and Seaside Sparrows nest in the marsh. Great Blue Heron, Great and Snowy Egrets, and Glossy Ibis are seen often here, American Bittern and Cattle Egret less often, and even Tricolored Heron has been found. In winter, the marsh provides a hunting ground for both Northern Harrier and Short-eared Owl.

At **Meig's Point,** you can scan the sound in winter for typical North Atlantic species such as Red-throated Loon; Horned and Red-necked Grebes; Double-crested and Great Cormorants; Brant; Greater Scaup; Surf, White-winged, and Black Scoters; Oldsquaw; Common Goldeneye; and Red-breasted Merganser. Purple Sandpiper is often found on rocks just offshore.

**39** From the intersection of US 1 and Conn. 117 east of Groton, drive west 0.3 mile and turn south on Depot Road to reach **Bluff Point State Park and Coastal Reserve,** an 806-acre park of specialized appeal. You may want to walk 1.5 miles along a trail to reach a bluff on Long Island Sound where you can scan for migrant and winter waterbirds, as well as a beach and a tidal salt marsh good for shorebirds. But it's the chance for a good fall concentration of migrant songbirds that attracts most birders here. Explore trails through woods and scrub in the north part of the reserve. On a good day you may find dozens of species, with possibilities including most of the eastern flycatchers, vireos, thrushes, warblers, and sparrows. It's important to be here in early morning for the best migration birding.

**40** Unlike coastal sites, many of which are at their best in migration, **Devil's Hopyard State Park,** about 7 miles east of East Haddam, is known for a variety of interesting breeding species (though spring migration can be

White Memorial
Foundation and
Conservation Center,
near Litchfield

excellent, too). In spring and summer, walk trails here—
especially those along the **Eight-Mile River,** bordered by tall
hemlocks—and look for Pileated Woodpecker; Acadian and
Least Flycatchers; Blue-headed, Yellow-throated, and
Warbling Vireos; Brown Creeper; Chestnut-sided, Black-
throated Green, Cerulean, and Worm-eating Warblers;
American Redstart; Ovenbird; Louisiana Waterthrush;
Scarlet Tanager; and Rose-breasted Grosbeak, among many
other nesting birds.

**41** One of the finest centers for nature study in northwestern Connecticut, **White Memorial Foundation
and Conservation Center** is located 2 miles west of Litchfield, south of US 202. With 35 miles of trails winding
through 4,000 acres of diverse habitats, the property of this
nonprofit education and research foundation offers

excellent birding throughout the year, with a notable list of nesting species. Obtain a map at the Nature Museum, and ask about programs offered by staff naturalists.

**Catlin Woods,** east of the museum, is a favorite birding spot—the hemlock woodland here has nesting Ruffed Grouse; Pileated Woodpecker; Red-breasted Nuthatch; and Yellow-rumped, Black-throated Green, and Blackburnian Warblers. Just north, **Little Pond** is home to such wetland-loving birds as Green Heron, Mute Swan, Wood Duck, Virginia Rail, Eastern Phoebe, Common Yellowthroat, Swamp Sparrow, and Red-winged Blackbird. Fields and scrubby areas nearby have Alder and Willow Flycatchers; Warbling Vireo; Eastern Bluebird; Blue-winged, Yellow, and Chestnut-sided Warblers; and Field and Song Sparrows.

Among the area's many other birding spots, easily found with the foundation map, **Laurel Hill** hosts several warblers including Blue-winged, Nashville, Chestnut-sided, Black-throated Blue, and Canada. **Point Folly,** a small peninsula extending into Bantam Lake, makes a good lookout from which to search the water for migrant Common Loon, Horned Grebe, and a variety of ducks.

**42** Just a few miles from the New York state line, **River Road** near Kent offers excellent spring-migration birding and interesting breeding birds along the Housatonic River. *(From jct. with US 7, take Conn. 341 W. Immediately after crossing the river, take Skiff Mountain Rd. N 1 mile to River Rd.)* Acadian Flycatcher and Cerulean Warbler are two of the special nesting birds of the area, and Yellow-throated Warbler has nested farther along, where the road ends and the Appalachian Trail continues. Black Vulture is seen occasionally, soaring overhead. Osprey and Bald Eagle fish along the river in migration.

During the spring and summer months, stop often along the road to listen for Blue-winged, Yellow, Chestnut-sided, Black-throated Blue, and Worm-eating Warblers. Ruffed Grouse drums in spring; the hoarse whistle of Scarlet Tanager, and the sweeter one of Rose-breasted Grosbeak, sound from treetops. At the peak of spring migration in May, possible sightings range over nearly the entire list of eastern songbirds.

# New England
## Information

**?** Visitor Center/Information    **$** Fee Charged    **‖** Food

**♿‖** Rest Rooms    **🚶** Nature Trails    **〰** Driving Tours    **♿** Wheelchair Accessible

*Be advised that facilities may be seasonal and limited. We suggest calling or writing ahead for specific information. Note that addresses may be for administrative offices; see text or call for directions to sites.*

### Rare Bird Alerts

Maine:
Statewide *207-781-2332, option 1*

New Hampshire:
Statewide *603-224-9900, option 2*

Vermont:
Statewide *802-457-2779, option 1*

Massachusetts:
Cape Cod *508-349-9464*
Eastern *781-259-8805*
Western *413-253-2218*

Rhode Island:
Statewide *401-949-3870*

Connecticut:
Statewide *203-254-3665*

### MAINE

**East Point Sanctuary**
*(Page 19)*
Maine Audubon Society
P.O. Box 6009
Falmouth, ME 04105
*207-781-2330*

🚶

### Scarborough Marsh
### Nature Center *(Page 20)*
Maine Audubon Society
P.O. Box 6009
Falmouth, ME 04105
*207-883-5100*

? ‖ ♿‖ 🚶 ♿

*Open June–Labor Day, with bird walks Wed. Also offers canoe tours*

### Acadia National Park
*(Page 21)*
P.O. Box 177
Bar Harbor, ME 04609
*207-288-3338*

? $ ♿‖ 🚶 〰 ♿

### Quoddy Head State
### Park *(Page 24)*
Rural Route 2, Box 1490
Lubec, ME 04652
*207-733-0911*

$ ♿‖ 🚶 ♿

### Baxter State Park
*(Page 24)*
64 Balsam Drive
Millinocket, ME 04462
*207-723-5140*

? $ ♿‖ 🚶

### NEW
### HAMPSHIRE

**Hampton Beach**
**State Park** *(Page 26)*
P.O. Box 606
Rye Beach, NH 03871
*603-926-8990*

? $ ‖ ♿‖ ♿

### Odiorne Point
### State Park *(Page 27)*
570 Ocean Boulevard
Rye, NH 03870
*603-436-8043*

? $ ♿‖ 🚶 ♿

### Great Bay National
### Wildlife Refuge *(Page 27)*
336 Nimble Hill Road
Newington, NH 03801
*603-431-7511*

♿‖ 🚶 ♿

### Sandy Point Discovery
### Center *(Page 28)*
89 Depot Road
Stratham, NH 03885
*603-778-0015*

? ♿‖ 🚶 ♿

*Open June–Oct.*

**White Mountain National Forest** *(Page 29)*
P.O. Box 638
Laconia, NH 03247
*603-528-8721*

*Fee for toll road to summit. Mount Washington Observatory maintains weather station and research facility on summit, as well as a museum open mid-May–late Oct.*

# VERMONT

**Wenlock Wildlife Management Area and Victory Basin Wildlife Management Area**
*(Pages 31, 32)*
Vermont Department of
Fish and Wildlife
103 S. Main Street
Waterbury, VT 05671
*802-751-0100*

**Mount Mansfield Natural Area** *(Page 32)*
Rural Route 1, Box 650
Waterbury Center,
VT 05677
*802-253-3000*

*Toll road open Mem. Day–Columbus Day. Trails closed mid-April–late May*

**Dead Creek Wildlife Management Area**
*(Page 32)*
966 Route 17W
Addison, VT 05491
*802-759-2398*

**Chimney Point State Historic Site** *(Page 33)*
7305 Vt. 125
Addison, VT 05491
*802-759-2412*

*Exhibit center open Mem. Day–Columbus Day*

# MASSACHUSETTS

**Joppa Flats Education Center and Wildlife Sanctuary** *(Page 36)*
Plum Island Turnpike
Newburyport, MA 01950
*978-462-9998*

*Visitor center with full facilities planned to open by 2000*

**Parker River National Wildlife Refuge** *(Page 37)*
261 Northern Boulevard,
Plum Island
Newburyport, MA 01950
*978-465-5753*

**Halibut Point State Park**
*(Page 39)*
16 Gaffield Avenue
Rockport, MA 01966
*978-546-2997*

**Mount Auburn Cemetery** *(Page 39)*
580 Mount Auburn Street
Cambridge, MA 02138
*617-547-7105*

**Monomoy National Wildlife Refuge** *(Page 40)*
Wikis Way, Morris Island
Chatham, MA 02633
*508-945-0594*

*Call regarding boat tours.*

**Cape Cod National Seashore** *(Pages 41, 43)*
99 Marconi Site Road
Wellfleet, MA 02667
*508-255-3421*

*Salt Pond Visitor Center open weekends Jan.–mid-Feb. and daily rest of year. Province Lands Visitor Center open daily mid-April–Nov.*

**Wellfleet Bay Wildlife Sanctuary** *(Page 42)*
291 US 6
South Wellfleet, MA 02663
*508-349-2615*

# RHODE ISLAND

**Block Island National Wildlife Refuge** *(Page 44)*
P.O. Box 307
Charlestown, RI 02813
*401-364-9124*

**Trustom Pond National Wildlife Refuge** *(Page 45)*
P.O. Box 307
Charlestown, RI 02813
*401-364-9124*

*Barrier beach closed April–mid-Sept.*

**Sachuest Point National Wildlife Refuge** *(Page 46)*
P.O. Box 307
Charlestown, RI 02813
*401-847-5511*

**Swan Point Cemetery**
*(Page 46)*
585 Blackstone Boulevard
Providence, RI 02906
*401-272-1314*

## CONNECTICUT

**Audubon Center in Greenwich** *(Page 47)*
613 Riversville Road
Greenwich, CT 06831
*203-869-5272*

**Connecticut Audubon Coastal Center** *(Page 47)*
1 Milford Point Road
Milford, CT 06460
*203-878-7440*

*Closed Mon.*

**Stewart B. McKinney National Wildlife Refuge**
*(Page 48)*
P.O. Box 1030
Westbrook, CT 06498
*860-399-2513*

**Lighthouse Point Park**
*(Page 48)*
1 Lighthouse Road
New Haven, CT 06515
*203-946-8005*

**East Rock Park** *(Page 49)*
Orange and Cold
   Spring Streets
New Haven, CT 06515
*203-946-6086*

**Hammonasset Beach State Park** *(Page 49)*
P.O. Box 271
Madison, CT 06443
*203-245-2785*

**Bluff Point State Park and Coastal Reserve**
*(Page 50)*
c/o Fort Griswold Battlefield
   State Park
57 Fort Street
Groton, CT 06340
*860-445-1729*

**Devil's Hopyard State Park** *(Page 50)*
366 Hopyard Road
East Haddam, CT 06423
*860-873-8566*

**White Memorial Foundation and Conservation Center**
*(Page 51)*
71 Whitehall Road
Litchfield, CT 06759
*860-567-0857*

# Mid-Atlantic

Here sprawls the southern part of one of the world's great urban corridors, the Washington-to-Boston supermetropolis. Here highways entwine with rail lines and more highways, and city and suburb alternate seemingly without end along Atlantic shore and harbors, until from an airplane the landscape seems one glowing band of light. Here in large part we have reconfigured the natural landscape to serve our own purposes, for better or worse.

Here, too, is Cape May, New Jersey, unquestionably one of America's top birding spots, where hawks pass overhead each fall by the thousands. Northern New Jersey holds Great Swamp National Wildlife Refuge, where conservationists fought off a proposed airport in the days before ecology was a buzzword. Here in the expansive tidal marshes along Delaware Bay, rails carry on their furtive affairs as they did in the days before the first Europeans appeared. To the north, herons, egrets, and shorebirds enthrall watchers

*Preceding pages:*
Snow and Canada
Geese and other
waterbirds, Jamaica
Bay Wildlife Refuge,
New York
*Above:*
Ruddy Turnstone
*Right:*
Green-winged Teal

next door to John F. Kennedy and Philadelphia international airports, at Jamaica Bay Wildlife Refuge and John Heinz National Wildlife Refuge, respectively.

Nature yet endures in our largest metropolitan agglomeration, and so do opportunities for birding. It can be a solitary pursuit—walking a trail in White Clay Creek State Park, in northern Delaware, or in Delaware Water Gap National Recreation Area, straddling the Pennsylvania-New Jersey border—or a sociable one, such as a Saturday morning in May at the Ramble in Manhattan's Central

Park, or an October morning on Hawk Mountain in Pennsylvania. It can be the pleasure of spring warblers in Rock Creek Park in Washington, D.C., or the excitement of chasing a rarity, say, a Ruff or a White-winged Tern at Bombay Hook National Wildlife Refuge in Delaware.

For a beginner, the great thing about the mass of people in the Northeast is the fact that there are just that many more birders, and a valuable body of collective expertise to

## Special Birds of the Mid-Atlantic

*Roseate Tern*

| | | |
|---|---|---|
| Cory's Shearwater | Tundra Swan | Curlew Sandpiper |
| Greater Shear- | Eurasian Wigeon | Ruff |
| water | King Eider | Pomarine Jaeger |
| Sooty Shearwater | Common Eider | Parasitic Jaeger |
| Wilson's Storm- | Surf Scoter | Little Gull |
| Petrel | White-winged | Iceland Gull |
| Northern Gannet | Scoter | Lesser Black- |
| Great Cormorant | Black Scoter | backed Gull |
| Glossy Ibis | Oldsquaw | Glaucous Gull |
| Brant | Spruce Grouse | Black-legged |
| Mute Swan | Black Rail | Kittiwake |
| | Piping Plover | Gull-billed Tern |
| | Purple Sandpiper | Roseate Tern |

| |
|---|
| Black Skimmer |
| Three-toed |
| Woodpecker |
| Black-backed |
| Woodpecker |
| Yellow-bellied |
| Flycatcher |
| Gray Jay |
| Boreal Chickadee |
| Bicknell's Thrush |
| Saltmarsh Sharp- |
| tailed Sparrow |
| Seaside Sparrow |

exploit. Gulls in their multifarious plumages can seem impossible to sort out, for example, but visit Niagara Falls or Maryland's Conowingo Dam in winter and you will find people peering through telescopes who will point out the darker underside of the primary feathers of the one Black-headed Gull in the middle of all those Bonaparte's. Spend a weekend at one of the region's excellent hawk-watch sites and you'll learn a lot about the shapes and sizes and wing-flapping patterns of raptors. While you'll encounter the inevitable can't-be-bothered birder who is single-mindedly pursuing some rarity, you'll find many more friendly folks who are willing and happy to share their knowledge with others. Take them up on it.

This chapter begins in western New York, heads over to the Atlantic coast, and turns south to finish in extreme western Maryland. ∎

# NEW YORK

**1** **Niagara Falls** (*Information Center 716-284-2000 or 800-421-5223*), famous the world over for its thundering walls of water, is celebrated by birders for a related phenomenon: The area from the rocky rapids above the falls down through the Niagara River Gorge to its outlet at Lake Ontario has been called "the gull capital of North America." In fall and winter, gulls attracted to the churning water, which remains mostly unfrozen through the coldest weather, sometimes congregate by the tens of thousands. Mixed in with the abundant Bonaparte's, Ring-billed, and Herring are always assorted uncommon to rare species, from Little and Black-headed to Iceland, Glaucous, and Great Black-backed—sometimes totaling a dozen or more species.

From the city of Niagara Falls, cross over to **Goat Island,** which separates the American Falls from the Horseshoe, or Canadian, Falls. Check the rapids above the falls for gulls and for ducks, which may include Canvasback, Greater Scaup, Bufflehead, Common Goldeneye, and Common and Red-breasted Mergansers. Many birders agree that the Canadian side of the river provides better views, so cross the border on the Rainbow Bridge and visit the many observation points in the park both above and below the falls.

Follow the river downstream about 5 miles and stop at the **Sir Adam Beck Power Plant** on the Canadian side, where flocks of gulls feed in the outflow. Then cross to the American side again and check the power-plant outlet between Niagara Falls and Lewiston. Finally, continue north to **Fort Niagara State Park,** where the river enters Lake Ontario, and scan the river and lake for gulls and waterbirds, which might include Red-throated Loon, Red-necked Grebe, Common or King Eider, Harlequin Duck, Oldsquaw, or Barrow's Goldeneye.

- Winter gulls at Niagara Falls
- Spring hawk-watching at Derby Hill Bird Observatory
- Fall shorebirds at Jamaica Bay Wildlife Refuge

Information section p. 93

Niagara Falls, on the United States–Canada border

**2** One of western New York's best all-around birding spots, **Braddock Bay** is an indentation in the Lake Ontario shoreline just west of Rochester. A mix of city park, state wildlife management area, and private property, the area offers marsh and wading birds, waterfowl, owls, migrant songbirds, and an exciting spring hawk-watch. To reach it, take the Lake Ontario State Parkway west from its intersection with N.Y. 390 to the second exit and follow East Manitou Road north. Watch for the city park entrance on the left. At a T junction, turn right to the hawk-watch platform. In spring, hawks pass along the lakeshore by the thousands: Sharp-shinned, Broad-winged, and Red-tailed are most frequent, but several other species are common as well. Also, scan the bay here for Double-crested Cormorant in spring, migrant and wintering waterfowl, migrant

Caspian and Common Terns in spring (plus Forster's in fall), and nesting Black Tern, a seriously declining species in the Northeast. Beginning near the hawk-watch platform, a nature trail leads to **Cranberry Pond,** where at times you can spot waders (including occasional American and Least Bitterns), ducks, rails, and migrant shorebirds. Continue north on East Manitou Road to Edgemere Drive and take this east about 3 miles to Island Cottage Road, stopping to check the ponds on the south as you go. Park and explore **Island Cottage Woods** (taking care to stay on the trails), where spring songbird migration can bring excellent numbers of vireos, thrushes, and warblers.

**Purple Sandpiper**

The Purple Sandpiper, which breeds in the Arctic, might better be called a "rockpiper," since in winter it's almost always found on wave-splashed rocks along the North Atlantic coast. This species especially favors rock jetties, and with the building of these structures where once there was only sand and marsh, it now winters much farther south than before. Look for this sandpiper at **Barnegat Lighthouse State Park** (see p. 72) in New Jersey and the **Ocean City** (see p. 88) jetty in Maryland.

**3** Spring hawk-watching has made the **Derby Hill Bird Observatory** one of the state's most famous birding sites (*from Mexico, 30 miles N of Syracuse, go N 3.5 miles on N.Y. 3. Turn left on N.Y. 104B, taking the next right onto Sage Creek Rd., for a little more than 1 mile N*). From this high point on the southeastern corner of the Lake Ontario shoreline, watchers tally the sometimes spectacular numbers of hawks that stream past from late winter into May. (Here, as at Braddock Bay, weather can make the hawk flight either exciting or slow. The best days have moderate southerly winds and a cloud cover.) Broad-winged Hawk is by far the most numerous species, but anything from Bald and Golden Eagles to Northern Goshawk and Peregrine Falcons might happen by. Osprey; Northern Harrier; Sharp-shinned, Cooper's, Red-shouldered, Red-tailed, and Rough-legged Hawks; and American Kestrel are all regular migrants at various times throughout the spring.

**4** Situated at the northern end of Cayuga Lake in New York's Finger Lakes region, the more than 7,000 acres of **Montezuma National Wildlife Refuge** protect marshland that can host well over 100,000 waterfowl in spring and fall migration, including Snow and Canada Geese, Tundra Swan, and up to 25 species of ducks, several of which remain to nest. Naturally, all this marsh attracts other types of birds, too: Breeding species include Pied-billed Grebe, American and Least (rare) Bitterns, Great Blue Heron, Black-crowned Night-Heron, Virginia Rail, Sora, Common Moorhen, Common and Black Terns, and Marsh Wren (and rarely Sedge). Scan the refuge **Main Pool** from the visitor center or nearby observation platform before beginning the 3.5-mile wildlife drive. Watch for Osprey and Northern Harrier, both of which nest here, and for various waterbirds including Double-crested Cormorant, herons, egrets, gulls, and terns. Where the wildlife drive crosses north of I-90, check **Tschache Pool** for nesting Bald Eagle, and **May's Point Pool** for fall migrant shorebirds, which sometimes take flight at the approach of a hunting Peregrine Falcon.

**5** One well-known spot to find many of the northern birds of the Adirondack Mountains is **Ferd's Bog,** a suitably boreal-looking spot near the small town of Eagle Bay *(from N.Y. 28, take Uncas Rd. NE 3.5 miles)*. A trail here leads into an open bog where pitcher plants, sundews, and orchids grow. Nesting birds in the vicinity are a roll call of mostly higher latitude species: Three-toed and Black-backed Woodpeckers; Olive-sided and Yellow-bellied Flycatchers; Blue-headed Vireo; Gray Jay; Boreal Chickadee; Red-breasted Nuthatch; Brown Creeper; Winter Wren; Golden-crowned Kinglet; Nashville, Magnolia, Black-throated Blue, Black-throated Green, Blackburnian, and Canada Warblers; Northern Parula; Lincoln's, Swamp, and White-throated Sparrows; Dark-eyed Junco; and Purple Finch. Osprey nests nearby, and Red Crossbill is an irregular visitor. Spruce Grouse occurs in the area, but you'll need luck on your side to see one here. Walk carefully, as the bog environment is fragile.

**6** Any list of New York's birding hot spots must mention one of the best, and seemingly unlikeliest, of them all. **Central Park,** right in the heart of Manhattan,

Ring-billed Gulls,
Central Park,
New York

is a magnet not only for migrants but for city-bound birders. The park's 840 acres must seem tremendously inviting to birds looking for shelter in a forest of buildings, and nearly any patch of trees or shrubs may host interesting species in spring and, to a lesser extent, in fall. Most favored is the **Ramble,** a wooded area near the Great Lawn. In late April and May, you will find plenty of birders exploring the pathways for flycatchers, vireos, thrushes, warblers, sparrows, and anything else that might drop in. Central Park isn't just a convenient urban substitute for a "real" birding trip. When a migrant wave hits, it can hold its own with nearly anyplace on the East Coast. While not as famous as Central Park, **Prospect Park,** across the East River in Brooklyn, deserves mention as another fine migrant site.

NEW YORK 65

Black-bellied Plovers and Common and Forster's Terns at East Pond, Jamaica Bay Wildlife Refuge, Queens

**7** Year-round, New York City's most rewarding birding site is the **Jamaica Bay Wildlife Refuge** in southern Queens, reached by taking Cross Bay Boulevard south from Belt Parkway. (The parking lot at the refuge visitor center is easy to miss, so watch carefully for it on the west side of the boulevard.) Waders, waterfowl, and especially shorebirds are the attraction at this preserve hard by John F. Kennedy International Airport; an amazing total of 330 species have been seen here. Stop at the refuge visitor center for information and a necessary free permit to walk the trails, and check the sightings book for interesting recent finds. Then walk around the **West Pond,** where depending on the season you will find waders (such as Great and Snowy Egrets, Tricolored Heron, Yellow-crowned Night-Heron, and Glossy Ibis), or geese and ducks, or shorebirds, gulls, and terns. American Oystercatcher, Willet, Marsh Wren, Saltmarsh Sharp-tailed and Seaside Sparrows, and Boat-

tailed Grackle are among the nesting birds. In winter, look for Brant in Jamaica Bay, for Northern Harrier and Short-eared Owl over the marshes, and for an occasional Snowy Owl perched regally on the ground. The "garden" area near the visitor center can be excellent for migrant land birds in spring and fall (especially).

This much visited refuge, part of **Gateway National Recreation Area,** is best known for shorebirds, especially in summer and early fall at the **East Pond,** across from the visitor center. High tide is most productive, and at times the mudflats may be crowded with hundreds of Black-bellied and Semipalmated Plovers, Greater and Lesser Yellowlegs, Semipalmated and Least Sandpipers, Red Knot, and Dunlin, to name just a few of the common species. Jamaica Bay's specialty is Curlew Sandpiper, a stray from the Old World that has been seen nearly annually.

**8** About 15 miles east of Jamaica Bay, take the Meadowbrook State Parkway south to **Jones Beach State Park,** one of the top sites on Long Island (actually on one of the barrier islands that parallel its southern coast). From fall through spring, follow Bay Parkway to the west end of the island. In fall—especially with a northwest wind, which pushes southbound migrants to the ocean's edge—the vegetation in this area can be alive with songbirds, often including western strays. Keep an eye out, too, for migrant raptors, including Merlin and Peregrine Falcon. Walk west along the beach, watching in winter for Northern Harrier, Snowy Owl, Horned Lark, the Ipswich race of Savannah Sparrow, and Snow Bunting. Check the jetty at the

Snow Buntings, Jones Beach State Park, Long Island

Fire Island National Seashore

end of the island for wintering Purple Sandpiper and scan the sea and inlet for seabirds.

Follow Ocean Parkway east about 15 miles and cross over to Fire Island and **Robert Moses State Park,** another excellent spot in migration. An annual hawk-watch here (*E from parking lot No. 5*) records good numbers of raptors, and here, as at Jones Beach, fall songbird migration can be exciting. Piping Plover and Least Tern, two species hurt by beach development and recreational use, nest along these barrier islands. In summer watch for Roseate Tern among flocks of the more common terns.

**9** At Long Island's eastern tip, where Block Island Sound meets the Atlantic Ocean, **Montauk Point** has long been a favorite—if often windy and chilly—spot from which to see waterbirds from fall through spring. Near the historic lighthouse, scan the waters and you may find hundreds of Red-throated and Common Loons; Northern Gannet; Common Eider; Oldsquaw; Surf, White-winged, and Black Scoters; Common Goldeneye; Red-breasted Merganser; and gulls of various kinds, to list only a sampling. Look for alcids (auks) such as Dovekie and Razorbill in the sea. Check fields, scrub, and dunes in nearby parklands for sparrows, Lapland Longspur, and Snow Bunting, and expect to see Northern Harrier and Rough-legged Hawk on the hunt, soaring and banking in the wind.

# NEW JERSEY

**10** To get right to the essential point: Fall migration at **Cape May** ranks with the most dramatic and rewarding birding adventures in the country. Credit goes, first of all, to geography. Situated at the end of a peninsula dividing Delaware Bay from the Atlantic Ocean, Cape May is home to seabirds or shorebirds throughout the year. In fall, southbound migrant songbirds following the coast (or pushed against it by westerly winds) arrive at the cape and face the challenge of flying at least 12 miles over water. Many stop to feed and rest before flying on—others, forced out to sea by north and west winds, fight their way back to land to regain their strength before continuing. In addition, tens of thousands of migrant hawks pass over the cape, their numbers concentrated by the funnel shape of the land.

All these birds, inevitably including rarities, attract top birders, who in turn use their expertise to find more rarities. Fall at Cape May now finds the woods and beaches full of binocular- and telescope-carrying people. Like a happy convention of migration-watchers, they leave few trees or fields or patches of sky unexamined and pass word rapidly of some outlandish discovery, perhaps a Calliope Hummingbird from the Pacific Northwest or a Swallow-tailed Kite from the Southeast or a Brown-chested Martin from South America. A major wave, or "fallout," of birds at Cape May is often dependent on the weather. In fall, the best wind is northwest, but anything between southwest and north-northeast can be good. In spring, the best flights occur with southwesterly wind and overcast conditions.

The logical place for a newcomer to begin exploration is the Northwood Center of **Cape May Bird Observatory,** where staffers are happy to give directions and advice, and where word of any rarities will be in the air. To get there,

- **Fall migration at Cape May**
- **Winter waterbirds at Barnegat Lighthouse State Park**
- **Year-round birding at Edwin B. Forsythe National Wildlife Refuge**

---

Information section p. 93

Birders at
Cape May Point

take the Garden State Parkway south to N.J. 109. At Perry Street drive west and continue on Sunset Boulevard, the main east-west road on the southern tip of the cape. From the stoplight at Broadway, drive west 1.7 miles to Lighthouse Avenue; turn south and take the second right onto East Lake Drive. Across from the observatory information center is **Lily Lake,** a popular birding spot. Returning to Lighthouse Avenue, drive south to **Cape May Point State Park,** where the observatory's hawk-watch is staffed from September through November. Usually 16 to 18 species of raptors are seen each fall, with peak numbers from late September to mid-October and the greatest diversity from late October to early November. On a good day with northwest winds, there can be huge numbers of Sharp-shinned Hawks, and often amazing flights of American Kestrel, Merlin, and Peregrine Falcon.

The beach at the state park is also a good place from which to scan for seabirds, and trails here—like anywhere on the lower cape with trees and shrubs—may have flocks of all sorts of vireos, thrushes, warblers, and other songbirds in fall.

Return to Sunset Boulevard and drive east almost a mile. The open area on the right, the Nature Conservancy's **Migratory Bird Refuge,** is another favorite birding spot, where Least Bittern, Virginia Rail, Piping Plover, and Least Tern nest. Wetlands attract waders and waterfowl, and beach access allows searching for shorebirds and seabirds. A bit farther east on Sunset Boulevard, take Bayshore Road north 1.2 miles to New England Road and follow it west to its end. **Higbee Beach Wildlife Management Area** here is Cape May's finest spot for migrant songbirds and hawks. Trails allow roaming throughout the area but for the best birding be sure to arrive here early, as on some days the show may pretty well be over by 9 a.m.

**11** New Jersey's second most famous birding site lies up the coast about 50 miles, just east of Oceanville off US 9: the **Brigantine Division** of the **Edwin B. Forsythe National Wildlife Refuge,** where an 8-mile wildlife drive circles two impoundments totaling 1,600 acres. Migrant shorebirds are the main attraction at Brigantine; they can be abundant in numbers and exciting in diversity both in spring and in late summer and fall, when 30 or more species might be found in the refuge's **West** and **East Pools** and in **Turtle Cove.** Uncommon to rare species such as Black-necked Stilt, Hudsonian and Marbled Godwits, Baird's and Curlew Sandpipers, and Ruff make occasional stops here.

Of course, all these wetlands attract wading birds and waterfowl: summer concentrations of herons, egrets, and ibises to Tundra Swan, Snow Goose, Brant (they rest on the bay but fly to the West Pool to drink fresh water), and more than 20 species of ducks from fall through spring (look for the rare Eurasian Wigeon in flocks of American Wigeon). Nesting birds include Osprey, Peregrine Falcon (reintroduced here), Gull-billed Tern, Black Skimmer, Fish Crow, Saltmarsh Sharp-tailed and Seaside Sparrows, and

Snow Geese, Edwin B. Forsythe National Wildlife Refuge, east of Oceanville

Boat-tailed Grackle. Winter sees many waterfowl leave when the water freezes, but Rough-legged Hawks and Short-eared Owls hunt over the fields.

**Barnegat Lighthouse State Park** is one of New Jersey's hot spots in the cold of winter. Reach it via N.J. 72 east from the Garden State Parkway to Ship Bottom and following Long Beach Boulevard/Central Avenue north; at Eighth Street in the town of Barnegat Light, swing left on Broadway. From the park or the long jetty that extends along **Barnegat Inlet,** scan for wintering birds including Red-throated and Common Loons; Double-crested and Great Cormorants; Common and King Eiders; Harlequin Duck; Oldsquaw; Surf, White-winged, and Black Scoters; and Black-legged Kittiwake (rare). Purple Sandpiper is usually present on jetty rocks in winter. In late fall and spring, look east across the Atlantic—you may find Northern Gannets fishing offshore.

**Northern Gannet**

With its pointed bill and tail and tapered body, the Northern Gannet seems as aerodynamic as a winged rocket ship as it flies over the ocean. Spotting a fish, it dives into the water with a spectacular impact from as high as 50 to 60 feet. From large nesting colonies in eastern Canada, gannets roam the East Coast from fall through spring, sometimes coming quite close to shore.

**12** Like Jamaica Bay Wildlife Refuge in New York (see p. 66), **Sandy Hook** is part of **Gateway National Recreation Area,** at the entrance to Lower New York Bay. A curving peninsula north of Highlands off N.J. 36, it's another good spot for wintering ducks and other waterbirds, and especially for spring and fall migrant songbirds, which rest and feed in any patch of trees or scrub. In addition, the narrowness of the spit here concentrates migrant raptors and can create a good hawk flight in spring and fall. Osprey, Piping Plover, and Least Tern are among the breeding birds.

As you enter the area, parking lots on the east offer views of the ocean, where some of the same sea ducks listed for Barnegat Lighthouse may be present in winter, and an east wind in spring or fall may bring Northern Gannet close in. Anywhere you find beach dunes, look for Snow Bunting and the Ipswich race of Savannah Sparrow in winter. Farther north, stop at the visitor center and walk west to **Spermaceti Cove** to check for waterbirds and (at low tide)

Belted Kingfisher, perched here, but often seen diving for fish

for shorebirds. A mile-long nature trail begins here. Ask staff members about summer programs, which often include bird walks. At parking lot L, check the woods to the north for migrant songbirds, visit the observation tower to scan **North Beach** for raptors and waterbirds, and walk the dune trail along **North Pond** for bitterns, waterfowl, rails, and passerines. **Horseshoe Cove** to the west is good for waterbirds, while the Boy Scout camp opposite the boardwalk is an excellent "migrant trap."

**13** The **Great Swamp National Wildlife Refuge** almost wasn't. Only earnest efforts by conservationists headed off a planned airport here. Today, the *who-cooks-for-you?* of Barred Owl and the *chur-lee* of Eastern Bluebird are heard instead of the whine of jet turbines. Located south of Morristown, just east of Basking Ridge (*take S. Maple Ave. to Lord Stirling Rd. and drive E*), the Great Swamp is a relict of a glacial lake formed after the last ice age. Its 7,425 acres of woods and wetlands offer an accessible spot for a good variety of breeders and migrants. Follow signs to the refuge

Great Swamp National Wildlife Refuge, south of Morristown

Wildlife Observation Center on Long Hill Road, where short trails and a boardwalk lead through forest and wet areas. Here Least Bittern, Great Blue and Green Herons, Wood Duck, Virginia Rail, Marsh Wren, Wood Thrush, Black-and-white Warbler, American Redstart, and Common Yellowthroat can be found in breeding season.

East of the road, the refuge wilderness area can be explored via nearly 8 miles of trails. Easier birding is available along Pleasant Plains Road to the west (*follow signs to refuge headquarters*), which is closed to through traffic and traverses open areas where Eastern Bluebird and Bobolink nest and through woods and second growth with breeding Wild Turkey, American Woodcock, Willow Flycatcher, White-eyed and Yellow-throated Vireos, Blue-winged and Yellow Warblers, and Baltimore Oriole.

**14** **Pequannock Watershed** (known to New Jersey birders as Clinton Road) is home to an excellent assemblage of nesting species in an area set aside to protect part of Newark's water supply. Before entry, you must obtain a permit; the office (973-697-2850) is reached via N.J. 23 just south of Newfoundland, then taking Echo Lake Road 1 mile north. After that preliminary, return north on N.J. 23 and turn right onto Clinton Road, less than a mile past Union Valley Road (County Road 513). Watch along the way over the next 7 miles or so for parking areas and trailheads, and visit as many different habitats as possible.

Moist wooded hillsides may have Worm-eating and Hooded Warblers, while second growth (especially power-line cuts) can host Golden-winged and Chestnut-sided Warblers. Listen for the scream of Red-shouldered Hawk or the whistle of Broad-winged Hawk. Wet areas near streams may host Acadian Flycatcher and both Northern and Louisiana Waterthrushes, while woodland hemlocks may have Blue-headed Vireo and Black-throated Green and Blackburnian Warblers. Clinton Road is excellent during winter finch invasion seasons.

**15** In northwestern New Jersey, **Delaware Water Gap National Recreation Area** makes a fine destination in winter, when numbers of Bald Eagles roost along the Delaware River, and also in breeding seasons. Stop at the Kittatinny Point Visitor Center (*Flatbrook/Millbrook exit from I-80. Weekends only in winter*) for a map, and sample the trails at the nearby **Dunnfield Creek Natural Area** before heading north on Old Mine Road, which parallels the river.

This road, one of the state's favorite birding routes, offers excellent possibilities over the next 12 miles. Some of the birds here are Pileated Woodpecker; Acadian and Least Flycatchers; Yellow-throated, Blue-headed, and Warbling Vireos; Cliff Swallow; Brown Creeper; Veery; Wood Thrush; Blue-winged, Chestnut-sided, Black-throated Green, Blackburnian, Pine, Cerulean, Worm-eating, and Hooded Warblers; Northern Parula; American Redstart; and Louisiana Waterthrush. To see a good selection, check as many different habitats as possible: shady ravines, tall riverside trees, conifers, hardwoods, and scrubby second growth. Stop along the road and at as many parking lots and picnic spots as you can. The recreation area encompasses the Pennsylvania side of the Delaware River, too (see p. 80).

# PENNSYLVANIA

**16** Good birding spots don't have to be far from civilization: Just ask people enjoying a warbler "fallout" in New York City's Central Park or Philadelphians walking the trails at **John Heinz National Wildlife Refuge** at **Tinicum,** just a mile north of the city's international airport. Tinicum (as most birders call it) attracts waders, waterfowl, shorebirds, and a good variety of other species to its wetlands and fields. From the visitor station (*from jct. of Pa. 291 and Island Ave., drive N on Island Ave. to Bartram Ave. Turn W on 84th St. and go N to Lindbergh Blvd.*), several miles of trails branch out alongside Darby Creek and adjacent marshes and impoundments.

In late summer, Great Blue and Green Herons, Great and Snowy Egrets, and Black-crowned Night-Heron feed in the wetlands, sometimes joined by Little Blue and Tricolored (rare) Herons, Yellow-crowned Night-Heron, and Glossy Ibis. Least Bittern, Common Moorhen, Marsh Wren, and Swamp Sparrow nest in these marshes, along with a selection of dabbling ducks, and in winter Northern Harrier hunts the open spaces along with an occasional Short-eared Owl.

When water levels are right in the tidal marshes and managed impoundments, you may find such common migrant shorebird species as Black-bellied Plover; Greater and Lesser Yellowlegs; and Semipalmated, Least, and Pectoral Sandpipers. As fall arrives, so do flocks of geese and ducks—mostly dabblers such as Northern Shoveler, Northern Pintail, and Green-winged Teal, with an assortment of divers intermixed.

**17** In Philadelphia's western suburbs, southwest of Newtown Square, **Ridley Creek State Park** is a favorite spot to see migrant and nesting songbirds. Pick up a map

American
Goldfinches in
their summer
plumage

at the park office south of Gradyville Road and head to the
**Multi-Use Trail** (the old Sycamore Mills Road) along the
creek. Nesting birds in the area include Yellow-billed
Cuckoo; Acadian Flycatcher; White-eyed and Yellow-
throated Vireos; Carolina Chickadee; Veery; Wood Thrush;
Blue-winged, Chestnut-sided, Yellow-throated, Prairie,
Cerulean, and Kentucky Warblers; Northern Parula; American Redstart; and Louisiana Waterthrush. Trails in the
park connect with the adjacent **Tyler Arboretum**, worth
checking in migration. Pine Warbler nests in the pinetum
here, where crossbills sometimes show up in November.

**18** Just south of Kleinfeltersville, **Middle Creek Wildlife
Management Area** ranks as one of the state's best
places to see concentrations of migrant Snow Geese and
Tundra Swans, with the possibility of finding Greater White-
fronted (rare) and Ross's Geese (seen annually in early
spring). Barnacle Goose, a stray from Greenland, has
recently appeared here, though the "wildness" of the birds
seen has been subject to debate. Late winter is the best time
for the swans, with good numbers of ducks present from fall
through spring. Though waterfowl are Middle Creek's claim
to fame, its nesting birds include Black-crowned Night-
Heron, Ruffed Grouse, Willow Flycatcher, Grasshopper

Fall at Hawk
Mountain Sanctuary,
north of Reading

Sparrow, and Bobolink. Shorebirds arrive in fair numbers
in migration with low water levels.

**19** Waterbirds make an impressive showing at **Lake
Ontelaunee,** just north of Reading. At the dam area
on Pa. 73, from fall through spring look for thousands of
Snow Geese, as well as loons, grebes, ducks, and gulls—a
long list of potential species indeed. Red-throated Loon;
Tundra Swan; Oldsquaw; Surf, White-winged, and Black
Scoters; Osprey; Bald Eagle; and Iceland and Lesser Black-
backed Gulls are just a few of the notable birds seen at times
from spring through fall. When the water is low, mudflats
on the upper part of the lake attract interesting waders and
shorebirds. To reach one viewpoint, take Maiden Creek
Road north from Pa. 73 along the east side of the lake. After
about 2.5 miles, turn left on Water Street to the lake.

**20** One of the greatest landmarks of the American conservation movement can be found on Kittatinny
Ridge about 25 miles north of Reading. Where gunners
once stood and killed migrating raptors by the thousands,
**Hawk Mountain Sanctuary** now attracts tens of thousands

of visitors each fall to experience the wondrous phenomenon of eagles, hawks, and falcons streaming along this Appalachian crest. Established in 1934 as the world's first refuge for birds of prey, Hawk Mountain endures as a birding pilgrimage site. While other locations such as Cape May, New Jersey (see p. 69), and Kiptopeke State Park, Virginia (see p. 103), may see more raptors, the camaraderie and history of Hawk Mountain make it a very special place.

Watchers begin gathering on the rocky outcrops of the sanctuary's **North Lookout** as early as mid-August, looking for southbound Osprey, Bald Eagle, and American Kestrel. In mid-September, thousands of Broad-winged Hawks pass by, and with October come thousands of Sharp-shinned and Red-tailed Hawks. Falcons are not as common here as along the Atlantic coast, but Northern Goshawk (most likely in November) and Golden Eagle (peak in early November) are Hawk Mountain specialties. Hundreds of Turkey Vulture, Northern Harrier, Cooper's and Red-shouldered Hawks, and American Kestrel are seen annually, with lesser numbers of Black Vulture, Merlin, and Peregrine Falcon. Weather is the vital factor in hawk flights: Try to be at Hawk Mountain in the days immediately after a cold front passes, with northwest winds following. To reach the sanctuary, take Pa. 61 from I-78, drive north about 7 miles to Drehersville, and take Hawk Mountain Road east.

**21** In the northeast, **Delaware Water Gap National Recreation Area** protects 40 often beautiful miles of the Delaware River. Named for the spot where the stream has eroded its way through Kittatinny Ridge, this long, narrow park includes areas in both Pennsylvania and New Jersey (see p. 75). It's famed for winter gatherings of Bald Eagles along the river, where a determined eagle seeker may find literally dozens of these magnificent birds perched along the shoreline in January. The parking lot at the Dingmans Ferry bridge is one of several good eagle lookout points. Watch, too, for waterfowl along the river. Common Merganser nests in the area and may be seen throughout the year.

For land birds, walk some of the 12 miles of trails at the **Pocono Environmental Education Center,** about 5 miles south of Dingmans Ferry. Both the **Scenic Gorge** and **Tumbling Waters Trails** pass through lovely ravines where hemlocks tower overhead and Acadian Flycatcher, Blue-headed Vireo, Red-breasted Nuthatch, and Blackburnian Warbler nest. In second-growth areas, look for both Blue-winged and Golden-winged Warblers—here, as in many other places, the latter is being pushed out of its nesting areas while the former expands its range. The center offers many special programs on birds and birding, from warbler weekends to eagle tours to hawk-watches. Also sample the trails near the recreation area's visitor center (*closed Nov.– April*) at Dingmans Falls, just west of Dingmans Ferry.

**22** The wooded hills and steep valleys of north-central Pennsylvania are home to a set of northern-affinity species seldom or never found as breeders in the rest of the state. A number of them are among the breeding birds of **Wyoming State Forest,** about 20 miles northeast of Williamsport. Fine northern hardwood-hemlock forest is home to Northern Goshawk; Northern Saw-whet Owl; Yellow-bellied Sapsucker; Alder (in shrubby wetlands) and Least Flycatchers; Blue-headed Vireo; Common Raven;

Winter Wren; Hermit Thrush; Magnolia, Black-throated Blue, Black-throated Green, Blackburnian, Mourning (in thickets in clear-cut areas) and Canada Warblers; Northern Waterthrush; White-throated Sparrow; Dark-eyed Junco; and Purple Finch. Unpaved roads throughout the forest provide access to good habitat. Stop at forest headquarters (*on Pa. 87*) for a map, essential for getting the most from your visit. To the east, Dry Run and Ogdonia Roads are easy places to begin exploring. Drive to the overlook at the end of Slab Run Road, north of headquarters via Mill Creek and Camels Roads, where road birding is good and a number of trails loop through woods and wetlands. The **Loyalsock Trail** meanders through the forest, intersecting roads often and allowing hikes of varying lengths.

Delaware Water Gap National Recreation Area, along the Pennsylvania–New Jersey border

**23** When it comes to variety and rarity, Pennsylvania's birdiest place is a 7-mile-long spit of land that extends into Lake Erie from the city of Erie. Though it's made of sand, **Presque Isle State Park** seems to have magnetic qualities for migrant birds, both regularly occurring eastern species and long-distance wanderers. More than 320 species have been found in this relatively minuscule sliver of beach, ponds, marsh, and woods. Though many records are of once-in-a-lifetime vagrants, the odds are better here than anywhere else in the state that something unusual will turn up.

In spring, northbound migrant songbirds following the Lake Erie shoreline move out onto the peninsula here and find themselves at the end of a cul-de-sac, nearly encircled by water. At the peak of migration, in mid-May, it's sometimes possible to see two dozen or more species of warblers while strolling only a few hundred yards.

In early spring, more than 25 species of waterfowl may occur in the lake, bay, or interior ponds of Presque Isle. Shorebirds appear along the beaches in spring and fall, and winter brings flocks of more common waterfowl species. A lucky visitor may sight such species as King Eider, Harlequin Duck, Purple Sandpiper, jaegers, Iceland or Glaucous Gulls, Snowy Owl, Northern Shrike, or Snow Bunting. While Presque Isle is home to some interesting nesting birds, it's also a very popular summer playground, and most birders seeking peace visit here from fall through spring.

Birding can begin immediately upon arrival, with an excellent opportunity to view Presque Isle Bay from the three parking lots on the right. A mile from the entrance (just past the third lot), an observation deck overlooks one of the peninsula's marshes, a good place for waterfowl and songbirds. Continue to West Fisher Drive and turn east—a keen eye along this stretch can spot wonderful nesting and migrant birds. At the end of this dead-end road, look for ducks in the marina to the left and Presque Isle Bay to the right. **Sunset Point** is the best place from which to scan the lake for passing migrant waterfowl. **Gull Point,** to the east, is partially closed to entry April through November, but a platform allows observation of shorebirds, gulls, terns, and anything else in the area. In winter, it's a good place to look for Snowy Owl, Horned Lark, and Snow Bunting.

Red-headed Woodpecker can be found along the **Sidewalk Trail,** and Prothonotary Warbler has nested in both natural and man-made cavities. To the south, the trees at **Frys Landing** can be excellent for warblers and other songbirds in spring.

# DELAWARE

The marshy convergence of water and land along the Delaware Bay shoreline, long resistant to human encroachment, encompasses some of the Atlantic coast's finest birding sites. Waterbirds of one sort or another, from loons to terns, are present throughout the year. This is one of the country's best places to find Curlew Sandpiper, a rare wanderer from breeding grounds in Siberia, and Ruff, another sandpiper that nests in Scandinavia and northern Asia. Even if no rarities are present, though, waders, massed shorebirds, or waterfowl will reward a visit.

● Concentrations of shorebirds along Delaware Bay

● Spring migration at White Clay Creek State Park

Information section p. 95

**24** **Bombay Hook National Wildlife Refuge** (*entrance off Del. 9, 2 miles N of Leipsic*) protects some 13,000 acres of tidal salt marsh, much of which is inaccessible to the casual visitor. A 12-mile auto tour route leads to impoundments managed for waterfowl, shorebirds, and other wildlife, and to walking trails and observation towers. A leisurely trip along the roads could quite profitably take several hours, especially in migration, when throngs of

Ruddy Turnstones, Red Knots, Sanderlings, and Laughing Gull, Delaware Bay

Geese in flight,
Bombay Hook
National Wildlife
Refuge, near Leipsic

shorebirds await study through a spotting scope. Peak shorebirding is in May and again from mid-July to late September. Common birds such as Black-bellied and Semipalmated Plovers, Greater and Lesser Yellowlegs, Ruddy Turnstone, Red Knot, Semipalmated Sandpiper, Dunlin, and Short-billed Dowitcher will be accompanied by many other species in the impoundments and marsh. In fall when adults and juveniles in their varying plumages are present, your field guide may get a real workout. Here's where one of the specialized guides concentrating on shorebird identification is invaluable.

Nesting birds at Bombay Hook include both bitterns; Bald Eagle; Clapper, King (check the **Boardwalk Trail**), and Virginia Rails; Black-necked Stilt; Willet; Forster's Tern; Acadian and Willow Flycatchers; Sedge (rare) and Marsh Wrens; and Saltmarsh Sharp-tailed Sparrow. In summer Great and Snowy Egrets, Great Blue and Little Blue Herons, Blacked-crowned Night-Heron, and Glossy Ibis roost in wetlands (especially **Bear Swamp**), and in fall huge numbers of Snow Geese, along with a long list of ducks, take up winter residence.

**25** South along the coast are two other wildlife areas also known for extraordinary shorebird viewing. From Bombay Hook, drive south 10 miles on Del. 9 to Little Creek and turn east on County Road 89 (Port Mahon Road). The tiny Black Rail, one of America's most sought-after and elusive birds, calls in the marshes along this road at night in spring. In about a mile, turn into the gravel lot on the right and scan the impoundment, part of **Little Creek Wildlife Management Area,** for shorebirds in spring and fall and waterfowl from fall through spring. Black-necked Stilt usually nests here, and the very rare Ruff has appeared at times. Continue east to the bay at **Port Mahon,** another excellent shorebird site in migration. Look for Royal Tern here in summer among the Caspian, Common, Forster's, and Least Terns. Black Tern and Black Skimmer can be found, too. In addition, the marsh vegetation just before you reach the bay is good for nesting Saltmarsh Sharp-tailed Sparrow, Nelson's Sharp-tailed Sparrow in fall, and Seaside Sparrow all year.

Return to Del. 9 and drive south just over a mile to the main entrance. Almost 3 miles in, an observation platform offers views of the wetland, host to summer waders and, from fall through spring, flocks of waterfowl; walk the dike for better views.

## Fuel for Flight

The fate of the hundreds of thousands of shorebirds that stop on the shores of Delaware Bay in northward migration is tied in large part to the horseshoe crab, the spiny "living fossil" arthropod whose females lay billions of eggs along the coast each spring. Ruddy Turnstone, Red Knot, Sanderling, and Semipalmated Sandpiper are the most common birds that use these eggs as essential fuel for their flight to Arctic breeding grounds. Many Red Knots, for example, arrive here after flying nonstop from Brazil, and so must replenish their energy reserves quickly and efficiently. In recent years shorebird numbers have declined; though several factors may be involved, commercial harvest of horseshoe crabs has come under serious criticism, and new laws have been proposed to limit the take.

**26** Back on Del. 9, drive south about 3.5 miles to Kitts Hummock Road on the east, just before intersecting US 113. Two miles east is the entrance to the **Ted Harvey Conservation Area** and more waterbird viewing. Some of the roads in this tract may be gated, but you can drive or walk to the various parking lots and viewing areas, especially the road leading to Delaware Bay, where migrant shorebirds can be diverse and abundant. White-winged Tern, another stray from the Old World, has appeared here and at Little Creek a few times in July and August, attracting eager listers from all over the country.

**27** Just east of Lewes, **Cape Henlopen State Park** occupies a thin spit of land pointing north where Delaware Bay meets the Atlantic Ocean. Nearly surrounded by water, this strategic location is a superb place from which to search ocean and bay for waterbirds. In addition, many of the raptors that leave Cape May, New Jersey, on their southbound migration in fall come ashore here. On certain days with northwest winds, Sharp-shinned Hawk, Merlin, Peregrine Falcon, and other species appear in good numbers. Spring, too, can bring good hawk-watching, especially for falcons.

As you enter the park, turn south past the campground to reach **Herring Point Overlook,** where from fall through spring it's often productive to scan the Atlantic. Seabird-watching can sometimes bring long periods of inactivity, but with an east wind pushing birds toward shore you may spot Red-throated and Common Loons, Northern Gannet, jaegers, and gulls. Sea ducks here can include Greater Scaup, Common Eider, Oldsquaw, and all three scoters. Back on the main park road to the cape, turn north to reach the fishing pier and a chance to search the bay and shore for winter loons, Great and Double-crested Cormorants, Brant, ducks, and gulls. Look for nesting Osprey and Least Tern in summer, and check the park's pinewoods for Brown-headed Nuthatch and Pine Warbler.

**28** Two spots in northern Delaware provide terrific birding for songbirds in spring migration, as well as interesting nesting species. In Newark, take Del. 896 north 3 miles to **White Clay Creek State Park,** where trails lead through woodland alive with flycatchers, vireos, thrushes, and warblers from mid-April into June. Continue east on Hopkins Road and north on Creek Road to the nature center, where you can pick up a bird list and maps showing more than 20 miles of trails. From this point, cars are not allowed on Creek Road, and walking it north can be productive.

Here and elsewhere in the park you might find nesting Wood Duck; Barred Owl; Acadian Flycatchers; White-eyed, Yellow-throated, and Warbling Vireos; Veery; Blue-winged,

Autumn at
Brandywine Creek
State Park, north
of Wilmington

Yellow, Cerulean (this park is Delaware's only breeding site), Kentucky, and Hooded Warblers; Northern Parula; and sometimes Black-and-white Warbler. Investigate not only the woods but also second-growth areas and fields where Prairie Warbler and Grasshopper Sparrow nest. Cerulean Warbler, the park's most notable nester, can be found reliably by returning south on Creek Road to the first bridge past Hopkins Road. Check the trees around the bridge and walk part of the blue-blazed trail.

North of Wilmington, **Brandywine Creek State Park** offers more great birding in spring migration. In addition, a marsh here is home to wetland species including Great Blue and Green Herons and Virginia Rail, which nests. From the intersection of Del. 100 and Del. 92, go east a short distance on Adams Dam Road and turn north into the park. Walk trails, especially those through the old-growth woods behind the visitor center and along the creek. A side road east of the main entrance leads to a hawk-watch spot where birders scan for migrant raptors in fall.

# MARYLAND

**29** From fall through spring, the area around the seaside town of **Ocean City** (*Visitor Information 410-213-0552 or 800-626-2326*) makes an excellent birding destination, primarily for seabirds and shorebirds, but including fall land birds, raptors, and waterfowl. As you approach along US 50 from the west, turn north on Md. 589 and, in about 0.5 mile, west on Griffin Road. Check the ponds on the south here for migrant and wintering waterfowl. Back on US 50, turn north on Golf Course Road, 0.3 mile east of the Md. 611 intersection, and scan the pond on the west for Black-crowned Night-Heron and other waders and waterfowl including wintering Tundra Swan and Canvasback.

After crossing the bridge to Ocean City, turn south on Philadelphia Avenue and drive to the jetty protecting the inlet here. Checking the surrounding waters from fall through spring will turn up loons, grebes, ducks (Common and King Eiders and Harlequin Duck, though rare, are seen most winters, and all three scoters are likely), and gulls. Purple Sandpiper winters on the rocks. East winds may bring Northern Gannet close to shore, or in May, a lucky sighting of Sooty Shearwater or Wilson's Storm-Petrel. Then head back north to Fourth Street, turn west, drive to the bay, and scan the mudflats and islands for Brown Pelican, shorebirds, waders, gulls, and terns. American Oystercatcher; Royal, Common, and Least Terns; and Black Skimmer are among the many possibilities.

**30** Return to the mainland and take Md. 611 south toward **Assateague Island National Seashore** and **Assateague State Park.** Stop at the Barrier Island Visitor Center just before the causeway over Sinepuxent Bay for a map, and park at the pedestrian bridge, from which you can scan the bay. On the island, beachside parking lots provide access across the dunes to lookout points for searching for seabirds. In the national seashore, turn west toward the Bayside camping area and walk the **Life of the Marsh Nature Trail.** In fall, especially after a cold front has passed, migrant songbirds can be abundant in trees and shrubs here and around the campground. A bit farther south, the **Life of the Forest Nature Trail** is also worth checking in migra-

American Wigeon, once called "baldpate" for its white crown

tion. Fall can also bring southbound hawks along the shore, with Peregrine Falcon occurring regularly from mid-September through October. (See p. 101 for Chincoteague National Wildlife Refuge on the southern part of Assateague Island.)

**31** A very different sort of environment attracts birders in spring to **Great Cypress Swamp** and its surroundings, about 15 miles northwest of Ocean City. To reach it, take Md. 610 north from US 50 a bit more than a mile and turn northwest on Sheppards Crossing Road. Follow this road about 4 miles to its crossing of the Pocomoke River. After looking here, retrace your route 0.5 mile and turn north on Nelson Road, driving 0.3 mile to Swamp Road, where you should turn east on Blueberry Road, taking that north to Ebenezer Road and returning east on it to Md. 610. Your reward for this complicated route will be roadside birding through the Pocomoke Swamp, where spring migrants can be abundant and exciting, and nesting birds

Roosting waterfowl at Blackwater National Wildlife Refuge, south of Cambridge

include Barred Owl; Pileated Woodpecker; White-eyed and Yellow-throated Vireos; Wood Thrush; Yellow-throated, Prothonotary, Worm-eating, and Hooded Warblers; Northern Parula; and American Redstart. The rarity of the area is Swainson's Warbler, found here irregularly in breeding season, though it has become even scarcer in recent years.

**32** While Pocomoke Swamp is usually visited only in spring and early summer, **Blackwater National Wildlife Refuge** south of Cambridge *(take Md. 16 to Md. 335 and turn E on Key Wallace Dr.)* offers fine birding all year. Look for wintering waterfowl, herons and egrets from spring through fall, and migrant shorebirds. Nesting species include Osprey, Bald Eagle (common year-round, with as many as 200 birds present in winter), Chuck-will's-widow, Prothonotary Warbler, Summer Tanager, Grasshopper and Saltmarsh Sharp-tailed Sparrows, and Blue Grosbeak. Refuge woodlands include both deciduous trees and loblolly pines. Look in the latter for Brown-headed Nuthatch and Pine Warbler and for the endangered Delmarva fox squirrel.

The refuge wildlife drive *(fee)* passes several freshwater impoundments and crosses woodlands and an extensive

area of brackish marsh beside the tidal Blackwater River. Along the way, the 0.3-mile **Marsh Edge Trail** offers the chance to see waders and waterfowl, nesting Osprey and Bald Eagle, and pinewoods birds. A nearby observation point provides another view of open water. Farther along, in the marshes, look for American and Least Bitterns (both uncommon), herons and egrets, rails, wintering waterfowl, and migrant shorebirds. Snow and Canada Geese and Tundra Swan are common, as are many species of ducks. Marsh Wren nests in the bulrush. Check tall, isolated loblolly pines for roosting Bald Eagle, and in winter watch for Northern Harrier, Rough-legged Hawk, and Short-eared Owl (at dusk) over fields.

**33** About 10 miles above the Susquehanna River's mouth at Chesapeake Bay, **Conowingo Dam** is renowned for immense concentrations of wintering gulls on the tailwater area below, and for large numbers of Bald Eagles in an easily accessible setting. From US 1 just west of the river, take Shuresville Road south. In 0.6 mile, turn east on Shures Landing Road and drive to the river. Park in the power plant parking lot and scan from just below the dam. While Bald Eagles are present all year, in winter 40 or more may be present along the river here. An occasional Golden Eagle makes an appearance, so don't dismiss all brownish birds as immature Balds. From spring through fall, look for Osprey fishing on the river or perched nearby.

Thousands of Ring-billed Gulls congregate below the dam beginning in late fall, when hundreds (and sometimes thousands, depending on the weather) of Bonaparte's and Herring Gulls will be present as well, along with Great Black-backed. Mixed in among this wheeling and calling multitude will be other uncommon to rare species, possibly including Black-headed, Iceland, Lesser Black-backed, and Glaucous. In late summer and fall, look here for shorebirds, and for terns in migration.

**34** Out where Maryland's western extension rises with the Appalachian Mountains, **Herrington Manor State Park** and nearby **Swallow Falls State Park** are home to an assortment of highland breeding birds, as well as to beautiful scenery of woodland and rugged gorges. Just northwest of Oakland, the parks' mixed coniferous-deciduous woods have nesting Ruffed Grouse, Black-billed Cuckoo; Blue-headed Vireo; Golden-crowned Kinglet; Magnolia, Black-throated Green, Blackburnian, and Canada Warblers; Northern Waterthrush; and Rose-breasted Grosbeak. Herrington Manor has more open habitats where Alder Flycatcher and Golden-winged Warbler nest, while Swallow Falls might be more reliable for Veery and Hermit Thrush. Maple Glade Road runs from Swallow Falls to Cranesville Road, which leads into West Virginia and Cranesville Swamp Nature Preserve (see p. 300), another excellent birding site less than 30 minutes away.

## Rock Creek Park

Birders in the nation's capital who enjoy spring migration in **Rock Creek Park** are following in a distinguished tradition: That great conservationist and sportsman Teddy Roosevelt liked to watch birds here, and, so the story goes, once arrived late at a Cabinet meeting only to announce excitedly that he had just seen a Chestnut-sided Warbler. That's just one of the 25 or more species of warblers, not to mention cuckoos, flycatchers, vireos, wrens, thrushes, tanagers, and sparrows, that might be seen in May in this 1,754-acre forested park, where tulip trees, white oaks, sycamores, black gums, and beech trees create a long green oasis in the city. Stop at the nature center on Glover Road just south of Military Road, and then walk the trails that lead south and east to Rock Creek. Though migration is the best time to visit, the lush woodland is home to typical nesting birds of eastern deciduous forest including Broad-winged Hawk, Yellow-billed Cuckoo, and Barred Owl.

# Mid-Atlantic
## Information

**?** Visitor Center/Information   **⑤** Fee Charged   **🍴** Food

**🚻** Rest Rooms   **🚶** Nature Trails   **🚗** Driving Tours   **♿** Wheelchair Accessible

*Be advised that facilities may be seasonal and limited. We suggest calling or writing ahead for specific information. Note that addresses may be for administrative offices; see text or call for directions to sites.*

### Rare Bird Alerts

New York:
Albany *518-439-8080*
Buffalo *716-896-1271*
Ithaca *607-254-2429*
Lower Hudson Valley
  *914-666-6614*
New York City
  *212-979-3070*
Rochester *716-425-4630*
Syracuse *315-668-8000*

New Jersey:
Statewide *908-766-2661*
Cape May *609-861-0466*

Pennsylvania:
Allentown *610-252-3455*
Central area *717-255-1212*
  *ext. 5761*
Philadelphia *215-567-2473*
Reading *610-376-6000*
  *ext. 2473*
Schuykill County
  *717-622-6013*
Western *412-963-0560*
Wilkes-Barre
  *717-825-2473*

Delaware:
Statewide *302-658-2747*

Maryland:
Statewide *301-652-1088*
Baltimore *410-467-0653*

District of Columbia:
  *301-652-1088*

## NEW YORK

### Fort Niagara State Park
*(Page 61)*
1 Maintenance Avenue
Youngstown, NY 14174
*716-745-7273*

**?** **⑤** **🍴** **🚻** **♿**

### Braddock Bay Fish and Wildlife Management Area *(Page 62)*
6274 East Avon-Lima Road
Avon, NY 14414
*716-948-5182*

**🚻** **🚶** **♿**

### Derby Hill Bird Observatory *(Page 63)*
36 Grand View Avenue
Mexico, NY 13114
*315-963-8291*

**?** **🍴** **🚻** **🚶** **♿**

### Montezuma National Wildlife Refuge *(Page 63)*
3395 US 20/N.Y. 5
Seneca Falls, NY 13148
*315-568-5987*

**?** **🚻** **🚶** **🚗** **♿**

### Jamaica Bay Wildlife Refuge *(Page 66)*
Gateway National
  Recreation Area
Floyd Bennett Field,
  Building 69
Brooklyn, NY 11234
*718-318-4340*

**?** **🚻** **🚶**

*Free permit required and available at visitor center*

### Jones Beach State Park
*(Page 67)*
P.O. Box 1000
Wantagh, NY 11793
*516-785-1600*

**?** **⑤** **🍴** **🚻** **♿**

### Robert Moses State Park *(Page 68)*
P.O. Box 247
Babylon, NY 11702
*516-669-0470*

**?** **⑤** **🍴** **🚻** **♿**

## NEW JERSEY

### Cape May Bird Observatory *(Page 69)*
P.O. Box 3
Cape May Point, NJ 08212
*609-884-2736*

**?**

**Cape May Point State Park** *(Page 70)*
Lighthouse Avenue
Cape May Point, NJ 08204
*609-884-2159*

🚻♿

**Higbee Beach Wildlife Management Area**
*(Page 70)*
2201 County Road 631
Woodbine, NJ 08270
*609-292-9400*

🚶

**Brigantine Division, Edwin B. Forsythe National Wildlife Refuge**
*(Page 71)*
Great Creek Road
Oceanville, NJ 08231
*609-652-1665*

🚻♿

**Barnegat Lighthouse State Park** *(Page 72)*
P.O. Box 167
Barnegat Light, NJ 08006
*609-494-2016*

♿

*Open Nov.–April*

**Sandy Hook** *(Page 72)*
Gateway National
   Recreation Area
P.O. Box 530
Fort Hancock, NJ 07732
*732-872-5970*

🚻♿

**Great Swamp National Wildlife Refuge** *(Page 73)*
152 Pleasant Plains Road
Basking Ridge, NJ 07920
*973-425-1222*

🚻♿

**Pequannock Watershed**
*(Page 74)*
New Jersey Audubon
   Society
P.O. Box 26
Tennent, NJ 07763
*732-780-7007*

🚶

*Also known as Clinton Road; permit required*

**Delaware Water Gap National Recreation Area** *(Page 75)*
River Road
Bushkill, PA 18324
*717-588-2451*

🚻♿

## PENNSYLVANIA

**John Heinz National Wildlife Refuge** *(Page 76)*
2 International Plaza,
   Suite 104
Philadelphia, PA 19113
*610-521-0662*

🚻

**Ridley Creek State Park**
*(Page 76)*
Sycamore Mills Road
Media, PA 19063
*610-892-3900*

🚻♿

**Tyler Arboretum**
*(Page 77)*
515 Painter Road
Media, PA 19063
*610-566-9134*

🚻♿

**Middle Creek Wildlife Management Area**
*(Page 77)*
Hopeland Road
Kleinfeltersville, PA 17039
*717-733-1512*

🚻♿

*Closed late Nov.–Jan.*

**Hawk Mountain Sanctuary** *(Page 78)*
1700 Hawk Mountain Road
Kempton, PA 19529
*610-756-6000*

🚻♿

**Delaware Water Gap National Recreation Area** *(Page 80)*
River Road
Bushkill, PA 18324
*717-588-2451*

🚻♿

**Pocono Environmental Education Center**
*(Page 80)*
Rural Route 2, Box 1010
Dingmans Ferry, PA 18328
*717-828-2319*

🚻

*Visitor center open May–Oct.*

**Wyoming State Forest**
*(Page 80)*
Rural Route 2, Box 47
Arbutus Park Road
Bloomsburg, PA 17815
*717-387-4255*

🚻

**Presque Isle State Park**
*(Page 81)*
P.O. Box 8510
Erie, PA 16505
*814-833-0351*

---

## DELAWARE

**Bombay Hook National Wildlife Refuge** *(Page 83)*
2591 Whitehall Neck Road
Smyrna, DE 19977
*302-653-6872*

**Little Creek Wildlife Management Area**
*(Page 85)*
89 Kings Highway
Dover, DE 19901
*302-739-5297*

**Ted Harvey Conservation Area** *(Page 85)*
2016 Kitts Hummock Road
Dover, DE 19901
*302-284-4795*

**Cape Henlopen State Park** *(Page 86)*
42 Cape Henlopen Drive
Lewes, DE 19958
*302-645-8983*

**White Clay Creek State Park** *(Page 86)*
425 Wedgewood Road
Newark, DE 19711
*302-368-6900*

**Brandywine Creek State Park** *(Page 87)*
P.O. Box 3782
Wilmington, DE 19807
*302-655-5740*

---

## MARYLAND

**Assateague Island National Seashore**
*(Page 89)*
7206 National
 Seashore Lane
Berlin, MD 21811
*410-641-1441*

**Assateague State Park** *(Page 89)*
7307 Stephen Decatur
 Highway
Berlin, MD 21811
*410-641-2120*

**Great Cypress Swamp**
*(Page 89)*
Delaware Wild Lands, Inc.
P.O. Box 505
Odessa, DE 19730
*302-378-2736*

*Call or write ahead to arrange on-site visits; otherwise bird from road.*

**Blackwater National Wildlife Refuge** *(Page 90)*
2145 Key Wallace Drive
Cambridge, MD 21613
*410-228-2692*

*Fee for wildlife drive*

**Herrington Manor State Park** *(Page 92)*
222 Herrington Lane
Oakland, MD 21550
*301-334-9180*

**Swallow Falls State Park** *(Page 92)*
222 Herrington Lane
Oakland, MD 21550
*301-334-9180*

---

## DISTRICT OF COLUMBIA

**Rock Creek Park**
*(Page 92)*
5200 Glover Road NW
Washington, DC 20007
*202-426-6828*

# South Atlantic

The natural world seems especially near on the Atlantic coastal islands, out on the sunrise frontier of America. Perhaps it's the elemental nature of the landscape—sea, sky, sun, wind, sand—or our awareness, conscious or not, that these are, by earth's measuring, fragile and transient places. But here our senses seem keener, the environment more immediate. The fecund smell of a salt marsh, the raucous cries of gulls, the stirring sight of a flock of Dunlins whirling in unison as they come to rest on a beach—we experience these and realize instinctively that we are witness to earth's grand and endless cycle of renewal.

If we look more closely we may see a pale little Piping Plover running along the sand, or a secretive Virginia Rail

*Preceding pages:*
Great Blue Heron,
Cape Charles,
Virginia
*Above:* Peregrine
Falcon
*Below:* Terns,
North Carolina's
Outer Banks

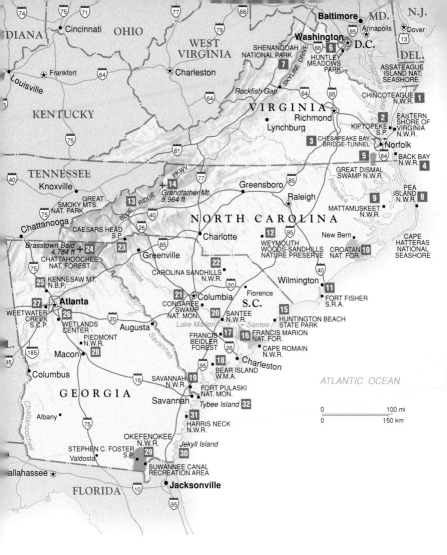

materializing in the marsh grass, or a fierce Merlin skimming over the dunes. Places like Assateague Island and Cape Hatteras, despite their great popularity among all sorts of recreationists, thankfully still offer the opportunity for solitary observation and contemplation of these and many other species.

This southern coast region brings birders some spectacular sights, including the fall hawk migration at Kiptopeke State Park and the gathering of thousands of Tundra Swans at Mattamuskeet National Wildlife Refuge. There will be more subtle encounters too, from a Black-throated Blue Warbler singing in a dark Appalachian hemlock forest to a Least Bittern picking its way through the cattails. Nesting birds here include southern Purple Gallinule and Painted Bunting and northern Red-breasted Nuthatch and Dark-eyed Junco. Habitats range from ocean beach to the highest mountain east of the Mississippi River. In

Band-rumped
Storm-Petrel

## Special Birds of the South Atlantic

| | | |
|---|---|---|
| Band-rumped Storm-Petrel | Wilson's Plover | Brown-headed Nuthatch |
| White-tailed Tropicbird | Purple Sandpiper | Swainson's Warbler |
| White Ibis | Royal Tern | Bachman's Sparrow |
| Wood Stork | Sandwich Tern | Nelson's Sharp-tailed Sparrow |
| Black-capped Petrel | Bridled Tern | Saltmarsh Sharp-tailed Sparrow |
| Cory's Shearwater | Black Skimmer | |
| Audubon's Shearwater | Swallow-tailed Kite | Seaside Sparrow |
| | Mississippi Kite | Painted Bunting |
| | Black Rail | |
| | Purple Gallinule | Common Ground-Dove |
| | | Red-cockaded Woodpecker |

between lie brackish estuaries, bottomland hardwood swamps, pine forests, the unique Sandhills ecosystem, lakes and ponds, and a correspondingly wide range of birds for us to enjoy.

Every season in the South Atlantic area has its own birding highlights. Spring sees waves of beautiful warblers heading up the Appalachian Mountains, a parade of color and movement through the treetops. From coastal lookouts, seabird migration can provide exciting viewing. In summer, heronries are full of noisy life, mountain breeders are singing, and regional specialties are nesting. Shorebirds throng beaches in fall, hawks move south, sometimes in huge numbers, and songbird migration can be excellent along the coast. In winter, waterfowl are in every watery environment from sea to marsh to lake, and birders check the Chesapeake Bay Bridge-Tunnel and other hot spots for rarities.

This chapter begins in northern Virginia and moves southward through the Carolinas to the Georgia coast, checking in at some of the finest birding spots in the East along the way. ■

# VIRGINIA

**1** One of the fabled places of East Coast birding, **Chincoteague National Wildlife Refuge** occupies the southern end of **Assateague Island National Seashore,** at the Virginia-Maryland border between the Atlantic Ocean and Chincoteague Bay. Birders have found more than 320 species here over the years. The refuge's mix of habitats and its strategic position on the coast make it an appealing destination for both single-minded rarity-hunters and casual birders who simply enjoy seeing such striking birds as swans, geese, herons, egrets, and ibises.

Several species of waterfowl nest at Chincoteague (Mute Swan, Canada Goose, Wood and American Black Ducks, and others), but in autumn swans, geese, and ducks begin arriving by the thousands. Refuge roads and the wildlife loop around **Snow Goose Pool** (*open to walkers and bikers before 3 p.m., to automobiles afterward*) may bring sightings of Tundra Swan, Snow Goose, Brant, dabbling ducks, and divers including Greater and Lesser Scaups, Bufflehead, Common Goldeneye (rare), and Ruddy Duck. In freshwater

- Year-round birding at Chincoteague National Wildlife Refuge
- Fall hawk migration at Kiptopeke State Park
- Appalachian specialties at Shenandoah National Park

Information section p. 133

Cattle Egret and horses, Assateague Island

Snowy Egret and
Great Blue Heron,
Chincoteague
National Wildlife
Refuge, Assateague
Island

impoundments and bays, watch for such rarities as Eurasian Wigeon and Common Eider. Fall is also when wooded areas, such as that found along the 1.6-mile **Woodland Trail** loop, may harbor good numbers of southbound warblers and other songbirds. Sharp-shinned and Cooper's Hawks, Merlin, and Peregrine Falcon pass in migration, and Red-throated and Common Loons and Horned Grebe arrive to spend the winter.

Shorebirds can be abundant in refuge impoundments and along the beach, especially from late summer through fall when two dozen or more species may be present, including large numbers of Black-bellied and Semipalmated Plovers, Greater and Lesser Yellowlegs, Ruddy Turnstone, and Dunlin, along with occasional Hudsonian and Marbled Godwits and Buff-breasted Sandpiper. Waders, too, congregate at wetlands in impressive numbers.

The threatened Piping Plover nests at the southern end of the island, closed to public access during breeding season. Other Chincoteague nesting birds include Osprey; American Oystercatcher; Black Skimmer; Common,

Forster's, and Least Terns; Chuck-will's-widow; Fish Crow; Brown-headed Nuthatch (check pinewoods); and sometimes Saltmarsh Sharp-tailed Sparrow, here at the southern edge of its range. Peregrine Falcon has nested on a hacking tower reached by taking the trail that leads north to Wash Flats—a long (and often solitary) but productive hike. Ask at refuge headquarters about commercial bus tours of the northern part of the area.

**2** In fall, following the passage of a cold front, southbound migrants often gather in great numbers near the tip of Cape Charles, where the narrowing peninsula and the birds' reluctance to cross the mouth of Chesapeake Bay can result in spectacular birding. **Kiptopeke State Park (Va. 704)** is a center of fall songbird migration-watching, beginning with the first Eastern Kingbirds and Blue-gray Gnatcatchers in July and continuing through straggling Gray Catbirds and Common Yellowthroats in late October. In between, Black-throated Blue and Yellow-rumped Warblers, American Redstart, and other species appear by the hundreds in woods, shrub lands, and fields. With 4,276 feet of Chesapeake Bay front, Kiptopeke is a good place to scan for Brant and ducks from fall through spring and for shorebirds, gulls, and terns year-round.

Peregrine Falcon

Fall hawk migration, though, may be Kiptopeke's biggest birding thrill: In recent years an average of 70,000 raptors have been counted from the park observation platform, sometimes including more than 20,000 Sharp-shinned Hawks, 9,000 American Kestrels, 5,000 Ospreys, and 2,300 Cooper's Hawks, as well as many hundreds of Merlins, Peregrine Falcons, and other species.

Nearby on Va. 600, the **Eastern Shore of Virginia National Wildlife Refuge** is also a fine spot for fall migrant songbirds and hawks. Roads provide access to ponds and wetlands where you'll find waders, ducks, and shorebirds. Take the wildlife trail through woods to a marsh overlook, checking the area for wintering American Bittern, Sora, American Woodcock, Sedge Wren (scarce), and Nelson's and Saltmarsh Sharp-tailed Sparrows. Waders, Clapper and Virginia Rails, Marsh Wren, and Seaside Sparrow are found here year-round. Out in Chesapeake Bay, the refuge's **Fisherman Island** has nesting Brown Pelican, White Ibis, and terns, but access is restricted to tours on Saturdays in fall and winter. Check with the visitor center for details.

**American Oystercatcher**

With its black-and-white pied plumage and blood-red bill, the American Oystercatcher stands out as one of our most attractive shorebirds. It's well named, too: The oystercatcher inserts its long, laterally compressed bill into oysters, mussels, clams, and other mollusks to cut the muscle that holds the halves of their shells together. With its prey helpless, the bird proceeds to feast on fresh seafood. Usually seen singly or in small groups, American Oystercatchers are fairly common all along the mid-Atlantic coast, but the sight of one of these striking birds is always a delight.

**3** The 17.6-mile **Chesapeake Bay Bridge-Tunnel** is one of the more unusual birding spots on the Atlantic coast. Four man-made islands, one at each end of the two tunnels, make excellent lookouts for seasonal shorebirds from fall through spring. The public is allowed only on the southernmost island, where there's a restaurant, but birders can obtain special permits for parking on the other three islands, where Red-throated Loon, Red-necked Grebe, Northern Gannet, Great Cormorant, King and Common Eiders, Harlequin Duck, all three scoters (Surf is most common), Oldsquaw, Red-breasted Merganser, and Purple Sandpiper (on rocks) are among the possibilities, along with jaegers, gulls, and other species. Many rarities have appeared here over the years, bringing birders back again and again to see what might turn up along this highway over the bay. For information about permits and the rules visitors must follow, write or call well in advance (see South Atlantic Information, p. 133).

**4** South of Virginia Beach, **Back Bay National Wildlife Refuge** protects a segment of coastline and bay encompassing sand beach, dunes, marsh, woods, bay islands, and impoundments enclosed by dikes. Access to the impoundments is limited in winter to create a water-

Chesapeake Bay
Bridge-Tunnel

fowl sanctuary, but in other seasons they host waders and shorebirds. Wooded and shrubby areas are full of migrant songbirds in spring and fall, and shorebirds, gulls, and terns are almost always present on the beach, where there's a chance of seeing an endangered Piping Plover in spring and early fall. No auto travel is allowed in the refuge, so be advised it's a walk of at least 0.25-mile to the beach from the visitor center and almost 0.5-mile to the bay via the **Bay Trail.** To visit the entire impoundment complex means a round-trip of at least 4 miles. Consult the refuge office for information and regulations.

**5** To leave the beach and drive inland 35 miles to **Great Dismal Swamp National Wildlife Refuge** (*I-64 to Va. 58W then follow signs*) is to travel to a different world indeed. Here bald cypress, Atlantic white cedar, tupelo, sweet gum, and red maple grow in a bottomland forest, which, though not at all dismal to a nature lover, is far removed from the windblown sea oats and marsh grass of Back Bay. The woods echo to the hoots of Barred Owl and the *zweet zweet zweet* whistle of Prothonotary Warbler, and at night to the calls of Chuck-will's-widow and Whip-poor-will. This is possibly the northernmost breeding area for the Wayne's subspecies of Black-throated Green Warbler, and a good spot to find Swainson's Warbler as well. At a parking

area off White Marsh Road (Va. 642) southeast of Suffolk you'll find a 0.75-mile boardwalk where you can see many of the typical nesting birds of this habitat, from Red-shouldered Hawk and Yellow-billed Cuckoo to Yellow-throated Vireo and Louisiana Waterthrush. Walking east along the Washington Ditch Road (named for our first President, who was involved with a logging company here) is a good way to find Black-throated Green and Swainson's Warblers. Other good spots are the trails along Jericho Ditch and

Yellow-crowned Night-Heron at Huntley Meadows Park, Alexandria

Lynn Ditch, reached from another parking area off Jericho Lane, about 5 miles north. Other breeding birds here include Red-headed and Pileated Woodpeckers; Acadian Flycatcher; Fish Crow; Wood Thrush; Yellow-throated, Worm-eating, Kentucky, and Hooded Warblers; American Redstart; and Summer Tanager.

**6** Just a few minutes south of the Capital Beltway (I-495), **Huntley Meadows Park** in Alexandria is one of the most popular birding areas in the greater Washington, D.C., region. Its 1,424 acres and more than 8 miles of trails make a fine respite from the traffic and bustle of the city. As you stroll here at dusk in early spring, you might hear an American Woodcock in display flight with its twittering call and rustling wings. In spring or summer you may flush up a Green Heron or see a family of Hooded Mergansers or King Rails, or in the evening hear the weird "pumping" call of an American Bittern. The park offers a half-mile boardwalk through a wetland area, which often provides

excellent looks at marsh birds. In addition, viewing areas, including a two-story observation tower, make it easy to sit and watch in summer for Great Egret and Yellow-crowned Night-Heron or for a migrant Virginia Rail or Sora. Other common nesting birds include Wood Duck, Barred Owl, Belted Kingfisher, Wood Thrush, Ovenbird, Scarlet Tanager, Eastern Towhee, and Song Sparrow.

View from Hawksbill Mountain, Shenandoah National Park, south of Luray

**7** The beauty of the Appalachian Mountains in 196,000-acre **Shenandoah National Park** makes it one of the most visited of America's parks. It's popular with birders, too, primarily as a place to see upper-elevation northern birds (see sidebar p. 122), which find in these highlands a facsimile of the main body of their ranges in New England or Canada. **Skyline Drive,** which begins in Front Royal, Virginia, runs for 105 miles through this long, narrow national park. The drive is dotted with overlooks and intersects more than 500 miles of hiking trails (the Appalachian Trail runs through the park), providing convenient access to fine birding. In addition, persons with limited mobility can find a good number of species simply by stopping, looking, and listening at Skyline Drive parking areas. Those who want to get away from the traffic and crowds along this scenic drive can find many longer walks.

South of Luray at Milepost 41.7 on Skyline Drive, keep an eye out for Peregrine Falcon. Forty-two of these magnificent predators were released in the park from 1989 to 1993, and recently a pair has nested each year on the cliffs of nearby Stony Man. A bit farther south, 4,049-foot **Hawksbill Mountain** (reached by two moderately strenuous trails) is a good hawk-watching spot in fall migration. Any place in the park can be excellent for warblers and other migrants in spring, as birds follow ridgetops on their northward journey.

Between Stony Man and Hawksbill, the **Limberlost Trail** at Mile 43 runs through a hemlock-dominated woodland good for nesting birds including Ruffed Grouse; Blue-headed Vireo; Common Raven; Veery; Cedar Waxwing; Chestnut-sided, Blackburnian, Kentucky, and Canada Warblers; Ovenbird; Scarlet Tanager; Dark-eyed Junco; and Rose-breasted Grosbeak. This 1.3-mile handicapped-accessible trail has only slight elevation changes and makes an excellent easy walk. The most popular birding location in the park may be the **South River Falls Trail** at Mile 63, where on a late-spring or summer visit you may find Yellow-throated and Blue-headed Vireos; Veery; Wood Thrush; Chestnut-sided, Black-throated Blue, Black-throated Green, Cerulean, Canada, and Hooded Warblers; Northern Parula; American Redstart; Scarlet Tanager; Eastern Towhee; and Dark-eyed Junco.

Skyline Drive reaches its southern terminus at **Rockfish Gap,** where local birders hold a hawk-watch in fall on the parking lot of a nearby motel. Here starts the 470-mile **Blue Ridge Parkway** (see p. 114), which winds southward to Great Smoky Mountains National Park in North Carolina. The parkway has 275 overlooks, 9 visitor centers, and miles of nature trails along the way where birders can enjoy highland birds as well as some of the most dramatic scenery in the eastern United States. One favorite birding location is **Peaks of Otter** at Mile 84, where the elevation ranges up to 4,004 feet at Flat Top Mountain.

# NORTH CAROLINA

The easternmost barrier islands of North Carolina, the legendary **Outer Banks,** have been known as a home to hardy fishing communities, a playground for beach lovers, and the Graveyard of the Atlantic, where storms and shoals have wrecked hundreds of ships. Birders know them as a place where sea, sand, and marsh combine to create exciting birding opportunities year-round. From tiny Piping Plovers to majestic Tundra Swans to powerful Peregrine Falcons, the birds of the Outer Banks are as varied as they are abundant and accessible.

**8** Located on Hatteras Island, **Pea Island National Wildlife Refuge** ranks with the top birding spots on the south Atlantic coast, encompassing 5,915 acres within

- Spectacular wintering Tundra Swans at Mattamuskeet NWR
- Appalachian specialties along the Blue Ridge Parkway

---

Information section p. 134

Cape Hatteras National Seashore

**Cape Hatteras National Seashore.** Approaching the refuge from the north along N.C. 12, stop first at the **Bodie Island Visitor Center,** where a nature trail provides access to wetlands excellent for herons, egrets, White and Glossy Ibises, waterfowl, rails, and shorebirds. As is usual in marshes, a quick scan won't reveal all that's here. However, patience may be rewarded with the sight of a Clapper Rail skulking through the vegetation, or in winter, of an American Bittern, Virginia Rail, or Sedge Wren.

The refuge begins across Oregon Inlet where, at the northern edge of its **North Pond,** an observation platform provides a view of this impoundment as well as of salt flats to the north where Snow and Canada Geese winter and Black-necked Stilt and Willet nest. Continue south to the refuge visitor center, where a half-mile nature trail runs along the southern edge of North Pond. The live oaks along this trail can be excellent for songbirds in fall migration. The pond itself has waders and wintering waterfowl, including Tundra Swan and several species of ducks. Look for Eurasian Wigeon, seen almost annually in flocks of American Wigeon, as well as shorebirds, including the possibility of such uncommon to very rare species as Marbled Godwit and Curlew Sandpiper. The observation tower at the end of the trail offers a view over Pamlico Sound. From there look for Brown Pelican and Royal and Sandwich Terns, which nest here.

Anywhere along the Hatteras Island beach, you can see an array of shorebirds, gulls, and terns. In fall, check the skies frequently for migrant raptors: Sharp-shinned Hawk is common, and Merlin and Peregrine Falcon are seen often. October is the best month for Peregrine, often with double-digit numbers of these impressive birds seen in a single day, though a single-digit number is more likely.

## Tundra Swan

To birders in many parts of the country, even a single wild swan makes for a red-letter day in the field. No wonder, then, that one of the birding highlights of the mid-Atlantic coast is its concentration of wintering Tundra Swans, which gather here after a long migration from breeding grounds in northern Canada and Alaska. North Carolina's **Mattamuskeet National Wildlife Refuge** (see p. 111) is the most famous winter home for Tundra Swans, offering tens of thousands of these magnificent birds from November through February. Swans may be seen just about anywhere waterfowl gather near the coast, from Chesapeake Bay south into northern South Carolina.

Thirty miles south of the refuge visitor center lies the "elbow" of Cape Hatteras itself, where, fall through spring, dedicated birders take four-wheel-drive vehicles or walk to the end of the point to watch for seabirds, from loons and grebes to shearwaters, storm-petrels, jaegers, and gulls. Even if you don't want to go that far, you should explore the salt flats here for shorebirds, gulls, and terns. Nesting birds may include Piping Plover (in small numbers); American Oystercatcher; Gull-billed, Common, and Least Terns; and Black Skimmer. This was once the site of a large breeding colony, but in recent years most birds have moved to the western tip of Hatteras Island—a 2-mile walk beyond the village of Hatteras.

Some of North Carolina's most exciting birding takes place on chartered boat trips into the Atlantic from marinas in Manteo and Hatteras village. Species seen on these pelagic trips, which usually last ten hours or more, vary with the season. Between late May and September, they can include Black-capped Petrel; Cory's, Greater, Sooty, and Audubon's Shearwaters; Wilson's, Leach's, and Band-rumped Storm-Petrels; Pomarine Jaeger; and Bridled and Sooty Terns.

American Bittern

Rarer possibilities include Herald Petrel, White-tailed Tropicbird, Masked Booby, South Polar Skua, and Parasitic and Long-tailed Jaegers. Every January the American Birding Association's newsletter, *Winging It*, includes a directory of pelagic expeditions, or you can check birding magazines for companies that advertise trips.

**9** Across Pamlico Sound, **Mattamuskeet National Wildlife Refuge** (*N.C. 264 E*) is famed for its tremendous population of wintering waterfowl, peaking in November at more than 100,000 birds. Tundra Swan is the highlight (see sidebar p. 110), with numbers varying from 15,000 to more than 40,000 in some winters. Snow and Canada Geese

(with occasional Greater White-fronted and Ross's) join more than 20 species of ducks on the waters of Lake Mattamuskeet and in surrounding fields. Several Bald Eagles are always present in winter as well. Good viewpoints are found along the N.C. 94 causeway across the lake and along the road leading southeast to the refuge headquarters. But be aware that Mattamuskeet isn't just a winter destination: Check the impoundment south of the entrance road for waders and shorebirds, especially in spring and fall migration. Osprey is abundant here in breeding season, with 60 to 80 nests scattered in bald cypresses around the lake.

**10** South of New Bern, **Croatan National Forest** is home to several notable birds, such as Red-cockaded Woodpecker, Brown-headed Nuthatch, the Wayne's subspecies of Black-throated Green Warbler, Swainson's Warbler, and Bachman's Sparrow. Before exploring, pick up a forest map at the Forest Service office in New Bern or the Croatan ranger station on US 70 about 8 miles southeast. Take County Road 1100 (Catfish Lake Road) west from US 70 about 4 miles to Forest Road 121 (Little Road). Areas both

north and south along this road are good for Red-cockaded Woodpecker (roost trees are marked with blue bands) and the Brown-headed Nuthatch. In breeding season, listen for the buzzy song of Black-throated Green Warbler. The Atlantic coastal Wayne's subspecies has a slightly smaller bill than the typical form of this bird, though you'll have to look hard to notice. Listen, too, in swampy places for the loud whistle of Swainson's Warbler. Continue west on County Road 1100 a little more than 3 miles, turning north on Forest Road 158 for 5 miles, and then east on Forest Road 3000 to reach **Catfish Lake Waterfowl Impoundment** (check with the Forest Service office for advice on visiting during fall hunting season). The "moist soils" impoundments here often host good numbers of herons, egrets, and shorebirds.

To reach another productive area, drive west from Morehead City on N.C. 24 approximately 8 miles to Broad Creek. Next, take County Road 1124 (Nine Foot Road) north 3 miles and turn west on Forest Road 128 (Millis Road). The open pinewoods along this route may have Bachman's Sparrow as well as Red-cockaded Woodpecker, and Swainson's Warbler is a possibility in appropriate habitat.

**11** Birders visit **Fort Fisher State Recreation Area,** south of Wilmington, for its beach, mudflats, ocean, and bay habitats, which attract a good variety of waders, shorebirds, gulls, and terns year-round. In nesting season, Painted Bunting is a good bet at the feeders of the North Carolina Aquarium. The **Hermit Trail** here provides access to marsh (look for rails), open water, and beach. In fall, warblers and other songbirds may throng shrubs and scrubby trees, and in winter loons, Northern Gannet, and ducks repay visitors who scan the Atlantic. Birders with four-wheel-drive vehicles or who are willing to walk can continue south more than 3 miles along a narrow spit of land where Brown Pelican, Wilson's Plover, American Oystercatcher, and Black Skimmer are among the many shorebirds and waterbirds present seasonally.

**12** **Weymouth Woods–Sandhills Nature Preserve,** just southeast of Southern Pines, preserves a 905-acre remnant of the Sandhills ecosystem once widespread in North and South Carolina. Though noted for its old-growth longleaf pines and pinewoods birds such as Red-cockaded Woodpecker, Brown-headed Nuthatch, and Pine Warbler, the preserve also encompasses bottomland deciduous woods, with good all-around birding accessible along more than 4 miles of trails. Red-cockaded Woodpecker can be found on the **Pine Barrens** and **Bower's Bog Trails** near the visitor center, and Brown-headed Nuthatch is common throughout pine areas. Bachman's Sparrow has recently begun nesting at the preserve, as controlled burning and other management techniques continue to restore the Sandhills habitat. The **Gum Swamp Trail** is good for Red-tailed Hawk, Wood Thrush, Prothonotary and Kentucky Warblers, Louisiana Waterthrush, and Ovenbird. Other nesting species here include Great Horned and Barred Owls, Chuck-will's-widow, Acadian Flycatcher, Blue-headed Vireo, Prairie Warbler, and Eastern Towhee.

**13** The rugged and beautiful Blue Ridge mountains of western North Carolina harbor many northern birds found nesting nowhere else in the state (see sidebar p. 122). Excellent access to birding sites can be found along the **Blue**

Autumn foliage along the Blue Ridge Parkway, western North Carolina

**Ridge Parkway,** administered by the National Park Service and unquestionably one of America's finest scenic drives. A good starting point is the area around the mountain town of Blowing Rock. Both **Moses H. Cone** and **Julian Price Parks** offer fine high-country forest and miles of trails to explore (particularly Moses H. Cone Park, which comprises 25 miles of carriage roads on what was once a wealthy businessman's estate). Here at about 4,000 feet, breeding birds include a mix of middle- and high-elevation species: Ruffed Grouse; Yellow-bellied Sapsucker; Blue-headed Vireo; Red-breasted and White-breasted Nuthatches; Golden-crowned Kinglet; Chestnut-sided, Black-throated Blue, Black-throated Green, Blackburnian, Black-and-white, Hooded, and Canada Warblers; Ovenbird; Louisiana Waterthrush; Scarlet Tanager; Eastern Towhee; Dark-eyed Junco; and Rose-breasted Grosbeak.

**14** Above the parkway, **Grandfather Mountain** rises to 5,964 feet, an elevation at which weather is often harsh, and where cold winds sculpt spruce and fir into "banner" trees with all limbs arrayed on the lee side of the trunk. Common Ravens soar above the cliffs, and lucky birders may hear the call of Northern Saw-whet Owl in March (they'd be luckier still to see one). Grandfather Mountain is privately owned (the first private commercial site to be named an International Biosphere Reserve) and a fee is charged for entry and to hike its trails. As the highest peak in the Blue Ridge, and with an acclaimed diversity of plant and animal life, it has long attracted naturalists' attention, and its highland species make it a rewarding stop for birders.

Grandfather Mountain, part of the Blue Ridge

The Blue Ridge Parkway winds around the mountain on the **Linn Cove Viaduct,** part of the last section to be completed and a road-building undertaking worth seeing in itself. The information center at Mile 304 (closed in winter) offers guidebooks and other information, and nearby trails, such as the 13-mile **Tanawha Trail,** provide more birding opportunities.

South along the parkway, N.C. 128 climbs into the Black Mountains to **Mount Mitchell State Park** and the summit of the highest mountain east of the Mississippi River. The red spruce and Fraser fir forest surrounding 6,684-foot Mount Mitchell has suffered from insect infestations and disease, but still can be rewarding to visit. Red Crossbill and Pine Siskin, both unpredictable nesting species in the southern Appalachians, have been seen in the park in summer.

South of Asheville, the parkway reaches its highest point near Richland Balsam at 6,053 feet. Here and elsewhere along the way, overlooks and short trails make convenient birding spots. The parkway ends at the edge of **Great Smoky Mountains National Park** (see p. 167).

# SOUTH CAROLINA

**15** The pleasing proximity of ocean, sandy beach, woodland, and marsh makes **Huntington Beach State Park** one of the top birding spots in South Carolina, not to say the south Atlantic coast. Marsh flanks the main entrance road—fresh on the right, salt on the left—and even a quick scan will reveal an assortment of waders and, in winter, ducks. A closer look (easy on the park's marsh overlooks and boardwalk) can turn up Pied-billed Grebe, Least Bittern (absent in winter), Black-crowned Night-Heron, Clapper Rail, Common Moorhen, Marsh Wren, or Seaside Sparrow. Follow the northern park road to its end and cross over to the beach, where shorebirds, gulls, and terns congregate. Look for Brown Pelican, Wilson's and Piping (mostly in winter) Plovers, American Oystercatcher, Willet, and Black Skimmer among a seasonally changing variety of birds.

From fall through spring, the mile walk north to the **Murrell's Inlet jetty** is a must, for it's here that birders look for Red-throated Loon, Great Cormorant, Greater Scaup, Common Eider, Harlequin Duck, scoters, Razorbill, Black Guillemot, and other coastal specialties that range from fairly common to very rare. The rock-loving Purple Sandpiper is common in winter on the jetty itself.

Among other species at Huntington Beach are Tundra Swan (winter), Osprey, Common Ground-Dove, and in breeding season, Yellow-throated and Prairie Warblers and Painted Bunting—but these are just a sampling of the birds in this diverse and productive park. Fall can bring excellent numbers of migrant songbirds, as well as Merlin and Peregrine Falcon along the beach. Fall also signals the arrival of the endangered Wood Stork, whose numbers at this site are increasing.

- Excellent year-round birding at Huntington Beach State Park
- Pinewoods birds in Francis Marion National Forest
- Wetland species at Savannah National Wildlife Refuge

Information section p. 134

Cape Romain
National Wildlife
Refuge, south
of Georgetown

**16** Farther south along the coast, **Francis Marion National Forest** and **Cape Romain National Wildlife Refuge** share the **Sewee Visitor and Environmental Education Center** on US 17 in Awendaw. Stop here for maps and advice about visiting these two areas before continuing south a short distance to Forest Road 228 (I'on Swamp Road). Drive north, looking for Mississippi Kite, Wild Turkey, Yellow-billed Cuckoo, Barred Owl, and warblers including Yellow-throated, Prothonotary, Swainson's (uncommon), Kentucky, Hooded, and Northern Parula. You may find the Wayne's Black-throated Green Warbler here, a subspecies found only along a small section of the Atlantic coast. The I'on Swamp's most famous bird, though, is a ghost: the extinct Bachman's Warbler, a swamp dweller once found here but not seen anywhere since the 1960s.

In about 4 miles, turn right onto Forest Road 202, which runs along a slightly higher ridge with open pinewoods. Look here for the endangered Red-cockaded Woodpecker (Francis Marion has the highest population of these birds in the state), Brown-headed Nuthatch, and Bachman's

Sparrow. Check scrubby areas and clear-cuts for Prairie Warbler and Painted Bunting.

Turn right onto S.C. 133 south and return to US 17. Driving north to S.C. 45 at McClellanville, keep north about 6 miles to the bridge over Wambaw Creek, a good lookout during nesting season for the beautiful Swallow-tailed Kite. Lucky birders might spot this species anywhere in this area, especially if they venture a bit farther to the north, where US 17 crosses the South and North Santee Rivers.

The **Moore's Landing** area of Cape Romain National Wildlife Refuge (*take See Wee Rd. S off US 17 to Bull's Island Rd.*) is an excellent place to see marsh birds, especially for persons with limited mobility. A pier extends into a salt marsh where American Oyster-catcher, Gull-billed Tern, and Black Skimmer can be found, along with shorebirds when the tide is low. This is a good spot for Marbled Godwit in winter, and Painted Bunting nests around the parking lot.

Wild Turkeys, Francis Beidler Forest Sanctuary and Center, near Harleyville

Visitors to Charleston will find two nearby spots of special interest. Across the Cooper River in Mount Pleasant, the **Pitt Street Causeway** (*Royall St. SE from US 17 Bus., then SW a block to Pitt St., following it to SE end*) provides easy access to salt marsh and tidal mudflats where Clapper Rail, Marsh Wren, and Seaside Sparrow breed and both Saltmarsh and Nelson's Sharp-tailed Sparrows have been found in winter. Waders and American Oystercatcher are present all year. For another worthwhile site, take S.C. 171 southwest of Charleston to **Folly Beach** and drive to the east end of Ashley Avenue, where you can walk along a closed road excellent for songbirds during fall migration after a cold front. Painted Bunting breeds here, and nearby are lookout points (including a public pier) where you can scan the Atlantic in winter for Northern Gannet and sea ducks.

**17** The National Audubon Society's **Francis Beidler Forest Sanctuary and Center,** off US 178 near Harleyville, protects 11,000 acres of bald-cypress-tupelo swamp, including 1,800 acres of old-growth forest. Like the Francis Marion National Forest to the east, the Beidler Forest was damaged by Hurricane Hugo in 1989. Today, visitors can watch the slow but steady recuperation of this splendid natural area. Among the birds seen often along its 1.5-mile boardwalk are Anhinga; Yellow-crowned Night-Heron; White Ibis; Red-shouldered Hawk; Barred Owl; Red-headed and Pileated Woodpeckers; Yellow-throated Vireo; Fish Crow; Yellow-throated, Prothonotary, Swainson's, and Hooded Warblers. Ask about bird walks and canoe trips, as well as night walks that allow even the timorous to enjoy the nocturnal sights and sounds of a great southern swamp.

White Ibis, Savannah National Wildlife Refuge, near Hardeeville

**18** **Bear Island Wildlife Management Area** is a terrific location for waders and marsh birds, with 12,000 acres of wetlands, woods, and fields where nesting birds include Least Bittern, White and Glossy Ibises, Mottled Duck, Bald Eagle, Clapper and King Rails, Common Moorhen, Black-necked Stilt, Marsh Wren, and Painted Bunting. Wood Stork is commonly seen among the throngs of herons, egrets, and ibises. Waterfowl and shorebirds are seasonally abundant and easily seen from roads. Bear Island is closed Sundays and from November to late January, though some impoundments can still be seen from a viewing platform adjacent to Bennett's Point Road (S.C. 26), which runs through the area south off US 17, just west of Ashepoo.

**19** Large areas of marsh, both freshwater and tidal, can also be found at **Savannah National Wildlife Refuge,** where former rice plantations dating from the 18th century have been converted to wildlife habitat. Part of the refuge can be readily seen from pull-offs along S.C. 170 southwest of Hardeeville, and the 4-mile **Laurel Hill Wildlife Drive**

south of the highway provides more viewpoints. Energetic birders can walk or bicycle along dikes throughout the refuge's 3,000-acre impoundment area. Thousands of ducks winter on the impoundments, and close views of waders (including egrets, herons, and ibises) are possible year-round. The striking Purple Gallinule is a breeding specialty, and the endangered Wood Stork is frequently seen (summer) along with the King Rail and wintering Virginia Rail and Sora. Shorebirds can be abundant in impoundments with low water. Near-constant scrutiny by local birders has turned up such rarities as Fulvous Whistling-Duck; Limpkin; Ruff; Red-necked and Red Phalaropes; Sprague's Pipit; and Yellow-headed Blackbird.

## Painted Bunting

The flamboyantly beautiful Painted Bunting is one of the South's most sought-after birds, looking, with its multicolored plumage, like some escapee from a zoo's tropical aviary. The South Carolina and Georgia coasts are a nesting-season population center for this species, which prefers scrubby areas with dense thickets. Good spots include **Carolina Sandhills** (see p. 123) and **Santee National Wildlife Refuges** (see this page), **Huntington Beach State Park** (see p. 117), and the **Francis Marion National Forest** (see p. 118) in South Carolina; **Jekyll Island** (see p. 131) in Georgia; and the **Fort Fisher** (see p. 114) area in North Carolina. Brilliant as the Painted Bunting is, it often perches inconspicuously. To find one, it helps to know their short, rather patternless warbling song.

**20** Flanking I-95 on the shores of Lake Marion, 15,095-acre **Santee National Wildlife Refuge** is usually considered the best place in South Carolina to find wintering geese. On the refuge's **Bluff Unit,** west of I-95, stop first at the visitor center, where you can pick up a map and, on weekdays, get advice from refuge staff. The nearby **Wright's Bluff Nature Trail** leads to an observation tower from which Canada Geese, along with Snow, occasional Greater White-fronted, and—if you're lucky—the rare Ross's, can be seen from late fall to spring. Around a hundred Tundra Swans also winter on or near the refuge and may be seen from the tower. The nature trail leads to viewpoints over Cantey Bay, where waterfowl gather, and passes swampy and marshy spots good for waders and other wetland birds. Osprey and Bald Eagle nest on the lake, and depending on (unpredictable) water levels, Cantey Bay may have good numbers of waders or migrant shorebirds on its shoreline.

**21** Protecting more than 22,200 acres of Congaree River bottomland just southeast of Columbia, **Congaree Swamp National Monument** was designated an International Biosphere Reserve in 1983 and the first Continentally Important Bird Area in South Carolina in 1998 —fitting honors for America's largest old-growth floodplain forest. Breeding birds here are those you'd expect in such a habitat: Yellow-crowned Night-Heron; Wood Duck; Red-shouldered Hawk; Mississippi Kite; Red-headed and Pileated Woodpeckers; Wood Thrush; Yellow-throated, Prothonotary, and Hooded Warblers; Northern Parula; and Summer Tanager among them. You'll find Brown-headed Nuthatch, Pine Warbler, and an occasional Bachman's Sparrow in the loblolly pines that remain after Hurricane Hugo in 1989.

Take the 0.75-mile elevated boardwalk close by the visitor center, watching for Barred Owl in the mature forest near the beginning. Passing through an area impacted by Hurricane Hugo, you'll arrive at Weston Lake, good for herons, egrets, and an occasional Anhinga. Listen along the trail for the uncommon Swainson's Warbler. More than 25 miles of trails wind through the western part of the preserve; the **Kingsnake Trail,** which traverses fine bottomland forest, is another favorite birding walk. However, with up to 80 percent of Congaree flooded at times, water travel is the only way to see much of it and a marked trail along Cedar Creek is available to those who provide their own canoes.

## North Meets South

In ecological terms, ascending one of the southern Appalachians' high mountains is like traveling more than 1,000 miles northward, with increasing elevation playing the part of increasing latitude. Birders who visit Georgia's **Brasstown Bald** (see p. 125) or North Carolina's **Grandfather Mountain** (see p. 116) are in some respects seeing a bit of Canada, with Common Ravens playing in the wind and the songs of Veeries fluting through the hemlocks. Other Appalachian species found south of their main ranges include Northern Saw-whet Owl, Yellow-bellied Sapsucker, Red-breasted Nuthatch, Brown Creeper, Winter Wren, and several warblers, including Black-throated Blue, Black-throated Green, Blackburnian, and Canada. The **Blue Ridge Parkway** (see p. 114), aside from being one of the country's most beautiful drives, provides access to trails, recreation areas, and other sites where, ornithologically speaking, North meets South.

**22** Making up a distinct geographic region in North and South Carolina, the Sandhills is a rolling landscape covered in deep sandy soil, with an ecosystem adapted to fire and periods of drought. A fine example is found in 45,000-acre **Carolina Sandhills National Wildlife Refuge,** northwest of Florence, where prescribed burning is restoring the longleaf pine and wiregrass habitat once widespread in the Southeast. Red-cockaded Woodpeckers are fairly common here, living in pinewoods in the family groups biologists call clusters, and aided by artificial cavities that encourage nesting. Brown-headed Nuthatch, another pine specialist, is common on the refuge, and Bachman's Sparrow, though uncommon, can usually be found when males are singing their sweet whistle-and-trill song (check the **Woodland Pond Trail** just north of headquarters).

Red-cockaded Woodpeckers are often seen in roost trees (marked with white bands) near headquarters, as well as in the Martins Lake area off the wildlife drive, also favored by many for all-around birding. The **Lake Bee Recreation Area,** about 2 miles north, is also good for Red-cockaded Woodpecker and Brown-headed Nuthatch. Wild Turkey; Northern Bobwhite (more often heard than seen); Chuck-will's-widow; Whip-poor-will; Red-headed Woodpecker; Pine, Prairie, Prothonotary, and Hooded Warblers; and Blue Grosbeak are among the refuge's nesting species. Ponds, streams, and fields provide habitat for a good variety of migrants and wintering birds.

The endangered Red-cockaded Woodpecker

**23** When out-of-staters think of South Carolina, they're more likely to picture Brown Pelicans and Black Skimmers than Common Ravens and Black-throated Blue Warblers. Nonetheless, the Palmetto State encompasses some Appalachian highlands where these and several other up-country birds can be found. One easily accessible spot is **Caesars Head State Park,** located within the 10,883-acre **Mountain Bridge Wilderness,** northwest of Greenville on the North Carolina state line, where trails wind over hills and through valleys in some of the state's most beautiful country.

Nesting species include Ruffed Grouse; Blue-headed Vireo; Chestnut-sided, Black-throated Green, Blackburnian (rare), Black-and-white, Worm-eating, and Hooded Warblers; Scarlet Tanager; and Dark-eyed Junco. Red Crossbill has nested here, and Cerulean Warbler has been

seen in summer, though breeding hasn't been confirmed.
The **Raven Cliff Falls Trail** is a good place to look for many
of these species. Local birders also recommend hiking the
**Pinnacle Pass Trail** for 2 miles east of US 276 to the Oil
Camp Road area. Color-coded, topographical trail maps are
available at the park office, where you can also ask for information about the region.

    **Caesars Head,** the 3,208-foot rock formation for which
the park was named, can be a productive hawk-watching
site in autumn migration, when more than 2,000 raptors
are occasionally seen in a day. Most are Broad-winged
Hawks, but Sharp-shinned, Cooper's, Red-tailed, and
others are spotted as well. Here at the Blue Ridge Escarp-
ment, raptors enter thermal updrafts and form "kettles," so
observers often watch birds soar for some time before they
gain height and set off again on their southward journey.

# GEORGIA

**24** From sea level along its southeastern Atlantic coastline, the Georgia landscape sweeps up through the central piedmont region to the rugged Appalachian highlands of its northern border. The state's highest point is 4,784-foot **Brasstown Bald,** east of Blairsville in the **Chattahoochee National Forest**—one of many Appalachian peaks called balds, whose treeless or sparsely wooded summits are mysterious in origin. More accessible than some similar areas, Brasstown Bald is approached by a spur road off Ga. 180 leading up to a parking area. From here in summer a shuttle bus runs to the visitor center on the summit, though most birders prefer to walk the half-mile trail to the top.

Along this trail and others that radiate from the Brasstown area, nesting birds include Ruffed Grouse, Blue-headed Vireo; Common Raven; Winter Wren; Veery; Chestnut-sided, Black-throated Blue, Black-throated Green, Blackburnian, and Canada Warblers; Ovenbird; Scarlet Tanager; Dark-eyed Junco; and Rose-breasted Grosbeak. Buy a National Forest Service map at the visitor center or the gift shop at the parking lot and explore nearby public lands for a wider range of species. **Lake Winfield Scott** and **Cooper Creek Recreation Areas** and **Vogel State Park,** all located within 20 miles west of Brasstown Bald, offer the chance for some highland species as well as Broad-winged Hawk, Eastern Wood-Pewee, Acadian Flycatcher, Wood Thrush, Black-and-white and Kentucky Warblers, and many other birds more typical of this latitude.

**25** In the Atlanta suburb of Kennesaw, **Kennesaw Mountain National Battlefield Park** commemorates an 1864 Civil War clash in which Confederates gained a

- Spring migration at Kennesaw Mountain
- Wetland species in Okefenokee Swamp
- Shorebirds and seabirds at Jekyll and Tybee Islands

---

Information section p. 135

View of the Appalachians from Brasstown Bald visitor center, east of Blairsville

short-lived victory against Sherman's Union forces. In spring, and to a lesser extent in fall, the park acts as a magnet for migrant songbirds and for metropolitan-area birders who enjoy them. From the visitor center, walk the mile-long road to the top of the 1,800-foot mountain and watch for migrants of dozens of species, from treetop birds such as Blackburnian and Cerulean Warblers to ground dwellers such as Swainson's Thrush and Ovenbird. On peak days in late April or early May, 20 or more species of warblers may be seen or heard here. Trails cross much of the 2,884-acre park, and checking as many areas as possible will lead to more diverse sightings. On weekends, birders unable to climb can take a shuttle bus, bird at the summit, and ride or walk back down to the visitor center.

**26** Some of Atlanta's best birding is found a short drive south of the city at the Clayton County Water Authority's **Wetlands Center** and **E.L. Huie Land Application Facility,** components of a wastewater treatment complex. Check the sightings list at the Wetlands Center, then take the nature trail and boardwalk through woods and wetlands that are excellent for warblers and other songbirds in spring and fall migration. Red-shouldered Hawk;

126      SOUTH ATLANTIC

Eastern Screech-, Great Horned, and Barred Owls; Prothonotary, Kentucky, and Hooded Warblers; and Louisiana
Waterthrush nest here. The Huie site is Atlanta's best spot
for shorebirds and wintering ducks. Birders can drive on levees around five ponds to scan water and mudflats; ducks are
always present in winter, but shorebird numbers depend on
water levels creating the mudflats they need. In spring and
summer, check nearby Blalock Lake, where Osprey nests.
To reach the area, take the Jonesboro Road exit off I-75 and
drive west about 7 miles toward Lovejoy. Turn right on Freeman Road and follow this to the entrance for the Wetlands
Center. Shamrock Road, which leads to Blalock and Shamrock Lakes, runs north off Freeman Road just west of the
Wetlands Center. The entrance to the Huie ponds is about
2 miles farther ahead, at the intersection of Freeman Road
and Dixon Industrial Boulevard.

**27** West of Atlanta, just 2 miles south of I-20, **Sweetwater Creek State Conservation Park** encompasses
215-acre **Sparks Reservoir,** a fine place to look for loons,
grebes, ducks, and gulls in winter. Scan the water from a
parking lot on Mount Vernon Road at the park's north
entrance, from the park office, and along Factory Shoals

Road, at the south entrance. Wintering or migrant species may include Common Loon, Pied-billed and Horned Grebes, Wood Duck (nests here), several dabbling ducks, Ring-necked Duck, Lesser Scaup, Bufflehead, Red-breasted Merganser, Ruddy Duck, American Coot, and Ring-billed and Herring Gulls. Great Blue Heron is present year-round, Green Heron spring through fall, and an occasional Osprey stops in migration. Unusual species seen here have included Greater Scaup, Harlequin Duck, and Oldsquaw. Seven miles of trails loop through the southern part of the park, offering pleasant woodland birding. Take the path from the picnic grounds up the Jack Hill area as well as the trails alongside Sweetwater Creek for a variety of habitats, from woodland to open places.

**28** About 25 miles north of Macon, **Piedmont National Wildlife Refuge** is known for good all-around birding as well as for the southern pinewoods specialties of Red-cockaded Woodpecker, Brown-headed Nuthatch, and Bachman's Sparrow. The woodpeckers can be found at several spots in the refuge, including along the 2.5-mile **Red-cockaded Woodpecker Trail,** north of headquarters. Look for Bachman's Sparrow here and elsewhere in open pine forest with grassy understory.

The 6-mile **Little Rock Wildlife Drive** passes a variety of habitats, including a pond, bottomland hardwoods, and scrubby openings where nesting species include Northern Bobwhite, Prairie Warbler, Yellow-breasted Chat, Field Sparrow, Blue Grosbeak, and Indigo Bunting. Another productive road begins off the main east-west refuge road nearly opposite the wildlife drive entrance and runs north toward Allison Lake. In woodland, watch for Red-shouldered Hawk; Wild Turkey; Blue-headed Vireo (here at the southern limit of its range); Pine (in pines), Kentucky, and Hooded Warblers; and Orchard Oriole.

**29** The fabled **Okefenokee Swamp,** one of America's most important wetland areas, lies on the Florida state line in southeastern Georgia, its dark waters giving birth to the Suwannee and St. Marys Rivers. Nearly 400,000 acres of the swamp are protected as **Okefenokee**

**National Wildlife Refuge.** Of that, more than 350,000 acres are officially designated wilderness. Within the swamp are wooded islands of slightly higher ground, expanses of open water, "prairies" where marsh vegetation spreads across thousands of acres, vast areas of flooded pond bald-cypress-tupelo woodland—and few ways to see much of it.

The major gateway to the swamp is the **Suwannee Canal Recreation Area,** at the refuge's east entrance, about 10 miles southwest of Folkston. You'll find a Red-cockaded Woodpecker cluster (family nesting group) near the entrance station, and more Red-cockaded Woodpeckers, along with Brown-headed Nuthatch and Bachman's Sparrow, at the **Upland Discovery Trail** on the Swamp Island Drive south to **Chesser Island.** Watch for Wild Turkey along the road. At Chesser Island, a 0.75-mile boardwalk leads to an observation tower; a few Great Blue

Okefenokee Swamp, southeastern Georgia

Herons and Sandhill Cranes usually nest near the boardwalk. Here the resident Sandhills are joined in winter by hundreds of cranes that migrate from northern states and Canada. You'll see waders here, though recent drought conditions have hurt populations of herons, egrets, and ibises. Anhinga, Wood Stork (formerly nested, but not in recent years), Osprey, Swallow-tailed Kite (rare, but believed to nest in the area), Red-shouldered Hawk, Barred Owl, and

Jekyll Island, southeast of Brunswick

Red-headed and Pileated Woodpeckers are a few of the many other possibilities.

To get closer to the swamp, return to the concession area and rent a canoe or johnboat or take a commercial tour out into the **Suwannee Canal** and its side channels. In addition, tours are also available, and boats can be rented at the park's west entrance at **Stephen C. Foster State Park,** 18 miles northeast of Fargo. Your chances of seeing Osprey and Purple Gallinule may be better here than on Okefenokee's east side.

**30** Georgia's coastal islands are a potpourri of resort communities, golf courses, and, thankfully, wild places as well. One accessible birding spot that also offers plenty of amenities for the traveler is **Jekyll Island,** southeast of Brunswick. Before crossing the causeway to the island, stop at the welcome center *(912-635-3636)* and check the mudflats behind it for waders and shorebirds. A few hundred yards ahead (still before the final bridge to the island), a wetland beyond the trees on the right may have White Ibis, Roseate Spoonbill (rare), Wood Stork, and other waders.

On the island, turn south on South Riverview Drive and continue to the **St. Andrew Picnic Area,** one of many spots on the perimeter roads where you'll find beach access and views of loons, grebes, American White Pelican, waterfowl in winter, and Brown Pelican, Double-crested Cormorant, waders (often including Wood Stork), shorebirds, gulls, and terns all year. Wilson's Plover, American Oystercatcher, Willet, Laughing Gull, Royal

Purple Gallinule, a colorful inhabitant of southern swamps and marshes

Tern, and Black Skimmer are among the nesting birds on the coast, and numbers of migrant shorebirds stop in spring and fall. The extreme southern end of Jekyll is most favored by birds and birders; to reach it, turn south on Macy Lane, park at the corner of Andrews Drive, and follow the path and boardwalk to the beach. Don't neglect the island's woods and marshes, where nesting birds include Wild Turkey; Clapper Rail; Brown-headed Nuthatch; Yellow-throated, Prairie, and Hooded Warblers; and Painted Bunting. In addition, more than 20 miles of bike and jogging trails access a wide variety of habitats.

**31** Up the coast about 45 miles, **Harris Neck National Wildlife Refuge** is reached by driving east 7 miles from US 17 at South Newport. Once a military base (the 4-mile auto route traverses part of the abandoned airstrip), the refuge is well worth a visit any time of year. Thousands of waders and waterbirds nest here, including Anhinga; Great, Snowy, and Cattle Egrets; Little Blue, Tricolored, and Green Herons; Black-crowned Night-Heron; White Ibis; Wood Duck; Clapper Rail; Purple Gallinule; and Common

Moorhen. Of special interest is the endangered Wood Stork, which has increased here since refuge staff erected artificial nesting platforms and discovered that decorating them with artificial vegetation encouraged the birds to breed. Breeding Painted Buntings are common throughout the summer, while in winter dabbling ducks such as Gadwall, American Wigeon, Mallard, Blue-winged Teal, Green-winged Teal, Northern Shoveler, and Northern Pintail are common on ponds, along with divers such as Ring-necked Duck, Bufflehead, and Ruddy Duck. Grassy fields host a good variety of sparrows.

Tybee Island, east of Savannah

**32** Just east of Savannah, **Tybee Island** is another easily accessible spot to look for seabirds and shorebirds. Approaching the island, stop first at **Fort Pulaski National Monument,** a Civil War fort constructed of more than 25 million bricks. Birders will look beyond the amazing edifice to trails and dikes that provide access to brackish marsh that is good for waders, waterfowl, rails (Clapper year-round, Virginia and Sora in winter), Sedge (winter) and Marsh (year-round) Wrens, and Saltmarsh Sharp-tailed and Nelson's Sharp-tailed (both in winter), and Seaside Sparrows (resident). **McQueen's Trail,** an old rail line alongside US 80, has been made into a hiking trail that runs west from Fort Pulaski beside more marshland.

On Tybee, look first along the northern end of the island, less developed than the middle section. In winter, scan rock jetties for rare Purple Sandpiper. Black Skimmer is common throughout the year, and American Oystercatcher is seen fairly often among the mixed flocks of shorebirds changing with the seasons. The southern end of Tybee also has beach and mudflats worth checking. Large rafts of wintering ducks are sometimes found offshore. In spring and fall, look skyward for migrant Peregrine Falcon, zooming along the beach in search of a hapless plover or sandpiper for lunch.

# South Atlantic
## Information

**?** Visitor Center/Information    **$** Fee Charged    **ᵮ** Food

**ᴪ** Rest Rooms    **↗** Nature Trails    **↻** Driving Tours    **♿** Wheelchair Accessible

*Be advised that facilities may be seasonal and limited. We suggest calling or writing ahead for specific information. Note that addresses may be for administrative offices; see text or call for directions to sites.*

## Rare Bird Alerts

Virginia:
Statewide *301-652-1088*

North and South Carolina:
Statewide *704-332-2473*

Georgia:
Statewide *770-493-8862*
Southern *912-244-9190*

## VIRGINIA

### Chincoteague National Wildlife Refuge
*(Page 101)*
8259 Beach Road
Chincoteague Island,
   VA 23336
*757-336-6122*

**? $ ᴪ ↗ ↻ ♿**

### Kiptopeke State Park
*(Page 103)*
3540 Kiptopeke Drive
Cape Charles, VA 23310
*757-331-2267*

**$ ᴪ ↗ ♿**

### Eastern Shore of Virginia National Wildlife Refuge
*(Page 103)*
5003 Hallett Circle
Cape Charles, VA 22310
*757-331-2760*

**? ᴪ ↗ ♿**

### Chesapeake Bay Bridge-Tunnel
*(Page 104)*
P.O. Box 111, Dept. OPS
Cape Charles, VA 23310
*757-331-2960*

**$ ᮮ ᴪ ♿**

*Birders are advised to write or call well in advance for information about permits and rules.*

### Back Bay National Wildlife Refuge
*(Page 104)*
4005 Sandpiper Road
Virginia Beach, VA 23456
*757-721-2412*

**? $ ᴪ ↗ ↻ ♿**

*No autos allowed. Trails closed Nov.–March*

### Great Dismal Swamp National Wildlife Refuge
*(Page 105)*
White Marsh Road
Suffolk, VA 23439
*757-986-3705*

**ᴪ ↗ ♿**

### Huntley Meadows Park
*(Page 106)*
3701 Lockheed Boulevard
Alexandria, VA 22306
*703-768-2525*

**? ᴪ ↗ ♿**

*Closed Tues.*

### Shenandoah National Park *(Page 107)*
3655 US 211 East
Luray, VA 22835
*540-999-3500*

**? $ ᮮ ᴪ ↗ ↻ ♿**

### Blue Ridge Parkway
*(Pages 108, 114-116)*
Route 1, Box 798
Spruce Pine, NC 28777
*828-765-6082*

**? ᮮ ᴪ ↗ ↻ ♿**

# NORTH CAROLINA

### Pea Island National Wildlife Refuge
*(Page 109)*
N.C. 12 South
P.O. Box 1969
Manteo, NC 27954
*252-473-1131*

### Cape Hatteras National Seashore *(Page 109)*
Route 1, P.O. Box 675
Manteo, NC 27954
*252-473-2111*

### Mattamuskeet National Wildlife Refuge
*(Page 111)*
Route 1, Box N-2
Swan Quarter, NC 27885
*252-926-4021*

### Croatan National Forest
*(Page 112)*
141 East Fisher Avenue
New Bern, NC 28560
*252-638-5628*

### Fort Fisher State Recreation Area
*(Page 114)*
State Road 1628
Carolina Beach, NC 28428
*910-458-8206*

### Weymouth Woods–Sandhills Nature Preserve
*(Page 114)*
1024 Fort Bragg Road
Southern Pines, NC 28387
*910-692-2167*

### Blue Ridge Parkway
*(Pages 108, 114–116)*
See Virginia listing p. 133.

### Grandfather Mountain
*(Page 116)*
P.O. Box 129
Linville, NC 28646
*828-733-2013*

### Mount Mitchell State Park *(Page 116)*
Rural Route 5, Box 700
Burnsville, NC 28714
*828-675-4611*

# SOUTH CAROLINA

### Huntington Beach State Park *(Page 117)*
16148 Ocean Highway
Murrells Inlet, SC 29576
*843-237-4440*

### Francis Marion National Forest and Cape Romain National Wildlife Refuge
*(Page 118)*
Sewee Visitor and
  Environmental Center
5821 US 17 North
Awendaw, SC 29429
*843-928-3368*

*Visitor center open
Thurs.–Sun.*

### Francis Beidler Forest Sanctuary and Center
*(Page 119)*
336 Sanctuary Road
Harleyville, SC 29448
*843-462-2150*

### Bear Island Wildlife Management Area
*(Page 120)*
Bennett's Point Road
Green Pond, SC 29446
*843-844-8957*

*Closed Sun. and
Nov.–late Jan.*

### Savannah National Wildlife Refuge
*(Page 120)*
Parkway Business Center,
  Suite 10
1000 Business Park Road
Savannah, GA 31405
*912-652-4415*

*Portions of refuge may be
closed in Oct. for wheelchair-
dependent hunters and
Dec.–Feb. to reduce
disturbance to wintering birds.*

**Santee National Wildlife Refuge** *(Page 121)*
Route 2, Box 370
Summerton, SC 29148
*803-478-2217*

**Congaree Swamp National Monument**
*(Page 122)*
200 Caroline Sims Road
Hopkins, SC 29061
*803-776-4396*

**Carolina Sandhills National Wildlife Refuge**
*(Page 123)*
Route 2, Box 100
McBee, SC 29101
*843-335-8401*

**Caesars Head State Park** *(Page 123)*
8155 Geer Highway
Cleveland, SC 29635
*864-836-6115*

*Caesars Head is part of and provides access to trails into the 10,883-acre Mountain Bridge Wilderness.*

# GEORGIA

**Brasstown Bald**
*(Page 125)*
P.O. Box 9
Blairsville, GA 30514
*706-896-2556 or*
*706-745-6928*

*Part of the Chattahoochee National Forest*

**Kennesaw Mountain National Battlefield Park**
*(Page 125)*
900 Kennesaw
   Mountain Drive
Kennesaw, GA 30152
*770-427-4686*

**CCWA Wetlands Center and E.L. Huie Land Application Facility**
*(Page 126)*
2755 Freeman Road
Hampton, GA 30228
*770-603-5606*

**Sweetwater Creek State Conservation Park**
*(Page 127)*
P.O. Box 816
Lithia Springs, GA 30122
*770-732-5871*

**Piedmont National Wildlife Refuge**
*(Page 128)*
Rural Route 1, Box 670
Round Oak, GA 31038
*912-986-5441*

**Okefenokee National Wildlife Refuge**
*(Page 128)*
Rural Route 2, Box 3330
Folkston, GA 31537
*912-496-7836*

*Also provides information on Suwannee Canal Recreation Area*

**Stephen C. Foster State Park** *(Page 130)*
Rural Route 1, Box 131
Fargo, GA 31631
*912-637-5274*

**Harris Neck National Wildlife Refuge**
*(Page 131)*
Parkway Business Center,
   Suite 10
1000 Business Center Drive
Savannah, GA 31405
*912-652-4415*

*Portions of refuge periodically closed for hunting and to reduce disturbance to wildlife*

**Fort Pulaski National Monument** *(Page 132)*
US 80 East
Savannah, GA 31410
*912-786-5787*

# Florida

Perdido

•Pensacola
**15** FORT
PICKENS• GULF ISLANDS
NATIONAL SEASHORE
Panama City

ST. JOSE
PENINSULA

10

98

*The flocks of birds that covered the shelly beaches,
and those that hovered overhead, so astonished us that
at first we could scarcely believe our eyes.*

This was John James Audubon's reaction on visiting the Florida Keys in the early 1830s, and it's still the vision that appears to many travelers when they think of Florida: masses of herons, egrets, ibises, spoonbills, and storks feeding in shallow wetlands or flying to roost at dusk, in a setting of lush, subtropical vegetation. In places this is just what you'll find, an avian spectacle that still has the power to astonish.

Unfortunately, persecution in the late 19th and early 20th centuries and, lately, the burgeoning population of South Florida and the attendant loss and degradation of habitat mean that never again will we see numbers of wading birds comparable to those that once throve here. It's sobering to imagine, as you look out over a teeming, colorful flock of waders in Big Cypress National Preserve or the famed J.N. "Ding" Darling National Wildlife Refuge, that once there were many more of these birds—in some cases ten times as many—and many more places where they could nest and feed.

Florida has more to entice birders than flashy herons and egrets, beautiful as they are. As a continental extremity, the peninsula is home to species seldom or never found elsewhere in the United States. Apart from regularly occurring specialties, Florida also sees rare strays that wander from the Bahamas and the Caribbean islands. Among the sought-after regular species are Swallow-tailed and Snail

*Preceding pages:*
Roseate Spoonbills
and Snowy
Egrets, Key Largo
*Above:* Swallow-
tailed Kite

**138** FLORIDA

GEORGIA

19

75

95

St. Marys

Suwannee

Ochlockonee

★Tallahassee

10

●Jacksonville

ATLANTIC

OCEAN

APALACHICOLA NATIONAL FOREST

**14**

98

EDWARD BALL WAKULLA SPRINGS S.P.

ST. MARKS N.W.R. **13**

19

F L O R I D A

St. Johns

■ST. GEORGE ISLAND S.P.

98

41

●Gainesville

●PAYNES PRAIRIE STATE PRESERVE **12**

Micanopy■

*Lake George*

CANAVERAL NATIONAL SEASHORE

Gulf of

Mexico

98

4

19

75

Orlando●

●PLAYALINDA BEACH

MERRITT ISLAND N.W.R. **11**

41

*FLORIDA'S Lake*

95

Tampa●

4

27

*Kissimmee*

AVON PARK AIR FORCE RANGE

TURNPIKE

275

Avon Park●

■

●Fort Pierce

**10**

MYAKKA RIVER S.P.

*Kissimmee*

Sarasota●

●

72

Arcadia●

70

*Lake Okeechobee*

JONATHAN DICKINSON S.P.

OSCAR SCHERER STATE PARK

75

74

●Babcock

*Caloosahatchee*

**9** J.N. "DING" DARLING N.W.R.

*Sanibel Island*

●Fort Myers

**8**

ARTHUR R. MARSHALL LOXAHATCHEE N.W.R. **5**

Boca● Raton

HUGH TAYLOR BIRCH S.R.A.

CORKSCREW SWAMP SANCTUARY

BIG

75

JOHN U. LLOYD BEACH S.R.A.

27

**4**

Naples●

CYPRESS

THE CONSERVANCY BRIGGS NATURE CENTER

NATIONAL **7**

●**Miami**

FAKAHATCHEE STRAND STATE PRESERVE

PRESERVE

**6**

41

94

SHARK VALLEY VISITOR CENTER

**1**

EVERGLADES

●Cutler Ridge

NATIONAL

27

●Homestead

0        50 mi

0        75 km

PARK

1

Key Largo

905

FLAMINGO VISITOR CENTER

1

**3** DRY TORTUGAS NATIONAL PARK

*Sugarloaf Key*

Marathon●

*Florida Keys*

**2**

Key West●

Kites, Short-tailed Hawk, Limpkin, Roseate Tern, White-crowned Pigeon, Mangrove Cuckoo, Smooth-billed Ani, Antillean Nighthawk, Gray Kingbird, Black-whiskered Vireo, the endemic (and threatened) Florida Scrub-Jay, and Shiny Cowbird. The pinelands, scrub, and prairies of central and northern Florida harbor Crested Caracara, Sandhill Crane, Red-cockaded Woodpecker (endangered), and Bachman's Sparrow, among other species. And beaches (less than two hours away no matter where you are in the state) host an array of shorebirds that changes with the seasons.

This chapter begins in extreme southern Florida and moves northward up the peninsula. ∎

# SOUTHERN EVERGLADES REGION AND THE KEYS

**1** By now, those with an interest in conservation know the story of **Everglades National Park,** at once sad and hopeful. Despite its 1.5-million-acre size, this portion of the "river of grass" and its inhabitants have suffered enormously from pollution and changes in water flow brought about by agriculture, urban growth, and other human activities. New public awareness, though, has led to massive and far-ranging efforts to restore the Everglades ecosystem. Time will tell of their effectiveness.

Most people get acquainted with the park at the Ernest F. Coe Visitor Center southwest of Homestead on Fla. 9336, or the Royal Palm Visitor Center, 4 miles farther inside the park. The 0.5-mile **Anhinga Trail** at the latter center is excellent for close views of alligators and various waterbirds, including Anhinga, a pelican relative that looks something like a sharp-billed cormorant. Many other waders and waterbirds are found here as well, from Green Heron and Purple Gallinule to White Ibis and Yellow-crowned Night-Heron.

As you drive through the park, watch for the South Florida race of Red-shouldered Hawk, smaller and much paler than birds elsewhere in the country. A Swallow-tailed Kite, one of the world's most beautiful and graceful raptors, may sail overhead during spring and summer. But the bird of prey most sought after here is Short-tailed Hawk, a small *Buteo* (the same genus as Red-shouldered and Red-tailed) that often eludes visiting birders. Short-tailed is easier— though not necessarily easy—to find in winter when birds from farther north migrate to the tip of the Florida peninsula. Take time to check all soaring hawks and vultures; Short-tailed often soars quite high, above other birds.

One of the most famous birding locales in Everglades National Park is **Snake Bight Trail,** a couple of miles past

- Varied waterbirds in Everglades wetlands
- Seabirds and exciting spring migration in the Dry Tortugas

---

Information section p. 160

Whitewater Bay,
Everglades
National Park

the canoe ramp and rest rooms at West Pond. One reason
it's famous, unfortunately, is its almost indescribably dread-
ful mosquitoes. (In truth, this could apply to nearly all the
Everglades from spring through fall, but birders suffer the
plague most often here.) The 2-mile trail leads alongside
an old borrow ditch to Snake Bight (a shallow bay), which,
short of taking a boat out into Florida Bay, is the likeliest
place in the United States to see Greater Flamingo. High
tide pushes the birds closer to shore to feed, making them
easier to sight, and the birds are seen most often from late
summer through midwinter. Don't be fooled by Roseate
Spoonbills, which are smaller with a much longer bill. The
origin of these flamingos has long been debated, with continuing disagreement over whether they're truly wild or
descendants of birds escaped from captivity. Snake Bight
is also a good place to see throngs of herons, shorebirds,
gulls, terns, and Black Skimmers, again with high tide being
by far the best time to visit—otherwise the birds will be far
out on the mudflats in the heat haze.

White-crowned Pigeon, an attractive South Florida

specialty, is seen often here. Mangrove Cuckoo, one of Florida's most prized birds, also occurs, but is quite elusive—hard to see even when located by its call. If you miss this species on your first trip to Florida, you'll be joining a very large club; just think of it as an excuse to come back again.

At the park's **Flamingo Visitor Center,** at the end of the main park road on the shore of Florida Bay, look for the white-plumaged form of Great Blue Heron, once considered a separate species. Its larger size, body shape, and leg color (yellow, not black, for "Great White Heron") help distinguish it from Great Egret. Reddish Egret, Roseate Spoonbill, Osprey, Bald Eagle, and a variety of shorebirds are likely, and in winter this is another spot to watch for Short-tailed Hawk.

Shiny Cowbird, a rarity found sporadically throughout Florida and occasionally seen here, is a recent invader from the Caribbean that is not illustrated in most field guides. The male is shiny purplish in color; the female is very difficult to differentiate from the common Brown-headed Cowbird Female. Check around the campground and other grassy areas for this irregularly occurring species.

Near **Homestead** and **Cutler Ridge,** south of Miami, watch from February through summer for Cave Swallows, which nest very locally in highway culverts and under bridges in the area. These birds belong to the distinct West Indian race of Cave Swallow, darker on the undersides and on the rump than the southwestern race, which may some-day be designated as a separate species. One favorite spot is near the S.W. 216th Street overpass of Florida's Turnpike (Fla. 821).

## Special Birds of Florida

*Mangrove Cuckoo*

Masked Booby
Brown Booby
Magnificent
  Frigatebird
Roseate Spoonbill
Wood Stork
Greater Flamingo
Fulvous Whistling-
  Duck
Swallow-tailed Kite
Snail Kite
Short-tailed Hawk
Crested Caracara
Limpkin
Sandhill Crane
Roseate Tern
Bridled Tern
Sooty Tern
Brown Noddy
Black Noddy

White-crowned
  Pigeon
Mangrove Cuckoo
Smooth-billed Ani
Burrowing Owl
Antillean
  Nighthawk
Red-cockaded
  Woodpecker
Gray Kingbird
Black-whiskered
  Vireo
Florida Scrub-Jay
Cave Swallow
Yellow Warbler
  (golden race)
Bachman's
  Sparrow
Shiny Cowbird

**2** Begin your exploration of the **Florida Keys** by taking Card Sound Road east from US 1 at Florida City, crossing the bridge to north Key Largo and Fla. 905. Because of crimi-nal activity (not only drug smuggling but, perhaps surprisingly, theft of the state's rare plants, butterflies, and even snails) law-enforcement officers are very strict about trespassing in this area. Bird only along roads unless pub-lic access is clearly permitted, such as at a short nature trail at the botanic site less than a half-mile east of the inter-section with US 1. Black-whiskered Vireo and Mangrove Cuckoo nest here, and White-crowned Pigeon can be common except in winter. Gray King-bird is frequent along the highway in spring and summer.

Continuing south, you'll find Ospreys nesting along the road, and "Great White Heron" may be seen along the shore any-where. Keep an eye out for soaring Magnificent Frigatebird, as well as Short-tailed Hawk in winter. In summer, the air-port at **Marathon** can be a good spot for one of the keys' specialty birds, the Antillean Nighthawk, active beginning just before sunset. Though slightly smaller than Common Nighthawk, Antillean is best distinguished by its insectlike call, usually described as *pity-pit-pit*. Check Sombrero Beach Park for Burrowing Owl, a declining species in Florida. The

Marathon golf course also has a few nesting pairs.

At **Sugarloaf Key,** turn south at the blinking light at Milepost 17 and drive west at a T intersection; turn right and follow County Road 939A to its end. This drive passes through extensive mangrove habitat good for spotting White-crowned Pigeon, Mangrove Cuckoo, Gray Kingbird, and Black-whiskered Vireo. Check periodically all along the way.

As you approach Key West (and quite literally the end of the road), the parking lot at Florida Keys Junior College on **Stock Key** provides perhaps the best chance to find Antillean Nighthawk (especially at dusk). On **Key West** itself, the species feeds at night over the Key West airport, in the southeastern part of the island. Roseate Tern, a bird with a very limited and disjunct breeding range in the United States, nests in the lower keys and should be looked for from April through summer anywhere you find terns gathering; **Fort Zachary Taylor State Historic Site** is a favorite spot.

**3** **Dry Tortugas National Park,** 68 miles west into the Gulf of Mexico from Key West, comprises seven tiny islands and about 100 square miles of ocean. The park centers on **Garden Key** and Fort Jefferson, a massive mid-19th-century fort never used in wartime. Most birders visit in spring, when an astonishing variety of migrants use these islands as a rest stop and several localized breeding specialties can be found.

"Great White Heron" form of Great Blue Heron

Visiting the Dry Tortugas is slightly more complicated than other excursions in this chapter, since you must arrange either a boat or seaplane trip. The best way to go is with a bird-tour company, several of which offer three-day boat trips that allow close reconnaissance of the islands, as well as the chance to see seabirds en route (including such species as Audubon's Shearwater, Northern Gannet, Pomarine Jaeger, and Bridled Tern). You can also set up a one-day trip with a boat or seaplane operating under a National Park Service permit; contact the park office for a list.

Bush Key and
Fort Jefferson,
Dry Tortugas
National Park,
west of Key West

The Dry Tortugas definitely rank on the short list of top U.S. birding sites. Sooty Tern and Brown Noddy nest by the thousands on **Bush Key,** just 200 yards or so from Garden Key. A few Black Noddies may also be found here, but are much more difficult to see. Lucky birders sometimes find a Black Noddy perched on the old coaling docks on Garden Key, allowing comparison with its abundant relative.

Magnificent Frigatebird and Masked Booby breed in the Dry Tortugas. The former is easily seen at Garden Key, but the latter is usually identified only on boat trips, as it nests on **Hospital Key** about a mile or so away. Brown Booby, while not a local nester, is sometimes seen around Garden Key roosting on buoys; its relative the Red-footed Booby is much rarer. The graceful White-tailed Tropicbird is seen as a very rare flyover.

In spring migration, thousands of trans-Gulf migrants use the Dry Tortugas as a rest stop. Good days (when north winds and/or rain make the ocean crossing difficult) can turn Garden Key into something resembling an overstocked aviary. Naturally, all this activity attracts raptors, so it's not unusual to find a Sharp-shinned Hawk, Merlin, or Peregrine Falcon trying to pick up an easy lunch. Such South Florida specialties as Gray Kingbird, Black-whiskered Vireo, and Shiny Cowbird are regularly found here as well.

# SOUTHEAST AND SOUTHWEST

**4** Hotels and tourist-thronged beaches haven't completely taken over the southeastern shoreline from Miami to Fort Pierce. Parks of varying sizes can still be found along the coast, and it's here that birders look not only for spring migrants but also for rare vagrants from the Bahamas (just 65 miles away) and the Caribbean, such as La Sagra's Flycatcher and Stripe-headed Tanager. Among the popular birding parks in the region are **John U. Lloyd Beach State Recreation Area** in Hollywood, **Hugh Taylor Birch State Recreation Area** in Fort Lauderdale, and **Jonathan Dickinson State Park** near Hobe Sound.

While the first two parks are productive mostly in migration and for vagrants, Jonathan Dickinson's size (11,500 acres) and diverse habitats make it a fine destination anytime. One specialty is Florida Scrub-Jay (formerly a race of the Scrub Jay shown in most field guides, now a separate species), a bird that has come to symbolize the Florida scrublands, a little-known and underappreciated Florida habitat. A sandy-soil, fire-dependent ecosystem with dozens of endemic plants and animals, Sand Pine scrub is threatened by development throughout the state. Florida Scrub-Jays

- Regional specialties in some of America's most famous natural areas
- Good sites for Florida Scrub-Jay

Information section p. 160

Florida Scrub-Jay

need areas with small oaks. Their family life incorporates a "nest-helper" system, in which a pair's older offspring help care for younger siblings. Jonathan Dickinson also hosts breeding Osprey and Bald Eagle, as well as Bachman's Sparrow in pinewoods.

**5** Just northwest of Boca Raton, **Arthur R. Marshall Loxahatchee National Wildlife Refuge** is a fairly reliable spot to find Smooth-billed Ani, a species that has declined greatly in population and has become harder to find in recent years. The impoundments here always have a good variety of waders and waterfowl, often including Fulvous Whistling-Duck, and occasionally a Snail Kite (endangered) spotted in slow, floppy-winged flight. This South Florida specialty is one of the many species harmed by human-caused disruptions in the Everglades water regime. Although the refuge does not allow boat tours, one option is **Swampland Tours** (941-467-4411), located on Fla. 78 on the north shore of Lake Okeechobee. The kite isn't guaranteed on every boat ride, but the odds are pretty good. Purple Gallinule and Limpkin are seen commonly.

### Snail Kite

The Snail Kite's distinctive bill is an adaptation for feeding on apple snails, large gastropods common in South Florida marshes that are essentially the kite's only food. The curved, pointed bill easily reaches inside the snail's shell, allowing the kite to remove the soft body. The kite's ability to find snails is greatly affected by water levels, so the birds wander widely in search of proper conditions for feeding. Once reduced to just a few pairs in Florida, the Snail Kite has made something of a comeback, though it remains vulnerable to drought and human-caused disruptions in water flow through the "river of grass."

**6** The northern section of Everglades National Park is accessible via the **Shark Valley Visitor Center,** on US 41 about 25 miles west of Florida's Turnpike (Fla. 821). Two walking trails often provide excellent looks at waders, but this area is best known as a good spot for the Snail Kite. Wood Storks are also common in winter. A paved 15-mile loop heads south through the vast saw-grass expanse of Shark River Slough (elevation 7 to 8 feet above sea level), where these medium-size hawks search for large apple snails. Don't be fooled by wintering Northern Harriers, which also fly low and slowly, and also have white rumps. The park operates

Big Cypress
National Preserve,
southeast of Naples

a tram tour along the loop, but if you have time, consider renting a bicycle. The path is as flat as a tabletop, and you'll be able to stop wherever you like to scan for kites. The roadside gators won't bother you if you don't bother them.

Across the highway from and just west of Shark Valley, the **Miccosukee Restaurant** (*305-223-8380*), operated by the Miccosukee Indians, has long been a favorite center for spotting Snail Kites. Find a clear view along the canal and check the marsh to the north, where the birds often roost. Keep your eyes open anywhere in this area, as kites are sometimes seen flying across the highway or along canals.

**7** Just a bit farther west on US 41, you'll enter **Big Cypress National Preserve,** which protects another 728,000 acres of the Everglades. Look for County Road 94 diverging to the left at the Tamiami Ranger Station. First paved, then unpaved and rough (*check with the preserve* *office for road conditions)*, this 26-mile route through swampy woods offers close views of herons and egrets before returning to US 41.

Ten miles farther west, turn north on unpaved County Road 839 (Turner River Road), which parallels a swampy canal and offers abundant waders and waterbirds, including Wood Storks. This beautifully homely wader, 3.5 feet tall, with a naked head and long, stout bill, has suffered as

Little Blue Heron and watchers at Corkscrew Swamp Sanctuary, west of Immokalee

much as any species from environmental changes in this century. Once breeding across much of the southeast, with a population as high as 50,000 in Florida alone, Wood Storks have declined to only a few thousand pairs nesting in Florida, Georgia, and South Carolina. Changes in Everglades water flow seriously affect nesting success. Some years thousands of young fledge, while other years may end with near-total nesting failure.

Continue north for 7 miles, turn west on County Road 837 for 3 miles, then south again to return to US 41. Seven miles west of the Fla. 29 intersection, stop at the Big Cypress Bend area of **Fakahatchee Strand State Preserve,** where a 2,000-foot-long boardwalk leads into a swamp forest with very old, very large bald cypresses. Bald Eagles nest here, and the big trees make this a good area to see Pileated Woodpecker, the crow-size woodpecker whose loud "laughing" call and oblong nest hole are signs of its presence.

If you haven't seen Shiny Cowbird, a favorite spot in winter has been the feeders at **The Conservancy Briggs Nature Center** (*from US 41, take Fla. 951 S for 2 miles, turning W on Shell Island Rd.*), southeast of Naples. Walk the trails through coastal mangroves for a chance to see Mangrove Cuckoo and, in spring and summer, Black-whiskered Vireo. Florida Scrub-Jays have been reintroduced here in recent years.

**8** The National Audubon Society's **Corkscrew Swamp Sanctuary,** off County Road 846 west of Immokalee, ranks among the state's finest natural areas. The sanctuary's 10,560 acres (with adjacent lands protected through Florida's Save Our Rivers campaign) is home to the country's largest colony of Wood Storks. The number of nests here has ranged in recent years from around 200 to nearly 1,000—but nests don't necessarily result in breeding success. In 1997 drought meant that no young fledged, and in 1998 El Niño brought flooding that again discouraged nesting.

Limpkin, a wading bird named for its "limping" walk

A 2.25-mile boardwalk loops through a splendid cypress swamp, where orchids adorn 6-foot-thick tree trunks, swamp lilies bloom abundantly, and alligators laze just a few feet away. You may see an Anhinga drying its wings beside the trail; a Little Blue Heron patiently waiting at a pond full of water lettuce for an unwary crayfish; a Limpkin searching for snails; or a small flock of White Ibis flying away, their plumage seeming to glow within the dark forest. Red-shouldered Hawks scream their evocative two-note call as they soar overhead.

**9** On Sanibel Island, near Fort Myers, lies one of America's most famous nature preserves, **J.N. "Ding" Darling National Wildlife Refuge,** where many a birder has seen his or her first Black-whiskered Vireo. As enticing as the refuge is, don't rush across the causeway between the mainland and Sanibel. Magnificent Frigatebird, Reddish

Egret, Wilson's Plover, American Oystercatcher, Black Skimmer, and a variety of terns can be seen along the way.

The main attraction at "Ding" Darling is its 5-mile wildlife drive (*closed Fri.*), where such impressive birds as American White and Brown Pelicans; Anhinga; Great Blue, Little Blue, Tricolored, and Green Herons; Great, Snowy, and Reddish Egrets; Yellow-crowned Night-Heron; White Ibis; Roseate Spoonbill; and Wood Stork are seen seasonally in varying numbers. Black-whiskered Vireo nests on the refuge and is usually easy to find along the wildlife drive and refuge walking trails in spring and summer, when males are singing. Mangrove Cuckoo nests, too, but is as elusive here as elsewhere.

Gray Kingbird, another goal of visiting birders, can be found anywhere on Sanibel, perching in plain sight far more cooperatively than the cuckoo or the vireo. Also quite conspicuous are Osprey, their bulky nests set atop all sorts of supports, from channel markers to platforms erected specifically to attract this popular raptor.

### South Florida's Exotics

With a huge pet trade, abundant fruit trees, and a subtropical climate that allows escaped birds to survive, southern Florida is home to a broad and colorful variety of free-flying exotic birds. Some, such as the Red-whiskered Bulbul (shown here) from southeastern Asia and the Spot-breasted Oriole from Central America, have established breeding populations in the Miami area. The Australian Budgerigar (the common "parakeet" of pet stores), once abundant in the Tampa-St. Petersburg area, has declined sharply in recent years. Several other species of parrots may be encountered anywhere in the southern peninsula, especially in the larger cities.

**10** Located off Fla. 72 about 9 miles east of I-75 in Sarasota, 28,875-acre **Myakka River State Park** repays a visit with some of the region's prettiest scenery. Palms, Spanish moss-covered live oaks, extensive marshes, open grassland, and 12 miles of the Myakka River attract a fine selection of species. Nesting birds include Anhinga, Least Bittern, Black-crowned and Yellow-crowned Night-Herons, Wood Duck, Osprey, Bald Eagle, Red-shouldered Hawk, Wild Turkey, Black-necked Stilt, and Common Ground-Dove. In addition, Glossy Ibis, Roseate Spoonbill, Wood Stork, Swallow-tailed Kite, Limpkin, and Sandhill Crane are seen regularly. Stop at the bridge where the main park road crosses the Myakka River, and don't miss the boardwalk at

Upper Myakka Lake. Nearby **Oscar Scherer State Park** (*off US 41*) is known for its population of Florida Scrub-Jays. The jays are usually easy to find and here, as elsewhere, often show a great curiosity toward their watchers.

The woodlands and prairies from Palmdale north toward Sebring and Avon Park are worth exploring for several special species. Crested Caracara, a strikingly marked large raptor, may be seen along Fla. 70 east of Arcadia, County Road 74 east of Babcock, or the part of US 27 connecting them. They're often seen scavenging on the ubiquitous road-killed armadillos. Short-tailed Hawk, difficult to find in the nesting season, is occasionally seen near Palmdale. Note that it occurs in both light and dark phases, and that when soaring its wing tips are often slightly upturned.

The **Avon Park Air Force Range** east of Avon Park is a good place to look for Swallow-tailed Kite, Short-tailed

Snowy Egret, Little Blue Herons, and White Ibis at J.N. "Ding" Darling National Wildlife Refuge, Sanibel Island

Sandhill Crane and chicks at Myakka River State Park, near Sarasota

Hawk (rare), Crested Caracara, Sandhill Crane, and Florida Scrub-Jay. The endangered Red-cockaded Woodpecker is found here, as is often the case, with Brown-headed Nuthatch and Bachman's Sparrow, which frequent the same open pine habitat.

As you drive along Kissimmee Road, watch and listen for Grasshopper Sparrow. This is the best place in Florida to find this species. It's also a great location for Wild Turkey. Call or check in at the range and visit the natural resources office on County Road 64 for a map and permission to bird, since the area is sometimes closed for military operations.

# NORTHERN PENINSULAR FLORIDA

**11** Less than an hour east of Orlando and adjacent to the Kennedy Space Center, **Merritt Island National Wildlife Refuge** *(4 miles E of Titusville Bridge on Fla. 402)* is famous for its varied birding opportunities. Encompassing Atlantic Ocean beach, marsh, oak scrub, pinelands, and grassland, the refuge has seen more than 310 species recorded since its establishment in 1963. You can pick up a map of the area at the refuge visitor center on Fla. 402, or at the Canaveral National Seashore office *(407-267-1110)* on US 1 in Titusville. Follow Fla. 406 east across the Intracoastal Waterway to the refuge.

Waders, Mottled Duck, Osprey, Bald Eagle, and Florida Scrub-Jay are among the many nesting species here. In fall, shorebirds are found on ponds and Atlantic beaches, while Peregrine Falcons are frequently seen hunting during their southbound migration. In winter, thousands of ducks congregate on the refuge; Tree Swallows sometimes feed in enormous flocks; Clapper, King, and Virginia Rails and Sora skulk along the edges of wetlands. Laughing, Ring-billed, and Herring Gulls are the common species, but a few Great Black-backed Gulls can also be found along with Caspian, Royal, and Forster's Terns and Black Skimmer. Northern Gannet is frequently seen offshore in winter, with dozens of birds sometimes sighted daily.

Just beyond the refuge visitor center, the **Oak Hammock Trail** is good for songbirds in spring migration. Next, drive along Fla. 402 to Playalinda Beach, where you can scan for seabirds, shorebirds, gulls, and terns. The 6-mile **Black Point Wildlife Drive,** north on Fla. 406, traverses marshes where waders are abundant. A hiking trail here leads to an observation tower with views over the surrounding wetlands.

● **Concentrations of waterbirds at Merritt Island National Wildlife Refuge**

Information section p. 161

Merritt Island
National Wildlife
Refuge, near
Titusville

**12** Located about 10 miles south of Gainesville, **Paynes Prairie State Preserve** comprises an expanse of wet prairie with pine flatwoods, hardwood hammocks, and wetlands intermixed, set within a basin formed by subsidence of the underlying limestone. Sandhill Cranes winter here in the thousands and can be seen from observation towers in various parts of the preserve, including at the visitor center north of Micanopy and just east of US 441 between Micanopy and Gainesville. Stop here for a bird checklist and a map locating several short hiking trails. Waders, Osprey, Bald Eagle, Wild Turkey, King Rail, and Purple Gallinule breed here, along with Sandhill Cranes of the resident Florida population.

# FLORIDA PANHANDLE

**13** **St. Marks National Wildlife Refuge** covers more than 68,000 acres along the Gulf of Mexico south of Tallahassee off Fla. 98. Around 60 percent of the refuge is classified as wetlands, both natural and diked impoundments; forested areas include pine flatwoods and hardwoods. The result is a fine variety of year-round birding opportunities.

A 7-mile road runs from the refuge entrance south past the visitor center (check nearby woods for Yellow-throated Warbler) to the Gulf, passing many marshy impoundments on the way to a historic 1829 brick lighthouse on the coast. Great numbers of ducks winter in these ponds, with the population peaking in December. Bald Eagle pairs begin nesting at St. Marks as early as November or December, while Ospreys wait until spring is nearer. You may find Brown-headed Nuthatch along **Mounds Trail** in the woods near the refuge fire tower. Waders are abundant year-round.

Several trails wind through the refuge, including some that follow dikes. These can be good places to see such marsh birds as rails, Purple Gallinule, Sedge (winter) and Marsh Wrens, and Nelson's Sharp-tailed Sparrow (winter). Marshes near the coast are home to Seaside Sparrow year-round, and the elusive Black Rail is sometimes heard calling. Wilson's Plover nests along the shore.

Just north of St. Marks, **Edward Ball Wakulla Springs State Park** is known as an excellent spot to find Limpkin, often seen on the river boat tours of this largest and deepest freshwater spring in the world. Anhinga, Swallow-tailed Kite, and Purple Gallinule also nest in the area.

**14** **Apalachicola National Forest,** just southwest of Tallahassee, encompasses some pinewoods where the endangered Red-cockaded Woodpecker nests.

● Red-cockaded Woodpecker at Apalachicola National Forest

● Spring "fallouts" at Fort Pickens

Information section p. 161

Apalachicola is home to more of these birds than any other area, with more than 500 active clusters (family groups) in 1998, and with a management plan in place intended to increase that number to more than 1,400. In the western part of the forest, Fla. 379 is a good place to look for the birds. This road, the Apalachee Savannahs Scenic Byway, is handy for those heading south to St. George Island or St. Joseph Peninsula State Parks (see p. 159). Southwest of Tallahassee, search along Forest Service Road 305 leading from Fla. 373 to Fla. 267, and along Forest Service Roads 367, 366, 360, 350, and 361, making a loop south of Fla. 267.

Watch for pines with white paint rings, indicating cavity trees, and also look for fresh flows of resin indicating an active site. Waiting before dusk for a Red-cockaded Woodpecker to return to its roost hole is a good way to see one, but observe from a distance—don't approach cavity trees too closely or in any other way harass individuals of this rare species. Brown-headed Nuthatch and Bachman's Sparrow are found in the same habitat as the woodpecker. In spring, listen in swampy areas for the song of the Swainson's Warbler, and check grassy areas in winter for Henslow's Sparrow.

**Pinewoods Woodpecker**

One of the few birds found only in the United States, the Red-cockaded Woodpecker is endemic to the pine forests of the southeast, where the loss of its particular habitat—it nests in small groups in mature pines with a fungal condition called red heart disease—has resulted in declining numbers and an endangered species status. Florida's **Apalachicola National Forest** is a center of the Red-cockaded Woodpecker population, and by driving the roads listed in the text, you'll have a good chance of finding the bird. Look for active roost trees, often marked by such extensive flows of whitish resin that they're called "candlestick trees." Old flows are dull, while fresh resin is sticky and shiny. The birds drill pits in the bark to create these sap flows, which may serve to repel predators that would climb the tree to feast on eggs or young. Early morning and late afternoon are the best times to look for the birds, which often spend the day foraging well away from their roost trees.

**15** South of Pensacola, on Santa Rosa Island, lies one of the most famous birding spots on the upper Gulf Coast: **Fort Pickens,** a part of the **Gulf Islands National Seashore.** Like Dauphin Island in Alabama and High Island in Texas, Fort Pickens is known primarily for spring "fallouts" of migrant songbirds. When north winds or rain make the Gulf crossing difficult, tired birds head for the first land they see, sometimes congregating in impressive numbers at coastal sites.

Anhinga drying plumage

The Fort Pickens area where most birders head is about 3 miles long by less than a mile wide. Drive on Fort Pickens Road to the campground, park at the store, and check spots with trees or shrubs, which from mid-March to mid-May can host vireos, warblers, thrushes, orioles, and other migrants. A biking trail parallel to the main road and several nature trails provide access to birding locations.

Back east along the Gulf Coast, several state parks can also provide great birding during fallouts. Two of the best known are **St. Joseph Peninsula State Park** near Port St. Joe and **St. George Island State Park** near Apalachicola. This area of Florida is also famous for having some of the highest quality beaches in North America—which often translates into summer crowds. Although Snowy Plover, Least Tern, Black Skimmer, and Gray Kingbird breed along the coast, birders most often visit from fall through spring, when the region is less populated. Fall can bring migrant songbirds, as well as southbound raptors. Sprague's Pipit is rare but regular on the causeway to St. George from mid-November through December, where some of the state's largest colonies of Least Tern and Black Skimmer breed.

# Florida
# Information

? Visitor Center/Information    ⑤ Fee Charged    🍴 Food

🚻 Rest Rooms    🚶 Nature Trails    🚗 Driving Tours    ♿ Wheelchair Accessible

*Be advised that facilities may be seasonal and limited. We suggest calling or writing ahead for specific information. Note that addresses may be for administrative offices; see text or call for directions to sites.*

## Rare Bird Alerts

Florida:
Statewide *561-340-0079*
Lower keys *305-294-3438*
Miami *305-667-7337*
Northern Florida
   *912-244-9190*

## SOUTHERN EVERGLADES REGION AND THE KEYS

### Everglades National Park *(Page 141)*
40001 State Road 9336
Homestead, FL 33034
*305-242-7700*

? ⑤ 🍴 🚻 🚶 🚗 ♿

### Dry Tortugas National Park *(Page 145)*
40001 State Road 9336
Homestead, FL 33034
*305-242-7700*

? 🚻 🚶 ♿

## SOUTHEAST AND SOUTHWEST

### John U. Lloyd Beach State Recreation Area
*(Page 147)*
6503 North Ocean Drive
Dania, FL 33004
*954-923-2833*

⑤ 🍴 🚻 🚶 ♿

*Site located in Hollywood*

### Hugh Taylor Birch State Recreation Area
*(Page 147)*
3109 East Sunrise
  Boulevard
Fort Lauderdale, FL 33304
*954-564-4521*

? ⑤ 🚻 🚶 ♿

*Guided walks Fri.*

### Jonathan Dickinson State Park *(Page 147)*
16450 SE Federal Highway
Hobe Sound, FL 33455
*561-546-2771*

⑤ 🍴 🚻 🚶 ♿

### Arthur R. Marshall Loxahatchee National Wildlife Refuge
*(Page 148)*
10216 Lee Road
Boynton Beach, FL 33437
*561-732-3684*

? ⑤ 🚻 🚶 ♿

### Big Cypress National Preserve *(Page 149)*
33100 Tamiami Trail East
Ochopee, FL 34141
*941-695-4111*

? 🚻 🚗 ♿

### Fakahatchee Strand State Preserve
*(Page 150)*
137 Coastline Drive
Copeland, FL 34137
*941-695-4593*

? 🚶 🚗 ♿

### The Conservancy Briggs Nature Center
*(Page 151)*
401 Shell Island Road
Naples, FL 34113
*941-775-8569*

? ⑤ 🚻 🚶 ♿

**Corkscrew Swamp Sanctuary** *(Page 151)*
375 Sanctuary Road
Naples, FL 34120
*941-348-9151*

🅿️♿🅷🍴🚶🐟♿

**J.N. "Ding" Darling National Wildlife Refuge** *(Page 151)*
1 Wildlife Drive
Sanibel, FL 33757
*941-472-1100*

🅿️♿🍴🚶🐟♿

*Wildlife drive closed Fri.*

**Myakka River State Park** *(Page 152)*
13207 State Road 72
Sarasota, FL 34241
*941-361-6511*

🅿️♿🅷🍴🚶🐟♿

**Oscar Scherer State Park** *(Page 153)*
1843 South Tamiami Trail
Osprey, FL 34229
*941-483-5956*

♿🍴🚶♿

**Avon Park Air Force Range** *(Page 153)*
29 South Boulevard
Avon Park Air Force
    Range, FL 33825
*941-452-4254*

🅿️♿🍴🚶♿

*Closed Tues.–Thurs. and at other times for training; call ahead.*

---

# NORTHERN PENINSULAR FLORIDA

**Merritt Island National Wildlife Refuge**
*(Page 155)*
P.O. Box 6504
Titusville, FL 32782
*407-861-0667*

🅿️🍴🚶🐟♿

**Paynes Prairie State Preserve** *(Page 156)*
Route 2, Box 41
Micanopy, FL 32667
*352-466-4100*

🅿️♿🍴🚶♿

---

# FLORIDA PANHANDLE

**St. Marks National Wildlife Refuge**
*(Page 157)*
1255 Lighthouse Road
St. Marks, FL 32355
*850-925-6121*

🅿️♿🍴🚶🐟♿

**Edward Ball Wakulla Springs State Park**
*(Page 157)*
550 Wakulla Park Drive
Wakulla Springs, FL 32305
*850-224-5950*

♿🅷🍴🚶♿

---

**Apalachicola National Forest** *(Page 157)*
Fla. 20, P.O. Box 579
Bristol, FL 32321
*850-643-2282*

🐟

**Fort Pickens** part of **Gulf Islands National Seashore**
*(Page 158)*
1801 Gulf Breeze Parkway
Gulf Breeze, FL 32561
*850-934-2600*

🅿️♿🅷🍴🚶♿

*Site located on Santa Rosa Island*

**St. Joseph Peninsula State Park** *(Page 159)*
8899 Cape San Blas Road
Port St. Joe, FL 32456
*850-227-1327*

♿🍴🚶♿

**St. George Island State Park** *(Page 159)*
1900 East Gulf Beach Drive
St. George Island, FL 32328
*850-927-2111*

♿🍴🚶♿

# South-Central States

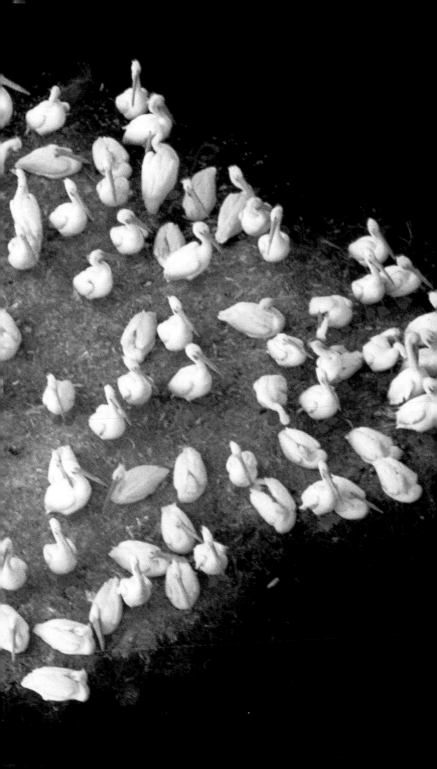

R oseate Spoonbill and Canada Warbler are seldom mentioned in the same paragraph, much less the same sentence. Here, though, they will be—to illustrate the avian extremes of this mid-southern chapter, which encompasses the salt marshes of Louisiana and the 6,000-foot peaks of eastern Tennessee, with a correspondingly broad range of birding possibilities. In one corner of the region, Fulvous Whistling-Duck and Purple Gallinule nest; in the other, Northern Saw-whet Owl, Common Raven, Black-capped Chickadee, and other northern birds extend their ranges south along the Appalachian Mountains.

*Preceding pages:* White Pelicans at Sabine National Wildlife Refuge, Louisiana *Above:* Wood Ducks *Below:* Brown Pelicans

Between these extremes lies the land that many people picture when they think of the South: meandering rivers lined with bald cypresses and tupelos, bottomland hard-

wood forests, and flat cropland. Southern birds favoring these temperate lands include Anhinga, Little Blue Heron, Swallow-tailed Kite, Prothonotary and Swainson's Warblers, and Painted Bunting.

Birders find rewards in other habitats, too. Pinewoods are home to Red-cockaded Woodpecker, Brown-headed Nuthatch, and Bachman's Sparrow, all southern specialties. Sandy beaches provide nesting sites for Snowy and Wilson's Plovers, Least Tern, and Black Skimmer. Some of America's most famous spring migration "fallout" sites lie along the Gulf Coast, and great inland reservoirs such as Alabama's Guntersville Lake attract wintering loons, grebes, waterfowl, Bald Eagles, and gulls.

Here, as in so many places, human activities have

worked immense changes on the landscape. The same rich alluvial soil that once grew huge oaks, hickories, and sweet gums now grows cotton, soybeans, and rice. Rivers and creeks that once annually overtopped their banks, spreading renewing silt and nurturing productive wetlands, are now ditched and leveed. Pine forests where trees once grew to staggering sizes are now planted and harvested like wheat or corn. The Carolina Parakeet is gone, as are the

## Special Birds of the South-Central States

*Scissor-tailed Flycatcher*

| | | | |
|---|---|---|---|
| | | Swallow-tailed Kite | Red-cockaded |
| | | Mississippi Kite | Woodpecker |
| Brown Pelican | White Ibis | Purple Gallinule | Scissor-tailed |
| Neotropic | Glossy Ibis | Snowy Plover | Flycatcher |
| Cormorant | Fulvous Whistling- | Wilson's Plover | Brown-headed |
| Anhinga | Duck | Royal Tern | Nuthatch |
| Magnificent | Ross's Goose | Sandwich Tern | Swainson's Warbler |
| Frigatebird | Mottled Duck | Common Ground- | Bachman's Sparrow |
| Reddish Egret | King Rail | Dove | Painted Bunting |

Ivory-billed Woodpecker and the Bachman's Warbler, all once widespread in the South.

On the other side of the scale, Ospreys and Bald Eagles are beginning to breed in places where they were long absent, their huge nests appearing beside lakes and rivers. Brown Pelicans have made a strong comeback after declines in population caused by pesticides. Colonies of wading birds, once vulnerable to hunting and harassment, enjoy strong protection. And a growing corps of conservationists works to safeguard the natural areas that remain in the South, from old-growth forests to lowland swamps. Many of them are among America's finest places to see birds, so read on, and plan a trip to enjoy them.

This chapter begins in the wild and rugged mountains of Tennessee, then heads south and west to the swamps of Louisiana. ■

# TENNESSEE

**1** The highlands of eastern Tennessee reach their pinnacle at 6,643-foot Clingmans Dome, the second highest point east of the Mississippi River, in **Great Smoky Mountains National Park.** For birders, this means the chance to see breeding species such as Northern Saw-whet Owl; Olive-sided Flycatcher (rare); Common Raven; Black-capped Chickadee; Red-breasted Nuthatch; Brown Creeper; Winter Wren; Golden-crowned Kinglet; Veery; Chestnut-sided, Black-throated Blue, Black-throated Green, Blackburnian, and Canada Warblers; Dark-eyed Junco; and Red Crossbill (irregular).

The best place to see many of these northern birds is the road from Newfound Gap, on US 441, up to Clingmans Dome (*closed in winter*). Although it can be very crowded, the parking lot at Newfound Gap can have interesting birds, and pull-offs and trail junctions along the ascending

- Northern species in the eastern mountains
- Migration hot spots in Knoxville and Nashville
- Excellent shore-birds in Memphis

Information section p. 197

Cades Cove in Great Smoky Mountains National Park

Rhododendrons on
Roan Mountain,
eastern Tennessee

road also offer birding opportunities. Saw-whets call here in spring, and you may hear the *jip-jip* notes of Red Crossbill, a species that's unpredictable but always present somewhere in the area. For a taste of hiking (and to get away from the road), walk the **Forney Ridge Trail** to Andrews Bald, a round-trip of less than 4 miles.

The beautiful **Cades Cove** area in the northwest part of the park is a good choice to see lower-elevation birds, including Ruffed Grouse, Wild Turkey, Acadian and Willow Flycatchers, Yellow-throated and Hooded Warblers, Blue Grosbeak, and Orchard Oriole.

**2** Many of the same highland birds can be found at 6,285-foot Roan Mountain, reached by taking Tenn. 143 south from the town of the same name. Visit **Roan Mountain State Park** for nesting birds such as Ruffed Grouse; Golden-winged, Chestnut-sided, and Worm-eating Warblers; Scarlet Tanager; and Rose-breasted Grosbeak. Continue 10 miles up to **Carver's Gap,** on the North Carolina state line, where a natural garden of pinkish purple Catawba rhododendrons attracts crowds at the peak of bloom, usually around the third week of June. In spring and

early summer, look and listen here for Alder Flycatcher (in alders) and Winter Wren. Hermit Thrush is heard singing in nesting season in this area, as is, rarely, Magnolia Warbler. Vesper Sparrow nests in grassy balds, where intrepid birders may find Snow Bunting in winter.

**3** Knoxville's favorite birding spot, **Sharp's Ridge Memorial Park** is an excellent place to observe songbird migration in spring and fall. To reach it, take Ludlow Avenue west from US 441 (Broadway). The technique here is simple: Walk the road along the ridge and look for warblers (sometimes more than 20 species a day in late April and early May), vireos, thrushes, tanagers, and other migrants. The wooded slopes mean you'll often have good views of birds usually seen only high in treetops. Fall migration can also be productive, although never as intense as spring waves.

**4** Varied habitats make the **Kingston Steam Plant** one of the best all-around birding spots in eastern Tennessee. Located 2 miles west of Kingston, north off US 70, this Tennessee Valley Authority facility encompasses ponds, marsh, grassy fields, and woodland. Check pines near the entrance road for the state's northernmost Brown-headed Nuthatches, as well as nesting Yellow-throated and Pine Warblers. Migration may bring Sora or Marsh Wren to marshy spots, or rarely Virginia Rail or Nelson's Sharp-tailed Sparrow. Ducks winter by the hundreds on ponds here; Snow Goose is rare but regular, and Greater White-fronted Goose is found occasionally. Osprey and Grasshopper Sparrow nest in the area, and late summer can bring good numbers of shorebirds, with Buff-breasted Sandpiper a regular visitor.

**5** Chattanooga's **Brainerd Levee** *(from Tenn. 153, drive W for 2 miles on Shallowford Rd.)* is popular with local birders for its easy access to wetlands good for sighting wintering waterfowl (especially dabbling ducks), migrant rails and shorebirds, and postbreeding waders. Walk the levee beside South Chickamauga Creek and look for Great Blue and Green Herons (both common), and such uncommon to rare visitors as Great and Snowy Egrets, Yellow-crowned Night-Heron, and White and Glossy Ibises. Least Bittern nests here, and American Bittern is seen in migration. When water levels are right, this can be the region's best shorebird spot, and grassy places can harbor sparrows and Sedge and Marsh Wrens in migration. Purple Gallinule is seen occasionally, and Common Moorhen is a nearly annual sighting.

Least Bittern, the smallest member of the heron family

**6** Off Tenn. 60 about 8 miles north of Georgetown via County Road 131, the **Blythe Ferry Unit** of the **Hiwassee Refuge** offers many of the standard attractions

of a waterfowl area: wintering ducks and geese (mostly Canada, with occasional Snow and rare Greater White-fronted) and wetlands that attract waders and shorebirds seasonally. In recent years, though, Sandhill Cranes have become the refuge stars, some wintering and others stopping in migration on their way from Florida and Georgia to breeding areas in the

north. From just a few birds, the concentration has grown to more than 6,000 at times, making this one of the state's premier wildlife spectacles from about November through March. Though closed through much of the winter, the area can be viewed from adjacent roads and an observation deck anytime.

Radnor Lake State Natural Area, Nashville

**7** Nashville birders treasure **Radnor Lake State Natural Area,** where more than 5 miles of trails wind through the wooded slopes surrounding an 85-acre lake. A fine spot to visit any time of year, the area is most popular in spring migration, when more than 20 species of warblers pass through, and in winter, when a good variety of ducks can be seen. Nature study and hiking are the focus here; even picnicking isn't allowed. American Woodcocks perform their courtship flights in late winter, when Ringnecked Duck, Lesser Scaup, Bufflehead, and Hooded Merganser cruise the lake. In summer, the songs of Wood Thrush, Prothonotary Warbler, and Summer and Scarlet Tanagers sound through the forest. Reach Radnor Lake by taking US 31 (Franklin Road) south of Nashville and turning west on Otter Creek Road.

**8** Located about 12 miles north of the small town of Big Sandy, the **Pace Point Area** of **Tennessee National Wildlife Refuge** can be one of the region's best birding spots from fall through spring. Here, where a wedge of land stretches north into immense Kentucky Lake, low water levels create shallows that attract large numbers of waders, shorebirds, gulls, and terns. In late summer Great Blue and Little Blue Herons and Great and Snowy Egrets congregate, and fall brings flocks of Black Terns to feed on small fish. Canada Geese and dabbling and diving ducks can be abundant at times. Check the small coves along the entrance road for mergansers; Barred Owl is seen often near the road down to the lake. In spring, woods west of the entrance road and near the refuge office are excellent for viewing flycatchers, vireos, and warblers. Both Osprey and Bald Eagle nest on the lake.

**9** Western Tennessee's most famous birding location, **Reelfoot Lake** typifies one image of the South—towering bald cypresses, muddy swamps dotted with water lilies, and Great Egrets wading quietly through the shallows, with the squeal of Wood Ducks, the scream of Red-shouldered Hawks, and the whistle of Prothonotary Warblers in the air. A national wildlife refuge, a state park, and a state wildlife management area offer birding locations around the lake, the most accessible of which is the auto tour route at **Reelfoot National Wildlife Refuge** off Tenn. 157 on the lake's eastern side. Nesting birds include Least Bittern, Black-crowned Night-Heron, Hooded Merganser, Osprey, Mississippi Kite, and Purple Gallinule. Migration brings shorebirds to muddy pools, late summer can see flocks of herons and egrets, and in winter thousands of ducks and geese mass on the lake and in fields (some years more than half a million, mostly Canada Goose, Gadwall, American Wigeon, and Mallard). The Black Bayou area, on the lake's west side, has marsh where Northern Shoveler and King Rail nest and grassy places where Short-eared Owl winters.

Reelfoot is known for its wintering Bald Eagles, with dozens of birds perched in the bald cypresses or soaring overhead. **Reelfoot Lake State Park** offers guided bus tours to see eagles (*call for information about these popular trips*). As

is true of many spots across the South, Reelfoot has in recent years seen the return of the Bald Eagle as a nesting species as well, with up to a half-dozen pairs breeding.

Ospreys nesting at Reelfoot Lake, western Tennessee

**10** The most famous birding site in Memphis, and justifiably so, is the **EARTH Complex** in the southwestern part of town *(Mitchell Rd. W from US 61; at T.O. Fuller State Park, bear left onto Plant Rd. to Riverport; then left on Riverport Rd. and first right on Plant Rd.)*. The air may not be fragrant at this sewage-treatment plant, but the shorebirds can be terrific. Check in at the office for advice on birding areas and road conditions; a spotting scope is essential to get the most from a visit. In spring and fall migrations (and for shorebirds, "fall" can begin in July), you can see Black-bellied and Semipalmated Plovers; Greater and Lesser Yellowlegs; Solitary, Spotted, Semipalmated, Western, Least, Pectoral, and Stilt Sandpipers; and Short-billed Dowitcher. Black-necked Stilt nests, and from fall through spring, ducks, gulls, and terns offer a break from the sometimes vexing task of trying to pin down which peep or dowitcher might be in your field of view.

# ALABAMA

**11** Alabama's most famous birding spot, **Dauphin Island** ranks among the top Gulf Coast spring migration "fallout" sites to which travelers make regular pilgrimages from late March through mid-May. A 14-mile-long barrier island at the mouth of Mobile Bay, linked to the mainland by a causeway (watch as you cross for waders, waterfowl, and Seaside Sparrow), Dauphin can be mobbed with migrants the day after a front brings north winds or rain. Beaches, bay, and Gulf waters make for productive birding at other times of year as well.

Many birders make their first stop the **Audubon Bird Sanctuary,** at the eastern end of the island on Bienville Boulevard. Several trails wind through this 164-acre woodland of pine, live oak, and magnolia; viewpoints overlook Gaillard Lake, and a boardwalk leads to the beach. Brown-headed Nuthatch can be found here year-round. Another equally favored location is the **Shell Mounds** area (*Iberville Dr., 2 blocks N of Bienville Blvd.*), named for the oyster shells left here during an occupation period (1100 to 1550) of Mississippian Indians. At either spot, when conditions are right, migrant songbirds—flycatchers, vireos, thrushes, warblers, tanagers, and other species—may be present in amazing concentrations.

Keep an eye out in spring for Black-whiskered Vireo, a regular visitor here north of its normal Florida range, and in open areas for Gray Kingbird from May through August. Also check the marshes south of the island's airport for wading birds, Mottled Duck, rails, American Oystercatcher, and sparrows. Explore the western end of the island by driving out Bienville Boulevard, scanning beaches for Reddish Egret, shorebirds (including Snowy, Wilson's, and Piping Plovers and American Oystercatcher), gulls, terns, and

Black Skimmer. Northern Gannet is seen often in the Gulf from fall through spring, and Magnificent Frigatebird soars overhead in summer.

A ferry runs from Dauphin Island to **Fort Morgan,** a national historic landmark on the mainland across the Mobile Bay ship channel that, like Dauphin, attracts not only the regular trans-Gulf migrants but frequent rarities. Western Kingbird and Scissor-tailed Flycatcher are regular here in October. The trees just east of the ferry landing can be productive in migration, as can the old stables area near the park entrance; check grassy areas around the fort for migrant Upland and Buff-breasted Sandpipers. The old airstrip is good for sparrows and migrant Bobolink. Walk to the westernmost point of the peninsula to search for shorebirds and seabirds in the Gulf.

Ala. 180 and 182 run eastward to Florida, providing more birding opportunities. The mostly undeveloped **Bon Secour National Wildlife Refuge** has nature trails at Mileposts 12 and 15 on Ala. 180, and **Gulf State Park** east of Gulf Shores offers more than 2 miles of beach to explore and a pavilion good for scanning for seabirds. Check the shoreline and waters around **Perdido Pass,** at the Florida state line, for waders and shorebirds. Snowy and Piping Plovers are often found here.

**Black Skimmer**

French speakers in south Louisiana call the Black Skimmer *bec à ciseaux*, or scissor-beak—an appropriate name considering its distinctive bill shape. This bird and other closely related species of skimmer are the only birds in the world with the lower mandible longer than the upper. Skimmers feed by flying just above the water, slicing the surface with their long lower bill. When they touch a fish or other prey, they quickly snap their beak closed to make the catch.

**12** The fields, woods, and water of **Eufaula National Wildlife Refuge** in eastern Alabama and western Georgia host a broad range of species, including abundant wintering ducks and geese as well as possible Wood Stork in late summer and Sandhill Crane in winter. Osprey and Bald Eagle nest around the lake, and the refuge has several rookeries where Anhinga, Great Blue and Little Blue Herons, and Great and Cattle Egrets nest. White Ibis appears regularly in summer. Drive the tour routes through the **Upland** and **Houston Units,** both accessed from the

Gulf State Park, along the Gulf of Mexico east of Gulf Shores

main refuge entrance off Ala. 285, to bird in a variety of habitats, including marshes on the Houston route that may have migrant rails and shorebirds as well as nesting Purple Gallinule and Common Moorhen. Least Bittern is an uncommon visitor. Some refuge roads are closed in winter, but two observation towers are always open. The platform at the Upland Unit is best to see wintering waterfowl.

**13** The long expanse of **Guntersville Lake** in northeastern Alabama is the state's best location to find wintering loons and grebes, and an excellent spot to see other waterbirds and Bald Eagles. **Lake Guntersville State Park** holds eagle-watches and programs, and its lakeshore is a good place from which to scan the water. A favorite lookout is the area behind Harbor House restaurant, at the southern end of the US 431 bridge. Several rare gulls have appeared here over the years. The best lookout, though, is the causeway where Ala. 69 crosses the lake just west of Guntersville. Stop carefully along the road and watch for loons (Common is most frequent, but Red-throated is seen almost annually, and even Pacific has showed up), grebes (both Red-necked and Western have been found), and waterfowl (scoters and Oldsquaw are rarities on the lake list). The **Guntersville Dam,** located 12.5 miles north of the US 431 bridge, makes another good viewpoint. Bald Eagles and gulls winter by the river below.

**14** Downstream on the Tennessee River, encompassing the middle part of Wheeler Lake, **Wheeler National Wildlife Refuge** sees some of Alabama's largest concentrations of wintering waterfowl. Several species of dabbling ducks are common, along with divers such as Canvasback, Common Bufflehead, Goldeneye, and Ruddy Duck. The refuge also hosts the state's largest population of wintering Canada Geese. Wood Duck and Hooded Merganser are common breeders.

At the Wheeler visitor center on Ala. 67, just 2 miles west of I-65, you'll find an observation building overlooking water where thousands of wintering ducks congregate in late afternoon. **Limestone Bay,** south of Mooresville, is a good spot for observing geese and the best spot for Snow Goose—and a few Ross's are found annually. Although the refuge is usually considered a winter birding site, good opportunities exist year-round. Swainson's Warbler has been found regularly near the headquarters, and trails provide access to woodland that is good for seeing spring migrants and common nesters.

Snowy Plover, an endangered shorebird of sandy beaches

**15** From fall through spring, visit **Wheeler Dam,** where Ala. 101 crosses the Tennessee River, and **Wilson Dam,** at Ala. 133 near Florence, to scan for gulls flying over the tailwaters. Bonaparte's, Ring-billed, and Herring are the common species, but concentrations here increase the odds of finding something unusual.

In migration, northern Alabama birders keep a watch on several small ponds near the town of **Leighton,** southeast of Florence. When water conditions are right, these ponds can be excellent places to see shorebirds. Rarities found here have included Roseate Spoonbill, Wood Stork, and Black-bellied Whistling-Duck. Take Ala. 22 west from Leighton to County Road 63 (Marthaler Lane), then turn

Northern Alabama's Bankhead National Forest

north another mile to ponds on both sides of the road. Black-necked Stilt has nested in this area. Continue north to Sixth Street, turn west, and check more ponds at County Road 61. Return east on Sixth Street about 8 miles to Mt. Stanley Road and drive north 3 miles to Town Creek Marsh, a wetland area on Wilson Lake that's good for rails and waders.

**16** Alabama's **Bankhead National Forest** invites exploration with a fine assortment of nesting birds, not to mention wild and rugged scenery. Here in the lower Cumberland plateau, wooded ravines with mature hemlock and hardwood forest are home to breeding warblers including Black-throated Green, Yellow-throated, Cerulean, Worm-eating, and Swainson's, and Northern Parula. Look for Blue-winged and Prairie Warblers in regenerating clear-cuts. Some of the best birding is found in and around the 35-acre **Brushy Lake Recreation Area** (*15 miles NE of Double Springs*) with a trail system that loops through a wide variety of habitats. A few miles north, Forest Road 208, running west from Ala. 33, has fine roadside birding, as does Forest Road 210, north from County Road 60 on the western edge of the wilderness.

# MISSISSIPPI

**Lower Pascagoula River Wildlife Management Area** may well be Mississippi's most important natural area, encompassing more than 30 miles of its namesake river and 40,000 acres of bottomland hardwood forest, oxbow lakes, bald-cypress-tupelo swamp, and tributary creeks. Breeding birds are those typical of such southern woods, including Yellow-crowned Night-Heron; Wood Duck; Mississippi Kite; Red-shouldered Hawk; Wild Turkey; Red-headed Woodpecker; and Prothonotary, Swainson's (uncommon), Kentucky, and Hooded Warblers. It's the beautiful Swallow-tailed Kite, though, that attracts birders from late spring through summer.

As is often the case with this sort of habitat, access is a bit problematical, with the few interior roads sometimes under water. From US 63, drive west on Miss. 614 (Wade-Vancleave Road) to the wildlife management area office on the south. Stop here for advice on road conditions and to bird in the surrounding area, especially in spring. Continue west to Deep Slough Road, a good (usually) unpaved road that leads north into woods productive for birding. Though there is a substantial population of Swallow-tailed Kites here, seeing one is not guaranteed. You may luck into a sighting anywhere, but your best chance is to watch for soaring birds just over the treetops in late morning. Several other old roads off Miss. 614, while usually not drivable, can be walked. This is also a popular hunting area—exercise caution in fall and winter.

**The Mississippi Sandhill Crane National Wildlife Refuge** preserves habitat for an endangered non-migratory subspecies of the gray, 4-foot-tall cranes. While most of the refuge is closed to visitation to protect the birds

- Nesting Least Tern at Gulfport
- Red-cockaded Woodpecker at Noxubee National Wildlife Refuge

Information section p. 198

Reddish Egret, found along the length of the Gulf Coast

(though the number of breeding pairs has risen to around 20, nesting success has been unaccountably low), tours are offered in January and February; call for information. At the refuge nature trail (*take Gautier-Vancleave Rd. exit from I-10 and drive 0.5 mile N*), Bachman's Sparrows sing their sweet song and Brown-headed Nuthatches squeak. Along the way, look for wading birds and migrant Osprey at **Bayou Castelle.** Both Henslow's and Le Conte's Sparrows may be found here in winter in weedy or tallgrass open areas.

**19** At Ocean Springs, visit the **Davis Bayou Unit** of **Gulf Islands National Seashore** for both land birding and waterbirding. A short nature trail passes through woods that may be full of birds in spring migration, especially during a "fallout" (see sidebar p. 181), and nearby marshes have wading birds and rails. A boat-launching area and a fishing pier provide lookout points over the bayou, where, depending on the season, loons, grebes, pelicans, ducks, waders, gulls, or terns may be present. Accessible by boat, the islands are also great places to see shorebirds, Ospreys, eagles, and spring and fall migrants. Check the visitor center for exhibits on Gulf ecology and maps of the area.

US 90 bordering the Mississippi Gulf Coast is lined with businesses, motels, and casinos. At **Gulfport,** sections of beach have been dedicated as Least Tern nesting areas, and here hundreds of these delicate little terns breed, along with Black Skimmers. Other beach, jetty, and harbor areas offer loons, shorebirds, gulls, and terns, as well as rare sightings of Northern Gannet from fall through spring and Magnificent Frigatebird, regular in summer. One favorite spot is the beach just east of Moses Pier, where US 49 intersects US 90. For a quieter beachfront, take US 90 west to Bay St. Louis and follow Beach Boulevard south through Waveland to **Buccaneer State Park,** which itself can be worth a visit in spring for migrant songbirds. Along the way you may find Reddish Egret or American Oystercatcher.

**20** Ten miles south of historic Natchez, **St. Catherine Creek National Wildlife Refuge** hosts an amazing number of wading birds in the postbreeding season from midsummer through fall. The thousands of birds present include such common species as Great Blue, Little Blue, and Green Herons; Great, Snowy, and Cattle Egrets; and White Ibis. Wood Stork is an annual visitor, and Roseate Spoonbill appears occasionally. The refuge can be productive for shorebirds, and waterfowl are abundant in winter.

### Migration Hot Spots

Heading northward in spring, eastern birds that have spent the winter south of the United States follow three main paths: island-hopping across the Caribbean to Florida, traveling up the eastern coast of Mexico to Texas, or flying directly across the Gulf of Mexico to the U.S. Gulf Coast. The fate of birds that take this last route is greatly affected by weather. With south winds it's an easy passage, and many birds travel far inland before stopping to rest and feed. When migrants encounter north winds or storms, though, they may struggle to reach land at all. Many die at sea, while the exhausted survivors home in on the first trees they see as they approach our southern shore. On some spring days, certain places along the Gulf Coast see fallouts of thousands of birds of dozens of species, creating a bonanza for birders. The **Peveto Woods Sanctuaries** (see p. 191) and **Grand Isle** (see p. 194) in Louisiana and **Dauphin Island** (see p. 174) and **Fort Morgan** (see p. 175) in Alabama are among the most famous of these migration hot spots.

**21** To the north, about 25 miles south of Greenville, **Yazoo National Wildlife Refuge** offers similar attractions: wintering flocks of ducks and geese (mostly Snow, with large numbers of Greater White-fronted and some Canada) and summer waders. Nesting birds at Yazoo include Pied-billed Grebe, Anhinga, Wood Duck, Hooded Merganser, Purple Gallinule, Common Moorhen, and Painted Bunting. The last can be difficult to find. It helps to learn its rather nondescript song, a series of warbling phrases. **Cox's Ponds,** a former catfish farm in the northwestern part of the refuge, is one of the region's top birding locations. Now managed as a "moist soils" area, it should be scanned any time of year for waders and shorebirds, especially in the peak fall migration period of August and September.

**Anhinga**

A southern swamp dweller, the Anhinga eats fish as do its pelican relatives. Instead of scooping them up, though, it spears its prey with its long, pointed bill. Three of its folk names derive from its appearance and behavior. "Black darter" comes from the Anhinga's ability to dart its head forward quickly and forcefully to stab fish; "snakebird" refers to its habit of swimming partially submerged with only its head and thin, sinuous neck showing; and "water turkey" comes from a fancied resemblance to the Wild Turkey, mostly because of its long, fanlike tail.

**22** The 48,000 acres of **Noxubee National Wildlife Refuge** south of Starkville combine extensive bottomland hardwood forest, lakes, and pinewoods to create one of Mississippi's finest birding areas. The refuge manages part of its pine forest for the endangered Red-cockaded Woodpecker, which has increased its population in recent years to more than 36 active clusters (family groups). Noxubee's short **Woodpecker Trail,** near the headquarters, passes through a cluster where the birds are usually found easily (early morning and late afternoon are best). Brown-headed Nuthatch, another pine specialist, can be seen here, too. In addition, a boardwalk at Bluff Lake leads to a deck offering a view of wintering waterfowl and a colony of 5,000 nesting Cattle Egrets and nonbreeding Wood Storks and White Ibises in late summer.

The 2-mile **Beaver Dam Trail** passes through the refuge's bottomland forest, where nesting birds include Yellow-throated Vireo; Yellow-throated, Black-and-white, Prothonotary, Kentucky, and Hooded Warblers; American

Redstart; and Louisiana Waterthrush. Swainson's Warbler is a rare breeder.

Bottomland forest at Noxubee National Wildlife Refuge, south of Starkville

**23** The 58,000 acres of **Sardis Lake** are easily accessible from I-55, just 9 miles east of Sardis on Miss. 315. Loons, grebes, waterfowl, and Bald Eagle can be seen from lookout points on the massive dam from fall through spring, and Osprey has begun to nest in the area. However, birding is often better on the lower lake, just below the dam, where American White Pelican and gulls feed on fish that have passed through the outlet channel. In addition to the usual Bonaparte's, Ring-billed, and Herring Gulls, rarities such as Black-headed Gull and Black-legged Kittiwake have appeared in late fall and winter. When the water level is down, sandbars in the lower lake can attract shorebirds (occasionally American Avocet), gulls, and terns. West of the Little Tallahatchie River, a side road leads to the **Clear Springs Nature Trail,** which passes through a bald-cypress-tupelo swamp where Red-headed Woodpeckers call year-round and Wood Thrushes sing their fluting song in breeding season.

MISSISSIPPI                    183

# ARKANSAS

- Excellent variety of waterbirds at Millwood Lake
- Winter waterfowl and raptors at Holla Bend National Wildlife Refuge

---

Information section p. 198

Red-headed Woodpecker

**24** You'll find some of Arkansas' finest birding near **Lake Chicot State Park,** in the southeastern corner of the state. Here in the flat landscape of the Mississippi Alluvial Plain, woods and wetlands provide habitat for a variety of breeding species along with locally rare wanderers from points south.

This small state park is located on 5,600-acre Lake Chicot, Arkansas' largest natural lake as well as the largest oxbow lake in the country. In late summer and early fall, Chicot attracts thousands of wading birds, which feed in nearby wetlands and roost in bald cypress trees in the lake's northern reaches. Part of this impressive gathering can be seen from shore, but for the best view sign up for a sunset boat tour with a park naturalist (*call ahead for schedule and reservations*). Great Blue and Little Blue Herons and Great and Cattle Egrets are abundant on this strikingly pretty lake, accompanied by smaller numbers of American White Pelican, Snowy Egret, Tricolored Heron, Black-crowned and Yellow-crowned Night-Herons, White Ibis, and Wood Stork.

Any time of year, drive the gravel road atop the tall Mississippi River levee for a look at waterbirds and other species. The state park office can provide directions and a brochure guide. In late summer the swampy borrow pits alongside the levee can teem with waders, including Wood Stork and rarely a vagrant Roseate Spoonbill. Pied-billed Grebe, Wood Duck, and Hooded Merganser breed here, and a variety of other ducks winter. In addition, Mississippi Kite, Painted Bunting, and Grasshopper Sparrow (rare) can be found from spring through fall, and you may see Red-shouldered Hawk, Wild Turkey, or Red-headed Wood-pecker anytime.

**25** Felsenthal National Wildlife Refuge, on US 82 west of Crossett, is known for hosting Arkansas' largest population of the endangered Red-cockaded Woodpecker. Much of this 65,000-acre refuge is swampy bottomland forest, but Pine Island and Shallow Lake Roads, both leading south from US 82, provide access to the pine forest the woodpeckers frequent. The birds often change roost sites from year to year, so be sure to ask at the refuge office for advice on current locations. Watch for pines with painted white bands, indicating trees with roost cavities, and look for the fresh flow of sap that marks an active tree. Explore roadsides for typical birds of southern woodlands, including Barred Owl; Red-headed and Pileated Woodpeckers; Acadian Flycatcher; Yellow-throated Vireo; Fish Crow (listen for its *cah-cah* call, higher than that of American Crow); Wood Thrush; Northern Parula; and Black-and-white, Prothonotary, Kentucky, and Hooded Warblers. Swainson's Warbler can be more elusive.

Felsenthal National Wildlife Refuge, west of Crossett

**26** The state's best location for waterbirds is **Millwood Lake,** a 30,000-acre reservoir located on Ark. 32 east of Ashdown in southwestern Arkansas. From fall through spring, hundreds of loons, grebes, cormorants, ducks, coots, and gulls can be seen from spots along the shore, especially the **Beard's Bluff** area at the eastern end of the huge dam. Bald Eagles have nested here; look for a mammoth nest in the top of a dead tree in the middle of the lake. In winter Rock Wren has been found several times on the rocky slope of the dam, and Sprague's Pipit is rare in the short grass on the opposite side. Osprey is common in spring and fall.

Millwood is most famous for its regional rarities, including Red-throated Loon; all three species of scoter; all three species of jaeger; Little, Laughing, Black-headed, Glaucous, and Sabine's Gulls; and Black-legged Kittiwake. Checking duck flocks of common species such as Gadwall, Mallard, Northern Pintail, and Lesser Scaup might turn up a Cinnamon Teal or an Oldsquaw. Greater Scaup, while uncommon, is regular, especially along the dam. Mid-October through early January is the optimal time for searching through the masses of Ring-billed, Bonaparte's, and Herring Gulls for the rarer gulls and jaegers. Sabine's Gull, perhaps Millwood's signature rare gull, tends to appear between mid-September and mid-October and doesn't necessarily associate with other species, except occasionally with Franklin's Gull. A spotting scope and a liberal amount of patience are required to study waterbirds here.

Although waterbirds created much of Millwood's reputation as a birding hot spot, land bird potential is excellent as well, especially at the **Okay Levee** off Ark. 355 for sparrows and such land bird rarities as Say's Phoebe, Vermilion Flycatcher, and Couch's and Western Kingbirds. At the parking area, scramble up onto the rock levee and walk westward. The levee stretches 2 miles along the lake, providing good scope views of waterfowl.

**27** For a chance to see three pinewoods specialists, Red-cockaded Woodpecker, Brown-headed Nuthatch, and Bachman's Sparrow, visit the **Buffalo Road Demonstration Area** in the **Ouachita National Forest.** From the town of Needmore, south of Waldron on US 71, go west on dirt County Road 892 for a bit more than 3 miles to an area of open pinewoods. Park along the road and listen for the woodpecker's raspy *sripp* call, the nuthatch's *bit bit bit*, and the accelerating whistles of the sparrow (spring and summer).

**28** The Ozarks of northwestern Arkansas encompass a beautiful landscape of deep, rugged valleys and clear streams. **Devil's Den State Park,** about 28 miles south of

The Ozarks at Devil's Den State Park, south of Fayetteville

Fayetteville, is a fine example of Ozarks geology (the region comprises an uplifted and eroded plateau) and a good place to see migrant and nesting birds. Watch for Greater Roadrunner along the highway as you approach the park. Down in the **Lee Creek Valley,** look for nesting species including Red-shouldered Hawk; Wild Turkey; Scissor-tailed Flycatcher (rare); Yellow-throated Vireo; Blue-winged (rare), Yellow-throated, Worm-eating, and Kentucky Warblers; Northern Parula; American Redstart; Ovenbird; Louisiana Waterthrush; Chipping and Field Sparrows; and American Goldfinch.

**29** Though hardly scenic, a favorite spot for local birders is the **Charlie Craig State Fish Hatchery,** just south of Ark. 102 at Centerton, a small town west of Bentonville. The ponds here, by far northwestern Arkansas' best shorebirding spot, also host numbers of ducks in

Bluff along the
Buffalo National River,
northern Arkansas

winter. Grassy spots along pond edges and in ditches
provide habitat for such uncommon migrants as American
and Least Bitterns, rails, and Sedge and Marsh Wrens.
Among the locally rare land birds that have been found
here are Prairie Falcon, Alder Flycatcher, Nelson's Sharp-
tailed Sparrow, and Yellow-headed Blackbird. Spring and
fall have seen shorebirds including Wilson's and Piping
Plovers, American Avocet, Willet, Whimbrel, Hudsonian
and Marbled Godwits (the former most likely in early May),
Ruff, and all three phalaropes.

**30** **Buffalo National River** surely ranks among the most
beautiful natural areas east of the Rockies. Established to protect 135 miles of free-flowing mountain stream,
the Buffalo also offers good spring and summer birding,

with possibilities of seeing locally uncommon breeding species such as Yellow, Cerulean, Worm-eating, and Swainson's Warblers and American Redstart. Look for Worm-eating on shady slopes, Cerulean in streamside trees and ravines with large trees. Swainson's is not a certainty, but has been seen near the Buffalo Point and Rush areas off Ark. 14, south of Yellville. Other good birding spots include the Steel Creek area off Ark. 74 west of Jasper and the Ozark campground off Ark. 7 north of Jasper. Chuck-will's-widow, Whip-poor-will, Wood Thrush, Ovenbird, Hooded Warbler, and Summer and Scarlet Tanagers are among the other nesting birds along the river, which is increasingly becoming important as a wintering location for Bald Eagles. It is also famed for canoeing, and floating quietly down the river can offer a different perspective on birding, as well as terrific scenery of forest and tall limestone bluffs.

**31** Though waterfowl and Bald Eagles make **Holla Bend National Wildlife Refuge** one of Arkansas' best known winter sites, its fields, lakes, and woods create fine birding opportunities year-round. Set along the Arkansas River near Dardanelle, the refuge hosts thousands of Snow and Canada Geese in winter. White-fronted Goose is occasionally found, and Ross's Goose, the look-alike smaller relative of Snow Goose, is rarely but regularly spotted.

Look for wintering Bald Eagles in large trees along the river or the oxbow lakes of the old channel. In spring and fall, American White Pelican, Osprey, and Caspian Tern migrate along the river. Northern Harrier is common in winter. Red-shouldered Hawk is often seen, and Broad-winged Hawk nests. Golden Eagle and Peregrine and Prairie Falcons are very rare visitors, and migrant Sandhill Cranes have occasionally stopped to feed. Holla Bend is also a good place to find Yellow-headed Blackbird in spring, and Long-eared Owl has wintered in thick stands of cedar.

Scissor-tailed Flycatcher, Bell's and Warbling Vireos, Lark Sparrow, Painted Bunting, and Dickcissel can be found in open areas in spring and summer. The refuge also offers some fine bottomland woods where Wood Duck, Wild Turkey, Barred Owl, Fish Crow, Northern Parula, and Kentucky Warbler breed. These habitats can be reached along the auto tour route, where side roads—most closed to vehicles but open to walking—provide access to good spots.

**32** Just off I-55, about 12 miles north of West Memphis, **Wapanocca National Wildlife Refuge** endures as an island of bottomland forest in a sea of agricultural land— a remnant of the "Great Swamp" that once covered much of eastern Arkansas and frustrated travelers for decades

Pair of Wood Ducks, the male among the most colorful of waterfowl

before the land was drained. A 6-mile auto tour leads alongside swampy woods where Wood Duck, Hooded Merganser, Mississippi Kite, Red-shouldered Hawk, Red-headed and Pileated Woodpeckers, Yellow-throated and Prothonotary Warblers, and Orchard and Baltimore Orioles nest. Geese winter in refuge fields, and marshy spots attract waders in late summer. Horned Lark, Yellow-breasted Chat, and Dickcissel breed in open places, and Bald Eagle winters in the big trees around Wapanocca Lake.

**33** To the south, **St. Francis National Forest,** near the historic Mississippi River town of Helena, is a fine place to find Wild Turkey, Red-headed Woodpecker (both year-round), and Swainson's Warbler (spring–summer). Ask about conditions at the U.S. Forest Service office in Marianna before exploring Forest Roads 1900 and 1901, which wind through hardwood forest that supports a variety of breeders, from Red-shouldered and Broad-winged Hawks to Yellow-billed Cuckoo, Wood Thrush, and Eastern Towhee.

# LOUISIANA

**34** The small patch of low, windswept woods just south of La. 82, 8 miles west of Holly Beach, may not seem impressive to the passing motorist, but acre for acre it's among the most exciting birding spots on the Gulf Coast. During spring migration songbirds can throng these trees at the **Peveto Woods Sanctuaries**—especially during a "fallout" (see sidebar p. 181), when north winds or rain force tired migrants to stop at the first shelter they see after crossing the Gulf of Mexico. Cuckoos, flycatchers, vireos, thrushes, warblers, tanagers, buntings, and orioles are among the species present from late March into May. The low vegetation here provides excellent looks at birds usually seen only in treetops. Fall migration doesn't offer the marvels spring does, but it still often brings good birding. To reach the sanctuary, turn south on Gulf View Avenue and watch for a left turn to the parking lot.

About 20 miles east along the Gulf Coast and just across the Calcasieu Ship Channel, the **east jetty** (*S on Davis Rd. off La. 27/82*) at Cameron is a great place to see concentrations of pelicans, wading birds, shorebirds, gulls, and terns. The long jetty extending out into the Gulf has created a large mudflat where you'll find birds feeding or resting, from common year-round residents such as Willet, Laughing Gull, Caspian and Royal Terns, and Black Skimmer to less frequent species such as Reddish Egret and Snowy and Wilson's Plovers, and a host of seasonal migrants and winter visitors. There's always something to see here, though spring and fall bring the greatest variety of species.

**35** Spend enough time in southwestern Louisiana and you could begin to believe that mountains are just a geological myth, so flat is this land of coastal marshes and

- Coastal hot spots for spring migration
- Vast marshlands in national wildlife refuges

----

Information section p. 199

rice fields. Great expanses of wetlands are encompassed within several wildlife refuges, but the nature of the landscape dictates that most of these preserves are more accessible to alligators and egrets than to humans. One place to get close to the marsh and some of its inhabitants is **Sabine National Wildlife Refuge** with its visitor center on La. 27 between Holly Beach and Hackberry. At Sabine's 1.5-mile **Marsh Trail,** 4 miles south of the visitor center, you may find Neotropic Cormorant, Least Bittern, White and White-faced Ibises (check for the occasional Glossy), Roseate Spoonbill, Mottled Duck, Clapper Rail, Purple Gallinule, and Marsh Wren among many other species.

East along La. 27, north of Creole, **Cameron Prairie National Wildlife Refuge** offers another way to observe the marsh with its 3-mile **Pintail Wildlife Drive,** which loops through fields and wetlands where waders and shorebirds are common. From fall into spring, Snow Geese are abundant (check for the uncommon Ross's), and more than a dozen species of ducks may be present.

**36** From Hayes, drive 3 miles east on La. 14 to Illinois Plant Road, then turn south to **Lacassine National Wildlife Refuge,** which is worth a visit to drive the gravel roads and walk the levees that skirt the vast marsh of Lacassine Pool, another spot to see waders, waterfowl (huge concentrations of ducks and geese), and marsh birds. Beautiful Purple Gallinules swim in roadside ditches. Equally beautiful Roseate Spoonbills feed in open water. Anhingas perch and spread their wings to dry; King Rails skulk in reeds; Gull-billed Terns hawk for insects above the marsh; and Least Bitterns clamber about vegetation. Fulvous Whistling-, Wood, and Mottled Ducks nest here. In addition, Lacassine is the center of the growing southwestern Louisiana population of Black-bellied Whistling-Duck.

**37** The **Atchafalaya Swamp** is one of America's great wild places, a wide stretch of river bottom with towering trees and lazy backwaters. But access to its untracked interior is difficult. To see a sample of this habitat, drive La. 975 between I-10 and US 190, skirting **Atchafalaya National Wildlife Refuge** (no facilities) and **Sherburne**

Bald cypress, Atchafalaya Swamp, west of Baton Rouge

**Wildlife Management Area** *(hunting or fishing license or Louisiana Wild Stamp necessary for entry)*, which has a short nature trail. You can see the stunning Swallow-tailed Kite in breeding season (watch for it soaring just above the tree-tops) or Wood Storks in post-nesting dispersal. The often elusive Swainson's Warbler is fairly common in this area, which is home to typical southern wetland birds from Anhinga to Mississippi Kite to Wood Duck to Prothonotary Warbler.

The lively, noisy spectacle that is an active heron rookery is easily accessible at the **Cypress Island Preserve** on the southern end of Lake Martin *(take La. 31 for 2 miles S of Breaux Bridge, then W on Lake Martin Rd.)*. From March through June, up to 11 species nest here, including the common waders as well as Anhinga, Black-crowned and Yellow-crowned Night-Herons, White Ibis, and Roseate

Spoonbill. Watch, too, for alligators hanging around under nests, waiting for young birds to misstep in the trees above.

**38** Spring birding can be fabulous at **Grand Isle,** a barrier island at the mouth of Barataria Bay (*follow La. 1 S to its end*), when trans-Gulf migrants drop in on its woods, fields, and beach. Residents of the small town here have become accustomed to birders wandering the streets, checking not only for typical eastern migrant songbirds but for strays such as Groove-billed Ani, Vermilion and Scissor-tailed Flycatchers, Western and Gray Kingbirds, Black-whiskered Vireo, Lark Bunting, Yellow-headed Blackbird, and Bullock's Oriole, all of which have made an appearance here. Along the long stretches of accessible beach, especially at **Grand Isle State Park,** you'll find Brown Pelican, Reddish Egret, Black Skimmer, and flocks of shorebirds, gulls, and terns to scan. Watch for Magnificent Frigatebird soaring above the Gulf in summer.

**Brown Pelican**

Of all the birds harmed by DDT and other pesticides used in the middle decades of the 20th century, the Brown Pelican certainly was among the most affected. In Louisiana, where tens of thousands of pairs once nested (and where it's the state bird), the species had disappeared as a breeder in the 1960s, and it was seen only rarely along the Gulf Coast. With the ban on the use of such chemicals, the Brown Pelican has made a strong comeback, and today these huge but graceful birds are again common, gliding over the Gulf or diving into its waters for fish.

**39** Rich swamp woodland can be explored along 9 miles of trails in the **Barataria Preserve Unit** of **Jean Lafitte National Historical Park and Preserve** just south of New Orleans. Stop at the visitor center on La. 45 (Barataria Boulevard) to gather maps and information, then head north 1 mile to the **Bayou Coquille Trail,** a short, handicapped-accessible, paved-and-boardwalk path that passes through several ecological zones on its way from live-oak forest through bald-cypress-tupelo swamp to marsh. Nesting birds in the swamp or in higher, drier forest include Yellow-crowned Night-Heron; Wood Duck; Red-shouldered Hawk; Great Horned and Barred Owls; Pileated Woodpecker; Acadian Flycatcher; White-eyed and Yellow-throated Vireos; Northern Parula; and Yellow-throated, Prothonotary, Swainson's (uncommon), and Hooded Warblers. Least Bittern, King

Rail, and Purple Gallinule nest in the marsh, where herons, egrets, and ibises are common, and Painted Buntings breed in scrubby places around the preserve.

**40** Another good birding spot convenient to New Orleans, **Bayou Sauvage National Wildlife Refuge** is a mostly undeveloped area on US 90 about 4 miles east of I-510. On the north side of US 90, the short **Ridge Trail**

Little Blue Heron with frog prey, Atchafalaya Swamp near New Iberia

winds through bottomland hardwoods and palmettos to an observation deck overlooking a lagoon, making it a fine place to see waders, ducks, and migrant songbirds. South of the highway, a boardwalk behind the refuge Learning Lab provides views of a marsh. Check with the refuge office about guided trips on spring weekends to view a rookery where thousands of herons and egrets nest. Other refuge breeding birds include Least Bittern; White, Glossy, and White-faced Ibises; Mottled Duck; Bald Eagle; Purple Gallinule; and Black-necked Stilt.

**41** Excellent bottomland forest is accessible at **Pearl River Wildlife Management Area** northeast of Slidell (*hunting or fishing license or Louisiana Wild Stamp necessary for entry*). Take I-59 north to the Honey Island Swamp exit and drive east about 2 miles to a nature trail that loops through a woodland of oak, sweet gum, sycamore, tupelo, and bald cypress. Among the birds typical of such habitat, two are especially noteworthy: Several pairs of Swallow-tailed Kites nest in the vicinity, though you may need patience (and a good viewpoint) to actually see one or more soaring just over the trees. Swainson's Warbler, that skulking swamp dweller, can also be seen here—more easily if you know its ringing song of slurred whistles.

Roseate Spoonbill, named for its odd but functional bill

**42** To find the southern pinewoods trio of Red-cockaded Woodpecker, Brown-headed Nuthatch, and Bachman's Sparrow, explore **Alexander State Forest,** south of Alexandria. Just minutes from I-49 (*Woodworth exit, drive W*), the forest also has nesting Prairie Warbler, Painted Bunting, and Blue Grosbeak in cutover and scrubby spots. In recent winters, Henslow's Sparrow has been found consistently in weedy and scrubby places. White rings on pines indicate roosting cavities of the endangered Red-cockaded Woodpecker. Listen for the sweet song of the Bachman's Sparrow in spring and summer, and for the squeaky call of the Brown-headed Nuthatch anytime. The road leading to the **Indian Creek Recreation Area** is a good place to begin.

Northeast of Alexandria, **Catahoula National Wildlife Refuge** offers good birding year-round, though it may be best known for its flocks of tens of thousands of wintering ducks (Mallard, Blue-winged Teal, Northern Pintail, and Wood and Ring-necked Ducks are the most common species). In late summer, flocks of postbreeding egrets and herons may include Tricolored Heron, White or Glossy Ibises, Roseate Spoonbill, or Wood Stork. A 9-mile loop drive around Duck Lake provides access to an observation tower and two woodland trails. **Catahoula Lake,** a Wetland of International Importance, is located just adjacent to the refuge.

# South-Central States
## Information

**?** Visitor Center/Information    **Ⓢ** Fee Charged    **🍴** Food

**🚻** Rest Rooms    **🧍** Nature Trails    **〜** Driving Tours    **♿** Wheelchair Accessible

*Be advised that facilities may be seasonal and limited. We suggest calling or writing ahead for specific information. Note that addresses may be for administrative offices; see text or call for directions to sites.*

## Rare Bird Alerts

Tennessee:
Statewide *615-356-7636*
Chattanooga
   *423-843-2822*

Alabama:
Statewide *205-987-2730*

Arkansas:
Statewide *501-753-5853*

Louisiana:
Statewide *877-834-2473*
Baton Rouge
   *504-768-9874*
Southeast *504-834-2473*
Southwest *318-988-9898*

## TENNESSEE

### Great Smoky Mountains
**National Park** *(Page 167)*
107 Park Headquarters
   Road
Gatlinburg, TN 37738
*423-436-1200*

### Roan Mountain
**State Park** *(Page 168)*
527 Highway 143
Roan Mountain, TN 37687
*423-772-3303 or*
   *800-250-8620*

### TVA Kingston
### Steam Plant Wildlife
### Observation
**Area** *(Page 169)*
Swan Pond Road
Kingston, TN 37763
*423-717-2000*

*Located off US 70;
closed to public access
mid-Oct.–Jan.*

### Blythe Ferry Unit of
### Hiwassee Refuge
*(Page 170)*
Route 3, Box 178
Decatur, TN 37322
*931-484-9571*

**♿**

*Except for perimeter viewing
sites, interior refuge closed
mid-Oct.–Feb.*

### Radnor Lake State
**Natural Area** *(Page 171)*
1160 Otter Creek Road
Nashville, TN 37220
*615-373-3467*

### Tennessee National
### Wildlife Refuge
*(Page 172)*
810 East Wood Street
Paris, TN 38242
*901-642-2091*

**〜**

### Reelfoot National
### Wildlife Refuge
*(Page 172)*
4343 Tenn. 157
Union City, TN 38261
*901-538-2481*

**? 🚻 🧍 〜 ♿**

### Reelfoot Lake State
**Park** *(Page 172)*
Route 1, Box 2345
Tiptonville, TN 38079
*901-253-7756 or*
   *800-250-8617*

**? 🍴 🚻 🧍 〜 ♿**

### EARTH Complex
### T.E. Maxson
### Wastewater Treatment
### Plant
*(Page 173)*
2085 Plant Road
Memphis, TN 38109
*901-789-4923*

## ALABAMA

### Dauphin Island Bird
**Sanctuaries** *(Page 174)*
P.O. Box 848
Dauphin Island, AL 36528
*334-861-2120*

**🍴 🚻 🧍 〜 ♿**

**Fort Morgan**
*(Page 175)*
51 Ala. 180 West
Gulf Shores, AL 36542
*334-540-7125*

**Bon Secour
National Wildlife
Refuge** *(Page 175)*
12295 Ala. 180
Gulf Shores, AL 36542
*334-540-7720*

**Gulf State Park**
*(Page 175)*
20115 State Highway 135
Gulf Shores, AL 36547
*334-948-7275*

**Eufaula National
Wildlife Refuge**
*(Page 175)*
509 Old Highway 165
Eufaula, AL 36027
*334-687-4065*

**Lake Guntersville
State Park** *(Page 176)*
7966 Ala. 227
Guntersville, AL 35976
*256-571-5444*

**Wheeler National
Wildlife Refuge**
*(Page 177)*
2700 Refuge
  Headquarters Road
Decatur, AL 35603
*256-350-6639*

**Bankhead National
Forest and Brushy
Lake Recreation Area**
*(Page 178)*
P.O. Box 278
Double Springs, AL 35553
*205-489-5111*

# MISSISSIPPI

**Lower Pascagoula
River Wildlife
Management Area**
*(Page 179)*
816 Wade-Vancleave Road
Pascagoula, MS 39581
*228-588-3878*

**Mississippi Sandhill
Crane National Wildlife
Refuge** *(Page 179)*
7200 Crane Lane
Gautier, MS 39553
*228-497-6322*

**Gulf Islands National
Seashore** *(Page 180)*
3500 Park Road
Ocean Springs, MS 39564
*228-875-9057*

**Buccaneer State Park**
*(Page 181)*
1150 South Beach Blvd.
Waveland, MS 39576
*228-467-3822*

**St. Catherine Creek
National Wildlife Refuge**
*(Page 181)*
76 Pintail Lane
Sibley, MS 39165
*601-442-6696*

*Areas of refuge flood in late
winter through spring.*

**Yazoo National Wildlife
Refuge** *(Page 182)*
728 Yazoo Refuge Road
Hollandale, MS 38748
*601-839-2638*

**Noxubee National
Wildlife Refuge**
*(Page 182)*
Rural Route 1, Box 142
Brooksville, MS 39739
*601-323-5548*

# ARKANSAS

**Lake Chicot State
Park** *(Page 184)*
2542 Ark. 257
Lake Village, AR 71653
*870-265-5480*

**Felsenthal National
Wildlife Refuge**
*(Page 185)*
5531 US 82 West
Crossett, AR 71635
*870-364-3167*

**Pine-Bluestem Buffalo
Road Demonstration
Area** *(Page 186)*
Poteau Ranger District
Ouachita National Forest
P.O. Box 2255
Waldron, AR 72958
*501-637-4174*

**Devil's Den State
Park** *(Page 187)*
11333 West Ark. 74
West Fork, AR 72774
*501-761-3325*

**Charlie Craig State Fish Hatchery** *(Page 187)*
977 West Fish Hatchery
Road
Centerton, AR 72719
*501-795-2470*

**Buffalo National River**
*(Page 188)*
402 North Walnut
Suite 136
Harrison, AR 72601
*870-741-5443*

**Holla Bend National Wildlife Refuge**
*(Page 189)*
Rural Route 1, Box 59
Dardanelle, AR 72834
*501-229-4300*

**Wapanocca National Wildlife Refuge**
*(Page 190)*
Highway 42 East
Turrell, AR 72384
*870-343-2595*

**St. Francis National Forest** *(Page 190)*
2675 Highway 44
Marianna, AR 72360
*870-295-5278*

# LOUISIANA

**Peveto Woods Sanctuaries** *(Page 191)*
Baton Rouge Audubon
Society
P.O. Box 82525
Baton Rouge, LA 70884
*225-768-9874*

*Formerly known as
Holliman Sheely*

**Sabine National Wildlife Refuge** *(Page 192)*
3000 Holly Beach Highway
Hackberry, LA 70645
*318-762-3816*

**Cameron Prairie National Wildlife Refuge**
*(Page 192)*
1428 La. 27
Bell City, LA 70630
*318-598-2216*

**Lacassine National Wildlife Refuge**
*(Page 192)*
209 Nature Road
Lake Arthur, LA 70549
*318-774-5923*

**Sherburne Wildlife Management Area**
*(Page 192)*
5652 La. 182
Opelusas LA 70571
*318-948-0255*

*Visitors must have hunting or
fishing license, or Louisiana
Wild Stamp.*

**Cypress Island Preserve** *(Page 193)*
The Nature Conservancy
of Louisiana
340 St. Joseph Street
Baton Rouge, LA 70802
*504-338-1040*

**Grand Isle State Park** *(Page 194)*
P.O. Box 741
Grand Isle, LA 70358
*504-787-2559 or
888-787-2559*

**Jean Lafitte National Historical Park and Preserve, Barataria unit** *(Page 194)*
7400 La. 45
Marrero, LA 70072
*504-589-2330*

**Bayou Sauvage National Wildlife Refuge** *(Page 195)*
17160 Chef Menteur
Highway
New Orleans, LA 70129
*504-254-4490*

**Pearl River Wildlife Management Area**
*(Page 195)*
District 7, P.O. Box 9800
Baton Rouge, LA 70898
*225-765-2360*

*Visitors must have hunting or
fishing license, or Louisiana
Wild Stamp.*

**Alexander State Forest**
*(Page 196)*
515 Forestry Road
Woodworth, LA 71485
*318-487-5172*

**Catahoula National Wildlife Refuge**
*(Page 196)*
Highway 84
P.O. Box Z
Rhinehart, LA 71363
*318-992-5261*

# Eastern Texas

In an election to choose the birding capital of the United States, the Texas coast would be a serious contender. The geographic range of this 370-mile sweep of Gulf of Mexico shoreline, combined with the subtropical environment of the lower Rio Grande Valley, attracts birders on regular pilgrimages the way avid theatergoers travel to New York City to check out each new season's Broadway shows.

Sandy beaches, salt marshes, and prairie make up much of the flat, geologically young Texas Gulf Coast. Some of the region's scattered woodlands, such as those at High Island, are famed for spring songbird migration, when vireos, thrushes, warblers, tanagers, buntings, orioles, and other species create one of the most colorful spectacles in American birding. Bolivar Flats, near the resort city of Galveston, has earned prominence as the best known of several excellent shorebird-watching sites, while rice fields and other agricultural areas west of Houston can attract impressive flocks of waterfowl from fall through spring, as well as migrant shorebirds. Farther south, an array of Mexican species are found at the northern limit of their ranges in the brushlands along the lower Rio Grande.

Every season has something to offer in this extensive and diverse region. Even midsummer, perhaps the least appealing time of year, affords visiting birders interesting breeding species, as well as such post-nesting wanderers as Magnificent Frigatebird and Wood Stork. Fall shorebird migration begins as early as July, when beaches and mudflats attract birds heading south from their Arctic nesting grounds. Huge flocks of Broad-winged Hawks pass over Hazel Bazemore County Park near Corpus Christi in fall, creating one of the great hawk-watching spectacles in the

*Preceding pages:*
Harris's Hawk
*Above:* Whooping
Crane

EASTERN TEXAS

country. Winter brings flocks of waterfowl to area fields, lakes, and marshes, as well as the annual return of Whooping Cranes to Aransas National Wildlife Refuge north of Corpus Christi. This is also a popular time for human refugees from northern blizzards to visit sites in the Rio Grande Valley, where the hot spots for birding are just plain warm as well. Spring means the excitement of migration, from warbler-watching on the upper coast to hawks moving north in huge flocks.

Making planning easier for the traveling birder, the Great Texas Coastal Birding Trail (see sidebar p. 212) directs visitors to excellent birding sites with maps and special road signs. Look for other states to emulate this rewarding concept in the future.

More and more, communities along the Gulf Coast and in the lower Rio Grande Valley are waking up to their

Observation platform at Santa Ana National Wildlife Refuge, near McAllen

birding possibilities, and working to spread the word about them. One of the ways they're doing this is by holding birding festivals, most of which feature field trips aimed at finding local specialties, guest speakers, and workshops on improving identification skills. The city of Rockport has long extended a special welcome to birders, publishing a local birding guide and holding its Hummer/Bird Celebration each September. Down in the valley, McAllen puts on its popular Texas Tropics Nature Festival in April, and nearby Harlingen holds the Rio Grande Valley Birding Festival in November. Attending any of these is a great way for out-of-state birders to get an introduction to the wonders of this marvelous area.

This chapter's route begins near the Louisiana border on the extreme northern coast, moving south to the brush-lands of the lower Rio Grande Valley. ■

# UPPER
# TEXAS COAST

Visually unexciting—mostly agricultural areas, marshes, scrubby fields, and small towns—the upper Texas coast more than makes up in avian diversity what it lacks in aesthetics. Interesting birds can show up almost anywhere in this region. Roseate Spoonbills feed in farm ponds; White and White-faced Ibises, Snowy Egrets, and Tricolored Herons stream by overhead; Gull-billed Terns flap with deliberate wingbeats over marshes, hunting insects; and American Bitterns or Yellow-crowned Night-Herons flush up from roadside ditches. Don't feel that you need to reach a particular destination to begin seeing things—keep your eyes open all the time in this delightfully birdy part of the world.

- Spring "fallouts" at Sabine Woods and High Island
- Shorebirds at Bolivar Flats

---

Information section p. 230

**1** Three spots near **Port Arthur** can be covered in a relatively short time, though travelers in a hurry might want to begin their exploration with Anahuac National Wildlife Refuge (see p. 206). South of Sabine Pass, **Texas Point National Wildlife Refuge** is an 8,952-acre expanse of marsh more accessible to waterbirds and alligators than to humans—an ocean of grass adjoining the real ocean to its south. Off Farm Road 3322, a dead-end road runs for several miles alongside the Sabine River nearly to the Gulf of Mexico, offering the chance to see some of the region's bird specialties. From Sabine Pass, drive west along Tex. 87 to reach a short refuge birding trail on the south side of the highway, where low trees and scrub can attract spring migrants. A bit farther west is **Sabine Woods,** a small open woodland on the north side of the road (watch for an inconspicuous sign 4 miles west of Sabine Pass). Owned by the Texas Ornithological Society, this spot can be terrific in spring migration, attracting much the same birdlife as High Island (see p. 208). Although a lot depends on weather conditions and luck, on a good day many local birders consider Sabine Woods even better than High Island.

Continue along Tex. 87 to **Sea Rim State Park,** best known among birders for its short marsh boardwalk, which often allows close views of rails, Least Bittern (the pretty black-and-buff bird that is America's smallest heron), and wintering Sedge Wren. Occasional close views of alligators provide another stimulating experience. Seaside Sparrows,

Great Egret, Anahuac National Wildlife Refuge, east of Houston

permanent residents in the marshes, are easy to see when males are singing in spring; their thin, buzzy song has much the same pattern as the Red-winged Blackbird's *konk-la-reeee*. The park's more than 5 miles of beach host birds ranging from Sanderlings chasing the waves back and forth to Reddish Egrets flouncing crazily here and there in pursuit of prey. Cliff Swallows nest in the park boathouse on the north side of Tex. 87, where a few Cave Swallows have been regular breeders in recent years.

**2** Thirty miles west, **Anahuac National Wildlife Refuge** provides easy vehicle access on 13 miles of gravel roads to coastal prairie and marshlands. Anahuac's fine birding is conveniently located just a short drive from legendary High Island (see p. 208), offering an alternative when birding is slow at the latter spot.

As you approach the refuge along Farm Road 1985, driving west from Tex. 124, check wet fields and cropland along the road. In spring and fall these fields can host throngs of shorebirds and waders. Watch to the south 3.1 miles from Tex. 124 for the **East Bay Bayou Tract,** where you can view songbirds in the narrow woodland along the bayou, as well as shorebirds and waders in bordering moist-soil units and rice fields. One specialty is Hudsonian Godwit, a shorebird that prefers inland areas to the shore. American Golden-Plover and Upland, White-rumped, Baird's, and Buff-breasted Sandpipers are among the other shorebird species more likely found here than along the coast's sandy beaches.

Neotropic Cormorant

### Special Birds of the Texas Coast

| | |
|---|---|
| Least Grebe | Yellow Rail |
| Northern Gannet | King Rail |
| Brown Pelican | Purple Gallinule |
| Neotropic | Sandhill Crane |
|   Cormorant | Whooping Crane |
| Magnificent | Snowy Plover |
|   Frigatebird | Wilson's Plover |
| Reddish Egret | Piping Plover |
| Roseate Spoonbill | American |
| Black-bellied |   Oystercatcher |
|   Whistling-Duck | Hudsonian Godwit |
| Fulvous Whistling- | Gull-billed Tern |
|   Duck | Sandwich Tern |
| Ross's Goose | Golden-fronted |
| Mottled Duck |   Woodpecker |
| Masked Duck | Cave Swallow |
| White-tailed Kite | Nelson's Sharp- |
| Harris's Hawk |   tailed Sparrow |
| White-tailed Hawk | Seaside Sparrow |
| Crested Caracara | Pyrrhuloxia |

Once you enter the refuge itself, turn right at the first road past the gate, drive a short distance, and check the willow trees on the north. Trees are scarce in these parts, so even this wee woods can attract migrant songbirds. Continue to **Shoveler Pond,** always watching road-side ditches for Mottled Duck (a Gulf Coast specialty), the beautiful Purple Gallinule (easily seen here from spring through fall), King Rail (a permanent resident, but not so easy to see), Least Bittern, and other waterbirds. A good variety of ducks is usually present on the pond from fall through spring, while surrounding grassy areas are home to wintering Greater White-fronted, Snow, Ross's, and Canada Geese. Ross's requires close study to be differentiated from the slightly larger Snow. Also in winter, Northern Harriers hunt over the prairies on upturned wings, and Bald Eagles watch the flocks of waterfowl for sick or injured birds. In addition, Sedge Wrens winter in the tall grass and begin to sing vigorously in spring before migrating north.

Alligators are abundant at Anahuac, sunning themselves in ponds and ditches. The venomous water moccasin is another common reptile, so watch your step before hopping out of your car for a closer look at a Roseate Spoonbill or Yellow-crowned Night-Heron.

Rails are as secretive at Anahuac as anywhere, but look for them along the edges of openings in the grass. Clapper Rail is most common in salt-water areas; King Rail generally prefers freshwater marshes. From fall through spring Virginia Rail and Sora are also seen. Yellow (wintering) and Black Rails are much rarer.

**Roseate Spoonbill**

The Roseate Spoonbill's odd-looking (in fact, spoon-shaped) bill is an adaptation to its feeding tactics. The bird swings its open bill back and forth in shallow water, using touch rather than sight; when it feels a small fish or crustacean, it quickly snaps up its prey. Immature birds are white and very pale pink, with feathered heads. The bright-pink and orange adults lose their head feathers, developing a masklike naked greenish face. Once nearly killed off along the Gulf Coast, spoonbills have made a strong comeback in recent decades.

**3** Though to most travelers **High Island** may seem to be just another small coastal town, this community east of Anahuac has long been one of the mythic places of American birding. A subterranean salt dome approaches the surface here, creating an area of slightly higher ground that early settlers called an "island." (Several similar islands are found to the east in Louisiana.) Oaks and other hard-woods—the only "forest" for miles around—offer rest and shelter to song-birds that have just completed their spring migration across the Gulf of Mexico. When conditions are right in April or early May, birds drop from the sky in numbers that are almost staggering—a phenomenon birders call a "fallout." Note the qualifier "when conditions are right": For every fabulous day at High Island there are ten or more when bird-ing ranges from very good to mediocre to slow. The best birding usually occurs after a front bringing north winds and/or rain has pushed through. Though fall migration doesn't match spring in numbers of birds or diversity, it often brings very good birding in its own right.

The Houston Audubon Society owns several tracts of woodland here, including the 50.9-acre **Boy Scout Woods** on Fifth Street and the 122.2-acre **Smith Oaks Bird Sanctuary** at the east end of Winnie Street. On any spring day both sanctuaries are likely to be full of birders from around the globe, but don't let the crowds deter you. People are generally quiet and well behaved; the birds are so exhausted that they pay no attention to their watchers; and the number of observers means that any rarity is almost certain to be seen, and news of it quickly circulated.

Birders at Boy Scout Woods, High Island

The list of possible species here includes virtually every eastern warbler, vireo, thrush, grosbeak, tanager, flycatcher, bunting, and oriole, and, not infrequently, western rarities as well. Species composition varies as the season progresses. In March, early migrants such as Eastern Kingbird; Yellow-throated Vireo; Northern Parula; Yellow-throated, Black-and-white, Worm-eating, and Hooded Warblers; and Louisiana Waterthrush begin showing up. The great mass of species arrives in April, but later migrants such as Mourning Warbler are more likely to be seen sometime in May.

Weather is the major factor in High Island spring birding. When a north wind makes migration difficult, tired birds home in on the High Island woods; with a strong south wind

aiding them, they often continue past the coast and find resting places much farther inland. The usual birding rule about getting up at dawn doesn't necessarily apply here. Because of the timing of their trans-Gulf flight (leaving the Yucatán Peninsula at dusk), a wave of migrants may not arrive at High Island until midmorning or, during a "fallout," even later.

A big day here may bring a tree full of Scarlet Tanagers, a shrub laden with Gray Catbirds, or more than 20 species of warblers in a couple of hours. If you're a beginning birder, don't be shy about visiting such a famously popular hot spot. High Island is a great place to see the field marks of lots of species in a short time, and there's always a friendly veteran around who's willing to share identification tips.

In Gilchrist, just a few miles west of High Island on Tex. 87, a small channel called **Rollover Pass** leads from the Gulf to East Galveston Bay. Pull off into the parking lot on the bay side and scan the mudflats and sandbars. Depending on the season and the state of the tide, you may see

American White Pelican, Neotropic and Double-crested Cormorants, Roseate Spoonbill, shorebirds (including American Oystercatcher, Black-necked Stilt, American Avocet, Marbled Godwit, and the ubiquitous Willet), several kinds of herons and egrets (including Tricolored Heron, Reddish Egret, and Black-crowned Night-Heron), gulls, terns (including Caspian, Royal, Sandwich, Common, Forster's, Least, and Black), and Black Skimmer.

American White Pelicans, Brown Pelicans, Black Skimmers, and other waterbirds at Bolivar Flats, near Galveston

**4** As diverse and abundant as birds may be here, it's just a preview of the scene at **Bolivar Flats,** about 16 miles west on Tex. 87. Turn south on Rettilon Road opposite Tex. 108 just before you reach Port Bolivar, drive to the beach, turn right, and park at the barrier. The 728 acres owned and leased by the Houston Audubon Society as a shorebird sanctuary and the adjacent tidal flats and Gulf comprise one of Texas' most famous birding locations. All the birds mentioned for Gilchrist can be seen here, and more. You may find all four small plovers—Snowy, Wilson's, Semipalmated, and Piping—within a few yards of each other, and be able to compare several of the small sandpipers known as peeps. Lift your eyes from the mud and sand occasionally and you may see Brown Pelicans fly by, a migrant Peregrine Falcon, or in late summer a Magnificent Frigatebird soaring overhead. In winter, scan the Gulf for Northern Gannet and scoters.

Here, as at High Island, continual scrutiny of the area means that few rare birds go unnoticed. Most gulls are the abundant Laughing and the common Ring-billed, Herring, and Bonaparte's (fall through spring), but such rare gulls as California, Thayer's, Lesser Black-backed, Glaucous, Great Black-backed, Black-legged Kittiwake, and Kelp have also been seen here or just across the bay on Galveston Island. Watch for Horned Larks in short-grass areas; the salt marsh can be good for Seaside and Nelson's Sharp-tailed Sparrow, the latter in winter and spring. In late winter and spring, American Avocets gather here in flocks numbering in the thousands.

**5** Next, take the free ferry across Galveston Bay to **Galveston Island,** where you'll find good shore-birding at **East Beach** (*go to the E end of Seawall Blvd. and turn S on Boddeker Dr.*). You can drive on the sand to find birds here, but watch for boggy places and mind the tide; summer, when the beaches are crowded with sunbathers, is not a good time to visit. On the western part of the island, beaches, pastures, and golf courses host such migrants as American Golden-Plover, Long-billed Curlew, Whimbrel, and Buff-breasted and Upland Sandpipers. North from Stewart Road

## Great Texas Coastal Birding Trail

Recognizing the Gulf Coast's fame among birders—and hoping to capitalize on the potential for birding tourism dollars—government agencies and private enterprise are cooperating to establish the Great Texas Coastal Birding Trail (GTCBT), an auto tour route that will eventually link some 300 sites from the Sabine River to the Rio Grande. Travelers can obtain special maps showing birding locations, and road signs depicting a Black Skimmer will point the way to sites ranging from such well-known areas as **Anahuac National Wildlife Refuge** (see p. 206) to small-town parks. The central coast section of the GTCBT is complete, with work progressing on the upper and lower parts. Several other states have expressed an interest in emulating the GTCBT formula—though few will be able to match its birding possibilities. For information, contact the GTCBT, 4200 Smith School Road, Austin, Texas 78744, or call 512-389-4800.

Birdwatching in Brazos Bend State Park, southwest of Houston

on 99th Street, the municipal golf course's perimeter streets provide good views. Farther west, take Eight-Mile Road north from Stewart and watch as you approach West Bay, the marsh locally famed for rails and waders. Check the beach and nature trail at **Galveston Island State Park** for waders, rails, and shorebirds.

**6** Farther down the coast, 28,000-acre **San Bernard National Wildlife Refuge** offers another chance to look for waders, waterfowl, and shorebirds you may have missed, and spring fallouts bring neotropical migrants. Almost any bird possible at Texas Point or Anahuac could show up here. In addition, you could spot a Crested Caracara, a handsome raptor near the northern edge of its range. Check trees for Barred Owl, and in spring and summer look in shrubby places for Painted Bunting. Wood Storks are sometimes seen here during their late-summer post-nesting wanderings, and, later, wintering flocks of Sandhill Cranes.

**7** Inland from the coast and north toward Houston, **Brazos Bend State Park** ranks as one of east Texas' most attractive parks as well as a very rewarding birding site. Once owned by a hunting club, Brazos Bend's nearly 5,000 acres encompass hardwood forest, coastal tallgrass prairie, extensive freshwater marsh and swamp, and several small lakes. Anhinga, Black-bellied Whistling-Duck, Wood Duck, King Rail, Pileated Woodpecker, Prothonotary Warbler, and Painted Bunting are among the park's breeding species. Waders such as American and Least Bitterns, Yellow-crowned Night-Heron, and Roseate Spoonbill are seen with varying regularity, as is the western Cinnamon Teal in winter. As noteworthy as its birds are, the park's most conspicuous wild inhabitants are alligators, which commonly rest near (and sometimes on) trails. Wise visitors will heed such signs as "Do not assume alligators are slow moving or sluggish" and "When an alligator stands its ground, opens its mouth and hisses, you have come too close."

Greater Prairie-Chicken at Attwater Prairie Chicken National Wildlife Refuge, near Eagle Lake

**8** Northeast of Eagle Lake, the 8,000 acres of **Attwater Prairie Chicken National Wildlife Refuge** protect a dwindling population of the critically endangered Attwater's race of the Greater Prairie-Chicken, a subspecies whose numbers have plummeted in recent years. Once, birders could view male birds "dancing" at a lek, or traditional courtship site, in early spring, but viewing has been prohibited as the resident prairie-chicken population has continued its decline despite intensive management and protection. Nonetheless, the refuge remains a popular and productive birding site. Both White-tailed Hawk and Crested Caracara are seen here, along with good numbers of wintering waterfowl and migrant shorebirds. Scan the sky often for a wide variety of raptors, from migrant Broad-winged and Swainson's Hawks to wintering Ferruginous Hawk and American Kestrel. Mountain Plover and Sprague's Pipit are two often elusive migrant or wintering species found along the refuge driving route, along with Northern Bobwhite; Sedge Wren; and Grasshopper, Le Conte's, and Harris's Sparrows. Check roadside ditches for King Rail and fields in spring for American Golden-Plover and Upland and Buff-breasted Sandpipers.

# CENTRAL
# TEXAS COAST

A transitional zone from wet east Texas to the drier, subtropical Rio Grande Valley, the central coast is crisscrossed by little-traveled highways through cattle farms and prairie. Long barrier islands protect its shoreline, and inshore waters offer fine fishing, the bounty of which can be sampled in any number of seafood restaurants.

**9** One of the most famous nature preserves in America, **Aransas National Wildlife Refuge** comprises more than 55,000 acres of woods, prairie, and coastal marsh along the Gulf Coast, about 50 miles south of Victoria. Aransas' prominence rests largely on its most famous winter visitor, the endangered Whooping Crane. Numbers of this magnificent, nearly 5-foot-tall bird had declined by 1941 to a tiny resident flock in Louisiana (extirpated by 1949) and 15 individuals whose sole wintering ground was a small area on the Texas coast. Their nesting home was unknown until 1954, when summering birds were found 2,400 miles away in Canada's Northwest Territories. The cranes make this long flight north each spring, returning to Texas in fall with the season's young birds. With protection Whooping Cranes in this flock grew to 76 birds by 1980, and the fall of 1997 saw a record 182 cranes return to Aransas and vicinity.

However, it must be said that visiting Aransas is not the best way to see a Whooping Crane. Instead, contact the Rockport-Fulton Chamber of Commerce *(512-729-6445 or 800-826-6441)* for a list of commercial boats that traverse the Intracoastal Waterway from about November through early April. Success is a near certainty on these trips, and travelers also see a variety of other species, including pelicans, waders, waterfowl, shorebirds, gulls, and terns.

- **Winter Whooping Cranes at Aransas National Wildlife Refuge**
- **Hawk migration at Hazel Bazemore Park**

Information section p. 231

Aransas is still a fine place to visit, even if the cranes don't make an appearance near areas with public access. The bird checklist here totals 394 species—second most of any site in the National Wildlife Refuge system. Refuge roads pass near ponds where Anhinga (spring and fall); Double-crested and Olivaceous Cormorants; King, Clapper, and Sora Rails; Purple Gallinule (spring through fall); Common Moorhen; and waterfowl may be found (along with alligators—be careful). The roads also travel the shoreline with the usual Texas assortment of waders and shorebirds. Additionally, several nature trails give access to oak woodlands that can provide excellent sightings during spring and fall migration, but be aware that the mosquitoes here can be horrific.

From the refuge observation tower views encompass an expanse of marsh where Whooping Cranes occasionally feed. Careless observers often mistake other birds for cranes, quite happily pointing out Great or Snowy Egrets or white-morph Reddish Egrets as the far rarer Whoopers. American White Pelican, White Ibis, and Snow Goose, white birds with black on their wings, are sometimes mistaken for cranes when flying, but all have much different shapes.

A 16-mile auto tour route through the refuge begins at the **Wildlife Interpretative Center.** Following it, you may spot various raptors including Red-tailed and White-tailed Hawks and Crested Caracara, and in winter the Whoopers' much more common cousin the Sandhill Crane.

Birding tour boat, Aransas Bay

**10** Follow Tex. 35 and Tex. 361 toward the town of Port Aransas, past beaches and bay fronts that may have pelicans, waders, gulls, terns, or flocks of shorebirds. Take the free ferry across the Intracoastal Waterway to "Port A," another town trying to attract its share of Texas birding tourists. A boardwalk at the **Port Aransas Birding Center** (*take Cut-Off Rd. to Ross Ave.*) leads into a wetland where you may find the diminutive Least Grebe (a south Texas specialty that nests here and quickly becomes rare farther north), Neotropic Cormorant, most of the

Great Blue Heron, Aransas National Wildlife Refuge, Gulf Coast

locally occurring herons and egrets (including nesting Least Bittern), Roseate Spoonbill, Black-bellied Whistling-Duck, and Mottled Duck. On the Gulf side of the island, the **Port Aransas jetty,** stretching several hundred yards from shore, provides a good lookout point for such oceanic birds as Northern Gannet (winter and early spring) and Magnificent Frigatebird (fairly common in summer and early fall).

**11** Continue driving south on Tex. 361 to **Padre Island National Seashore,** which protects one of America's longest stretches of undeveloped ocean shoreline, a nearly 70-mile sliver of beach and sand dunes with the Gulf of Mexico on one side and Laguna Madre on the other. Much of the park south of the Malaquite Beach visitor center is accessible only by four-wheel-drive vehicles, but there's still plenty of shoreline to search for shorebirds, gulls, and terns. This is well known as a great place to see migrating Peregrine Falcons in spring and especially, fall when several of

Mixed flock, including Northern Shovelers, American Coots, Black-necked Stilts, American Avocets, and Marbled Godwits, Corpus Christi Bay

these magnificent birds are likely to be seen cruising south along the beach daily. Keep your eyes open anywhere in this area for White-tailed Kite and White-tailed Hawk, beautiful raptors seen here and farther south.

**12** West of town, **Hazel Bazemore County Park** is the site of one of the country's premier hawk-watches. In 1998, of the more than a million birds seen between mid-August and mid-November, more than 90 percent were Broad-winged Hawks, with occasional daily totals in mid- to late September of more than 100,000 individuals. Lesser numbers of Osprey, Mississippi Kite, Sharp-shinned and Cooper's Hawks, American Kestrel, Peregrine Falcon, and other species are also seen. To reach the park, take US 77 south from I-37 for 0.8 mile; turn west on Farm Road 624, and in 0.8 mile turn north on County Road 69.

# LOWER COAST
# AND RIO GRANDE

South of Corpus Christi the land turns dry and scrubby, more western in its look than the upper coast. As you travel through the flat, mesquite brushland, you're entering a world that, uniquely in America, blends birds of east, west, and south—south as in Mexico, that is.

Eastern birds are represented especially well during spring migration, when any patch of trees may host an assortment of warblers, vireos, and thrushes (though migrants are not as abundant here as farther up the coast), and certain days bring the astounding spectacle of thousands of Broad-winged Hawks circling in "kettles," gaining height before continuing their northward trek. Western birds include White-tailed Kite, Harris's Hawk, Inca Dove, Black-chinned Hummingbird, Golden-fronted and Ladder-backed Woodpeckers, Ash-throated and Brown-crested Flycatchers, Verdin, Cactus Wren, Curve-billed Thrasher, Cassin's Sparrow, Pyrrhuloxia, Bronzed Cowbird, Hooded and Bullock's Orioles, and Lesser Goldfinch.

It's the Mexican species usually found only in south Texas that draw most birders, though. Some of these specialties—Plain Chachalaca, Great Kiskadee, and Green Jay among them—are easy to find, while others are rare or secretive. Some range northward up the coast; some are mostly confined to the immediate vicinity of the Rio Grande. With a bit of planning and luck, a birder can hope to see a good percentage of these species at the parks and refuges for which south Texas is famous.

**13** The town of Kingsville is famous, too, as the namesake of the legendary **King Ranch,** founded in 1853 by steamboat captain Richard King and now encompassing

- Mexican specialties along the Rio Grande
- Winter waterfowl at Laguna Atascosa National Wildlife Refuge

Information section p. 231

an area slightly larger than the state of Rhode Island. Cattle is the main King business, but to its other enterprises of oil, farming, quarter horses, leather goods, hunting, a museum, and bus tours, the ranch has recently added birding. While a fine assortment of south Texas birds have found a de facto refuge on the ranch, three species in particular—Ferruginous Pygmy-Owl, Northern Beardless-Tyrannulet, and Tropical Parula—are specialties. The little owl was once thought to be extremely rare in the United States, and birders sought it virtually exclusively near the Rio Grande. A thriving population was later discovered, however, on brushlands of ranches well north of the river. The tyrannulet and Tropical Parula can be found elsewhere in the area, but are probably easier to see here. Birders, who pay fees for a variety of guided tours of the ranch, will also see Wild Turkey in abundance, and probably White-tailed Kite, Harris's and White-tailed Hawks, Crested Caracara, and Green Jay, among many others.

Be on the lookout for raptors on the long stretch of US 77 between Kingsville and Raymondville. One recent winter Masked Ducks, rare vagrants from Mexico, settled in for a time at some of the small ponds on the east side of the highway here. Many a birder has seen his or her first Golden-fronted Woodpecker, Green Jay, Black-crested Titmouse (a race of Tufted Titmouse once considered a distinct species), Couch's Kingbird, or Hooded Oriole at the rest stops along US 77 south of Sarita, either the old one on the west side of the road or the new one in the median. Tropical Parula has nested with some regularity at both spots. Watch for both Cliff and Cave Swallows nesting in highway culverts, with small numbers of Cave Swallows seen even in winter.

Green Jay, a flashy specialty of the Rio Grande Valley

**14** East of Harlingen, **Laguna Atascosa National Wildlife Refuge** is yet another of Texas' highly and deservedly celebrated birding meccas. Its 45,000 acres include Laguna Madre shoreline, thorn forest, grassland, agricultural fields, and bays, lakes, and ponds of various sizes. Like most such refuges, Laguna Atascosa was established to provide a sanctuary for waterfowl, but its management mission has expanded to include nongame species as well.

Bluebird nesting box, King Ranch, near Kingsville

In recent years the refuge has been a release site for captive-raised Aplomado Falcons, raptors that were extirpated in Texas in the 1950s. This is also home to a small number of ocelots, rare and ultrasecretive cats barely holding on in the United States. (If you should happen to see an ocelot, go immediately and buy a lottery ticket, because the gods of fortune have chosen you as one of the luckiest people in the country.)

The roll call of Laguna Atascosa birds is very long, and only a few highlights may be noted here. Its shoreline can host nearly every type of waterbird listed previously in this chapter. Wilson's Plover nests here, and the refuge is an important winter home for the threatened Piping Plover. Marshy areas can harbor rails and other wetland species. Winter flocks of Sandhill Cranes and Snow Geese feed in fields, and ducks throng lakes and bays. (Laguna Madre is noted as the most important wintering ground for Redheads in the United States.) Least Grebe; Black-bellied Whistling-Duck; Plain Chachalaca; White-tipped Dove;

Bronzed Cowbirds and Great-tailed Grackles

Groove-billed Ani; Common Pauraque; Brown-crested Flycatcher; Great Kiskadee; Green Jay; Long-billed Thrasher; and Olive, Cassin's, and Botteri's Sparrows are some of the south Texas specialties that nest here, along with Greater Roadrunner, Ladder-backed Woodpecker, Verdin, Cactus Wren, Pyrrhuloxia, and Painted Bunting.

Laguna Atascosa's 15-mile **Bayside Drive** and 1.5-mile **Lakeside Drive** pass through varied habitats and lead to walking trails of from one-eighth to more than 3 miles. They also provide great birding for visitors unable to leave their vehicles. Don't speed around the loop drive on a hot, windy summer afternoon and expect to see a teeming host of birds, though. Arrive early from fall through spring, take time to explore, give yourself a midday break, and return in late afternoon—and you'll undoubtedly realize Laguna Atascosa deserves its distinguished reputation as one of the country's finest birding sites.

**15** Humans have greatly altered the environment of the lower Rio Grande Valley, but the natural areas that remain include some of the most famous and rewarding birding spots in the country. Here, among spreading suburbia and vegetable fields, pockets of woodland harbor birds that are more typical of the tropics than of temperate North America.

**Brownsville,** on the Rio Grande just a short stroll across the bridge from Mexico, offers several birding sites, but none is more famous than the place local tourism officials, tongue in cheek, call the "Mexican Crow Park"—actually the city dump. Birders usually go to landfills to see gulls, which happily feed on our abundant garbage, but here the attraction is the Tamaulipas (formerly Mexican) Crow, a small relative of the American Crow of the east and the Chihuahuan Raven, the common "crow" of south Texas. The **Brownsville Landfill,** located at the city's port off Farm Road 511, is the only reliable place in the United States to see Tamaulipas, and by now landfill workers have learned to tolerate birders who've made this one of the regular stops on the lower Rio Grande Valley circuit. The landfill is also a good place to look for gulls in winter; Lesser Black-backed is among the rarities that have been found here.

Brownsville is also known for its free-flying flocks of parrots, the origin of which has long been in dispute. Some are undoubtedly escaped cage birds, while others may be wild birds that have wandered north from Mexico. The flocks move around for food, of course, but one reliable spot to look for them has been on **Los Ebaños,** a street a block west of Central Boulevard; listen for the birds' harsh shrieks and chattering calls. Red-crowned Parrots and Green Parakeets are the most common species, but others may also show up.

Laughing Gulls at the Brownsville Landfill

**16** The **Sabal Palm Audubon Center and Sanctuary,** southeast of Brownsville off Farm Road 1419, ranks with Texas' most important natural areas. This 527-acre preserve protects the country's only significant remaining forest of sabal palms, a native species (as opposed to the exotic palms of sundry varieties ubiquitous in the valley) nearly extirpated in the United States by land clearing and damming. Birders know it as a beautiful spot to find Least Grebe, Plain Chachalaca, Buff-bellied Hummingbird, Green Jay, Long-billed Thrasher, Olive Sparrow, and many other species, occasionally including Tropical Parula. Here, as nearly anywhere along the valley, very rare vagrants from Mexico may show up at any time. Gray-crowned Yellowthroat, Golden-crowned Warbler, and Crimson-collared Grosbeak all have taken up temporary residence here in recent years. Those whose interests go beyond birds will find other rare animals and plants here as well, including the speckled racer, David's milkberry, and Barbados cherry (manzanita).

**17** Occasionally a famous golfer is asked which place he or she would play if restricted to just one course for life, and the answer is some legendary spot like Pebble Beach or Augusta National. Ask birders a comparable question about U.S. birding locations, and the choice would often be **Santa Ana National Wildlife Refuge,** off US 281 south of Alamo. These 2,088 acres bordering the Rio Grande host a great percentage of the region's specialties, attracted to an island of native forest and wetlands in an ocean of agriculture, cities, and suburbs.

Just a few of the birds found with some regularity here: Least Grebe; Anhinga; Black-bellied and Fulvous Whistling-Ducks; Hook-billed Kite; Gray and Harris's Hawks; Plain Chachalaca; King Rail; White-tipped Dove; Groove-billed Ani; Elf Owl; Common Pauraque; Buff-bellied Hummingbird; Ringed and Green Kingfishers; Northern Beardless-Tyrannulet; Brown-crested Flycatcher; Great Kiskadee; Couch's Kingbird; Green Jay; Long-billed Thrasher; Tropical Parula; Olive Sparrow; Bronzed Cowbird; and Hooded, Altamira, and Audubon's Orioles. With near-daily scrutiny from expert birders, Santa Ana has seen

the discovery of such rarities as Muscovy and Masked Ducks; Crane, Roadside, and Short-tailed Hawks; Ruddy Ground-Dove; Green Violet-ear; Elegant Trogon; Rose-throated Becard; Clay-colored and Rufous-backed Robins; Gray-crowned Yellowthroat; Golden-crowned Warbler; Crimson-collared Grosbeak; and Blue Bunting. In general, winter offers the best chance to see Mexican rarities.

Santa Ana National Wildlife Refuge, near McAllen

Santa Ana's official refuge bird list includes 9 vireos, 43 warblers, 24 flycatchers, and 29 waterfowl among its nearly 400 species. Remember, this is on a relatively tiny area, just 4 percent the size of Laguna Atascosa. Of course, no one can hope to see all these birds on a single visit, but the numbers indicate the refuge's potential. In short, go—and marvel.

Bentsen-Rio Grande Valley State Park, near Mission

Winter and spring are the most popular times to visit Santa Ana. To relieve traffic on refuge roads, private vehicles have been banned during the crowded winter season, when a tram makes a regular 7-mile circuit to drop off and pick up passengers. Some of the best birding areas are around **Willow** and **Pintail Lakes,** within easy walking distance of the refuge visitor center. Additionally, blinds in this area offer handicapped birders a chance to sit and wait for birds to come to them.

A note here about rarities in the valley: Because this area is so intensively birded, the odds are high that rare birds will be found and reported. It's especially important for visitors to check telephone rare bird alerts (see Eastern

Texas Information p. 230) as well as bulletin boards at parks and refuges, and to talk to other birders about what's been seen lately. Don't be shy about quizzing birders you meet at the various hot spots (and you will meet lots of them). You don't want to be walking the trail at Sabal Palm while a Crane Hawk is dining on a frog at Santa Ana.

**18** Twenty miles upstream from Santa Ana, **Bentsen–Rio Grande Valley State Park** provides a chance to find birds you may have missed at Santa Ana, though its list is not quite as lengthy. The elusive Hook-billed Kite is seen relatively often here; the orange eye-shine of the Common Pauraque is frequent on park roads at night; and a pair of tiny Elf Owls commonly nests in a cavity in a tree or telephone pole near the picnic area. Many of the "winter Texans" who park their RVs at Bentsen are enthusiastic bird feeders, which makes it easy to see White-tipped Dove, Green Jay, Bronzed Cowbird, and a variety of other species. Usually, one campsite becomes an informal birding center where news of the day's sightings is posted. One campground specialty is Blue Bunting, a rare but almost regular winter visitor to feeders; take care to distinguish this species from the more common Indigo Bunting. The park also offers naturalist-led birding tours in winter.

**Plain Chachalaca**

Like phoebes and chickadees, the pheasantlike Plain Chachalaca was named for its call: in this case a loud, harsh *cha-cha-lac* that begins with one individual and builds to a chorus of several birds that can be almost deafening in its intensity. With protection, chachalacas have expanded beyond the parks and refuges of the lower Rio Grande Valley into suburbs of McAllen and Brownsville, where their dawn calling serves as nature's own alarm clock—welcome to some, an irritant to late sleepers.

**19** About 10 miles north of Roma, turn south off US 83 to **Salineno,** where the road dead-ends at the Rio Grande. You can scan here for Muscovy Duck and for Hook-billed Kite, which often soars above the treetops as the air warms up in midmorning. The small trailer park here often has feeders where Audubon's Orioles appear regularly. Watch, too, for Groove-billed Ani in late spring and summer, and for Ringed Kingfisher along the river.

**20** **Falcon Dam,** which contains sprawling Falcon Reservoir, serves as another access point to the Rio Grande and good birding habitat. As you approach the dam on Tex. 2098, turn left onto a secondary road that runs below the large embankment. The expanse of short grass to your right is a fairly reliable spot for wintering Sprague's Pipit, an elusive species that has suffered in recent years from the destruction of its nesting areas in the prairies of the northern Great Plains. You'll have to walk the grassy area here and hope to flush up a bird (having a small group helps cover more ground), which will then circle high in the air before performing its astounding "death dive" back to earth. Once on the ground, the pipit may pause in a spot allowing you a good look, or it may scurry off to hide.

Continue to the parking area overlooking the dam's spillway where Ringed Kingfisher is often seen flying across the river, and Hook-billed Kite is a possibility. If you have the time, walk the old road downstream from the parking lot to search for other valley specialties, including the rare Ferruginous Pygmy-Owl.

Before the discovery of a substantial population in the King Ranch area (see p. 219), this was the best spot in the country to look for the owl, and countless people came here to play tapes, whistle, and otherwise try to attract the little bird. While ethical birders don't do such things nowadays when dealing with a small, isolated, or threatened population, there's no harm in strolling the road and hoping to find a Ferruginous Pygmy-Owl perched on a branch somewhere; they're often quite bold before a gaggle of excited, finger-pointing birders. In any case, this is a good walk to look for species such as Hook-billed Kite; Red-billed Pigeon (rare); Golden-fronted Woodpecker; Couch's Kingbird; Ash-throated and Brown-crested Flycatchers; Green Jay; and Altamira and Audubon's Orioles.

This far upriver from the coast, you're well into brushland that's home to such western species as Scaled Quail, Greater Roadrunner, Ladder-backed Woodpecker, Verdin, Cactus Wren, Curve-billed Thrasher, and Black-throated Sparrow. Habitat for these species abounds, but most is private, and Texas ranchers generally disapprove of trespassing. One accessible spot to look for these and other birds is **Falcon State Park,** located along the eastern shore of Falcon Reservoir. This small park is more oriented to boaters and anglers than birders, but its 2 miles of nature trails can be good for a variety of local specialties.

**21** One last bird, and two last sites, must be included in this section: The bird is the White-collared Seedeater, a tiny finchlike species

*Long-billed Thrasher*

### Special Birds of the Lower Rio Grande Valley

| | | | |
|---|---|---|---|
| Least Grebe | Purple Gallinule | | |
| Neotropic | Red-billed Pigeon | Golden-fronted | |
|   Cormorant | White-tipped Dove |   Woodpecker | Cave Swallow |
| Black-bellied | Green Parakeet | Northern Beardless- | Clay-colored Robin |
|   Whistling-Duck | Red-crowned Parrot |   Tyrannulet | Long-billed |
| Fulvous Whistling- | Groove-billed Ani | Brown-crested |   Thrasher |
|   Duck | Ferruginous |   Flycatcher | Tropical Parula |
| Muscovy Duck |   Pygmy-Owl | Great Kiskadee | White-collared |
| Mottled Duck | Elf Owl | Couch's Kingbird |   Seedeater |
| Masked Duck | Lesser Nighthawk | Scissor-tailed | Olive Sparrow |
| Hook-billed Kite | Common Pauraque |   Flycatcher | Botteri's Sparrow |
| White-tailed Kite | Buff-bellied | Green Jay | Pyrrhuloxia |
| Gray Hawk |   Hummingbird | Brown Jay | Bronzed Cowbird |
| Harris's Hawk | Ringed Kingfisher | Tamaulipas Crow | Altamira Oriole |
| Plain Chachalaca | Green Kingfisher | Chihuahuan Raven | Audubon's Oriole |

that's very common in brushy places throughout most of Mexico and Central America but that barely reaches the United States, where its irregular occurrence has frustrated many a birder hoping to add it to his or her list.

Seedeaters have been seen with some regularity in the cattails of a wetland adjoining the public library in the small town of **Zapata,** about 30 miles northwest of Falcon Dam, but the time-honored spot to find them is the even smaller town of **San Ygnacio,** 14 miles farther along US 83. From the highway, follow Washington Street west a few blocks to the Rio Grande and search the extensive area of reeds along the riverbank (where you might also find a Ringed Kingfisher). Early and late in the day are the best times, and it helps to bring a rabbit's foot.

# Eastern Texas
## Information

? Visitor Center/Information    $ Fee Charged    ⅋ Food

⚦ Rest Rooms    🏃 Nature Trails    ⇆ Driving Tours    ♿ Wheelchair Accessible

*Be advised that facilities may be seasonal and limited. We suggest calling or writing ahead for specific information. Note that addresses may be for administrative offices; see text or call for directions to sites.*

### Rare Bird Alerts

Texas:
Statewide *713-964-5867*
Northeastern *903-234-2473*
Corpus Christi
   *512-883-7410*
Lower Rio Grande Valley
   *956-969-2731*
Austin *512-926-8751*
San Antonio *210-308-6788*

## UPPER TEXAS COAST

### Texas Point National Wildlife Refuge
*(Page 205)*
Tex. 87
Sabine Pass, TX 77655
*409-971-2909*

⚦ 🏃

### Sabine Woods *(Page 205)*
c/o Texas Ornithological
   Society
7315 Cottonwood Drive
Baytown, TX 77521
*281-383-3955*

🏃

### Sea Rim State Park
*(Page 206)*
Tex. 87, P.O. Box 1066
Sabine Pass, TX 77655
*409-971-2559*

? $ ⚦ 🏃 ♿

### Anahuac National Wildlife Refuge
*(Page 206)*
509 Washington Street
Anahuac, TX 77514
*409-267-3337*

⚦ 🏃 ⇆ ♿

### High Island Sanctuaries and Bolivar Flats
*(Pages 208-211)*
Houston Audubon Society
440 Wilchester Boulevard
Houston, TX 77079
*713-932-1639*

? $ ⚦ 🏃 ♿

*Contact for Boy Scout Woods, Smith Oaks Bird Sanctuary, and Bolivar Flats Shorebird Sanctuary*

### Galveston Island State Park *(Page 213)*
14901 Farm Road 3005
Galveston, TX 77554
*409-737-1222*

? $ ⚦ 🏃 ♿

### San Bernard National Wildlife Refuge
*(Page 213)*
1212 North Velasco
Angleton, TX 77505
*409-964-3639*

⚦ 🏃 ⇆ ♿

### Brazos Bend State Park
*(Page 213)*
21901 Farm Road 762
Needville, TX 77461
*409-553-5101*

? $ ⚦ 🏃 ♿

*Visitor center open Sat.-Sun.*

### Attwater Prairie Chicken National Wildlife Refuge
*(Page 214)*
P.O. Box 519
Eagle Lake, TX 77434
*409-234-3021*

? ⚦ 🏃 ⇆

# CENTRAL TEXAS COAST

**Aransas National Wildlife Refuge**
*(Page 215)*
P.O. Box 100
Austwell, TX 77950
*512-286-3559*

⬛⬛⬛⬛⬛⬛

**Port Aransas Birding Center** *(Page 216)*
700 Ross Avenue
Port Aransas, TX 78373
*512-749-4158*

⬛

**Padre Island National Seashore** *(Page 217)*
9405 South Padre
  Island Drive
Corpus Christi, TX 78418
*512-949-8173*

⬛⬛⬛⬛⬛⬛

**Hazel Bazemore County Park** *(Page 218)*
P.O. Box 2608
Corpus Christi, TX 78468
*512-387-4231*

⬛⬛⬛

# LOWER COAST AND RIO GRANDE

**King Ranch** *(Page 219)*
Highway 141 West
Kingsville, TX 78363
*512-592-8055*

⬛⬛⬛⬛⬛

*Access via guided tour only*

**Laguna Atascosa National Wildlife Refuge** *(Page 220)*
P.O. Box 450
Rio Hondo, TX 78583
*956-748-3607*

⬛⬛⬛⬛⬛⬛

**Sabal Palm Audubon Center and Sanctuary**
*(Page 224)*
Sabal Palm Road
Brownsville, Texas 78523
*956-541-8034*

⬛⬛⬛⬛⬛

**Santa Ana National Wildlife Refuge**
*(Page 224)*
Route 2, Box 202A
Alamo, TX 78516
*956-787-3079*

⬛⬛⬛⬛⬛⬛

*Fee for winter tram tours only. Tour loop open to private vehicles Tues.–Wed.*

**Bentsen–Rio Grande Valley State Park**
*(Page 227)*
P.O. Box 988
Mission, TX 78573
*956-519-6448*

⬛⬛⬛⬛⬛

**Falcon State Park**
*(Page 229)*
P.O. Box 2
Falcon Heights, TX 78545
*956-848-5327*

⬛⬛⬛⬛⬛

Heartland

W hen birders think of the upper Midwest, one image often predominates in their collective imagination: A car winds slowly along a back road through a snowy forest, its occupants fighting off the cold with coffee, hot chocolate, and hopeful, half-hearted jokes. All eyes (including, most of the time, the driver's) are on the roadside trees, constantly scanning. Someone calls, "Stop! Stop! There it is!" and all look up to see another set of eyes staring back at them in the piercing yellow gaze of a Great Gray Owl, that huge, elusive predator of the North Woods. "He's so magnificent," someone says, and then there's simply silent admiration, because no one can argue with that.

*Preceding pages:*
Canada Geese,
Big Stone National
Wildlife Refuge,
Minnesota
*Above:* Great
Gray Owl
*Below:* Great Egret,
Crex Meadows
Wildlife Area,
Wisconsin

But perhaps this scenario is too specific. The subject here might be a Boreal Owl (even more elusive than the Great Gray), or a twittering band of Common Redpolls, or a flock of Bohemian Waxwings, sleek and elegant as guests at a fancy party. The glamour birds of this region are mostly the species of the far north, birds that barely reach the lower 48 states in their breeding ranges, or appear only as winter visitors. A trip to northern Minnesota or Wisconsin in winter is just as much a part of a birder's agenda as fall at Pennsylvania's Hawk Mountain or a spring visit to the Texas coast.

And this statement, too, begs an argument, for other seasons and other places have their own attractions. Spruce Grouse, Black-backed Woodpecker, and Gray Jay reward birders who venture north any time of year, and the much sought-after Connecticut Warbler nests here. Wisconsin's Crex Meadows ranks as one of the premier birding areas in the Midwest. Missouri's prairies are home to Greater Prairie-Chicken and Henslow's Sparrow. Refuges in Iowa and Illinois host migrant waterfowl and shorebirds. The Great Lakes attract gulls and other waterbirds. And even the crowded city of Chicago has several fine patches of green, one of which has earned the name "magic" for its ability to lure a variety of migrant species. All these, of course, are just highlights in a region of surprising diversity, of prairies and lakes, of spruce-fir forests and Mississippi River bottomlands.

This chapter covers the upper midwestern states, beginning in southern Missouri, on the border of the Deep South, and ending in Wisconsin. ■

## Special Birds of the Heartland

Northern Goshawk
Spruce Grouse
Sharp-tailed
  Grouse
Greater Prairie-
  Chicken
Yellow Rail
Sandhill Crane
Snowy Owl
Northern Hawk
  Owl
Great Gray Owl
Boreal Owl
Northern Saw-
  whet Owl
Three-toed
  Woodpecker
Black-backed
  Woodpecker
Yellow-bellied
  Flycatcher
Gray Jay

*Yellow-Bellied Flycatcher*

Common Raven
Boreal Chickadee
Bohemian
  Waxwing
Connecticut
  Warbler
Henslow's
  Sparrow
Chestnut-collared
  Longspur
Pine Grosbeak
Red Crossbill
White-winged
  Crossbill
Common Redpoll
Hoary Redpoll
Evening Grosbeak
Eurasian Tree
  Sparrow

# MISSOURI

**1** Once upon a time waterbirds would have been nearly as scarce as hen's teeth in the rugged Missouri Ozarks—before the creation of reservoirs like **Table Rock Lake** just west of Branson. Now in winter Common Loon, Pied-billed and Horned Grebes, and ducks both dabbling and diving can be seen, along with Bald Eagles perched in waterside trees and soaring overhead. The scarce Black Vulture also flocks here in winter with the common Turkey Vulture. **Table Rock State Park** (*Mo. 165 W off US 65*) provides one good lookout point, as do U.S. Army Corps of Engineers recreation areas scattered along the shore.

Table Rock was momentarily famous in the winter of 1990-91 when four species of loon (Red-throated, Pacific, Common, and Yellow-billed) appeared, but such a gathering is unlikely to be repeated before the next ice age. As you drive around the lake, especially on the many side roads, keep an eye out for Greater Roadrunner (year-round) and Painted Bunting (spring and summer), both at the northeastern edge of their ranges.

**2** West of Lamar, just a few miles from the Kansas state line, **Prairie State Park** offers a glimpse back to a time when tallgrass prairie still stretched across vast areas of the Midwest. Big bluestem and Indian grass grow head high here, and wildflowers such as Indian paintbrush, pale purple coneflower, and coreopsis bloom in lovely profusion. Northern Harriers soar over the grassland, and other nesting birds include Upland Sandpiper, Scissor-tailed Flycatcher, Loggerhead Shrike, Bell's Vireo, Grasshopper and Song Sparrows, Rose-breasted Grosbeak (near its southern range limit), and Dickcissel. The two breeding birds most sought, though, are Greater Prairie-Chicken and Henslow's Sparrow,

- Grassland birds in southwestern prairies
- Waterfowl at Squaw Creek National Wildlife Refuge
- Winter gulls at St. Louis's Riverlands area

Information section p. 269

Snow Geese at Squaw Creek National Wildlife Refuge, south of Mound City

both quite local in Missouri. In winter, Rough-legged Hawk and Short-eared Owl are possible. Check with the visitor center about areas closed because of bison reintroduction; after all, birding isn't supposed to be a contact sport.

**3** About 10 miles north of El Dorado Springs, **Taberville Prairie Conservation Area** hosts many of the same species. Though prairie-chickens have declined here in recent years, Henslow's Sparrows are fairly easily found in spring and summer. The elusive Smith's Longspur is a good possibility in March and November—look for it in areas of very short grass. A signed parking lot on County Road H provides a lookout point and access for walking into the prairie, as does a gravel road .75 mile north, running east from County Road H. Also drive a gravel road that heads south from County Road B, 2 miles east of its junction with County Road H.

A few miles west, **Schell-Osage Conservation Area** (*Cty. Rd. RA E from Cty. Rd. AA*) has long been a favorite of local birders. Its open water, bottomland forests, cropland, and marsh attract an excellent variety of birds. Geese and ducks can throng the wetlands from fall through spring (since this is a hunting area, access may be limited during waterfowl season). In spring, Yellow Warblers sing in waterside willows

and Prothonotary Warblers whistle from woods along the Osage River. Drive the gravel road along the north side of Schell Lake and check marshy pools for waders and shorebirds. At the east end of Schell Lake, a road leading east and north is good for migrant warblers in spring. At the west end of the lake, continue west along a dead-end road and check **H Pool,** where American Bittern may be found in migration and Black-crowned Night-Heron has nested.

**4** Visitors to the expanses of wetlands at **Squaw Creek National Wildlife Refuge** occasionally witness the presence of hundreds of thousands of Snow Geese and other waterfowl in migration. A 10-mile auto route provides excellent viewing of refuge pools and croplands. The list of possible species is long and varied here: American White Pelican can be common in migration; both bitterns have nested (Least is numerous here and can sometimes be seen from the observation platform at the beginning of the drive), as have both night-herons; Ospreys roost in open pool trees in migration. From late fall to early spring, Bald Eagles are sometimes present by the dozens. In addition, Common Moorhen is sometimes seen swimming through water plants and migrant shorebirds congregate in large numbers when water conditions are right (look for Hudsonian Godwit in

May). Le Conte's Sparrow is present in migration; Yellow-headed Blackbirds nest in the taller reeds. Few refuges are more conveniently located for travelers: It's just off US 159, only minutes west of I-29 south of Mound City.

**5** More centrally located in Missouri, **Swan Lake National Wildlife Refuge** (*30 miles S of Chillicothe, off US 65*) offers many of the same attractions as Squaw Creek, from big flocks of migrant pelicans and waterfowl to fine shorebirding in spring and fall.

**6** One of the best birding spots in central Missouri, **Eagle Bluffs Conservation Area** sits alongside the Missouri River south of Columbia (*from US 163, drive W on Cty. Rd. K to the headquarters, where you can pick up a map of the area*). A series of wetlands and adjacent woodlands has attracted an impressive list of birds, including rarities such as Tricolored Heron, Glossy Ibis, Ross's Goose, Cinnamon Teal, Prairie Falcon, Piping Plover, Black-necked Stilt, Red-necked Phalarope, Sprague's Pipit, and Cape May and Black-throated Blue Warblers. Great-tailed Grackle has nested here, on the eastern edge of its range.

Almost all the shorebird species on the Missouri list have been found here at one time or another, along with such marsh birds as American and Least Bitterns, Virginia Rail, Sora, Common Moorhen, and Sedge and Marsh Wrens. A road through the pond area provides good access for birders with physical disabilities. The adjacent **Katy Trail,** a section of abandoned rail line, passes woods where nesting warblers include Blue-winged, Yellow-throated, Black-and-white, Prothonotary, Worm-eating, and Louisiana Waterthrush.

Yellow-headed Blackbird, a summer breeder in midwestern marshes

**7** Diverse habitats, some natural and others man-made, make the **Shaw Arboretum,** an extension of the **Missouri Botanical Garden** (*from I-44 exit at Gray Summit to Mo. 100 E, about 35 miles W of St. Louis*), a popular birding destination near St. Louis. The arboretum's 2,400 acres include bottomland forest along the Meramec

River, fields (with areas of restored prairie), deciduous woods and conifer plantings, glades, wetlands, and scrubby second growth, all crisscrossed by 13 miles of hiking trails.

Conifer plantings near the visitor center can be good for winter finches. In spring and summer, areas of mixed woodland and open fields may have White-eyed Vireo, Eastern Bluebird, Blue-winged and Prairie Warblers, Common Yellowthroat, and Indigo Bunting. Henslow's Sparrow and Sedge Wren are occasional nesters in the prairie. In wetter woods near the river, look and listen for Red-shouldered Hawk; Barred Owl; Acadian Flycatcher; Wood Thrush; and Yellow-throated, Cerulean, Prothonotary, and Kentucky Warblers. Listen for the insectlike trill of Worm-eating Warbler, which may sound from these wooded slopes.

Shaw Arboretum, an extension of the Missouri Botanical Garden, near St. Louis

**8** North of St. Louis, **Riverlands Environmental Demonstration Area** encompasses grassland, marsh, and backwaters of the Mississippi River just upstream from a lock and dam. Accessed by turning east just before US 67 crosses the river into Illinois, this fine area has yielded a long bird list, including 18 species of gulls, from the regular Franklin's, Bonaparte's, Ring-billed, and Herring to single sightings of Slaty-backed, Glaucous-winged, and Ross's. In colder weather, especially when flocks are resting on ice, chances are good to pick out a Thayer's, Lesser Black-backed, or Glaucous.

In migration and/or winter, look for loons and grebes, pelicans, cormorants, herons (including occasional Snowy Egret), waterfowl of all kinds (including scoters and Oldsquaw), raptors (Bald Eagle is common), shorebirds, and terns. Alongside the many native sparrows in grass and brush, the region's most famous bird, Eurasian Tree Sparrow, can usually be found.

## Eurasian Tree Sparrow

Like its close relative the ubiquitous House Sparrow, the Eurasian Tree Sparrow was introduced into the United States from the Old World in the 19th century. The House Sparrow's expansion across the country was relentless, but the latter species still remains largely confined to the region around St. Louis, where the first individuals were released in 1870. Look for Eurasian Tree Sparrows at the **Riverlands Environ-men-tal Demonstration Area** (see p. 241) near St. Louis; around the East St. Louis Airport in Sauget, Illinois; and north of Burlington, Iowa *(Iowa 99 for 2.7 miles N of US 34; turn E on Tama Rd.).*

**9** Though its impressive forest suffered great damage in a 1993 storm, 21,675-acre **Mingo National Wildlife Refuge** *(off Mo. 51 NE of Poplar Bluff)* still offers birders access to some of the best bottomland woods —in part, a former channel of the Mississippi River. From spring through fall the beautiful and graceful Mississippi Kite soars over the forest. Bald Eagle has nested in recent years, and Red-shouldered Hawk is quite likely year-round.

Hooded Mergansers use refuge Wood Duck boxes (as do lots of Wood Ducks), and Least Bittern, Little Blue Heron, Yellow-crowned Night-Heron, Virginia Rail, and Sora might be seen in marshes. Other birds here range from Black Vulture (occasional), Wild Turkey, and Fish Crow to Willow Flycatcher, Northern Parula, and Worm-eating Warbler. Prothonotary and Hooded Warblers, two birds of surpassing beauty, give their respective *zweet-zweet-zweet* and wolf-whistle calls in breeding season. Winter brings waterfowl to Mingo, with thousands of geese and ducks gathering on wetlands, and Bald Eagles waiting patiently in tall trees, ready to swoop down and make a meal of any sick or wounded birds they notice among the gabbling and quacking flocks.

# ILLINOIS

"People in Chicago are spoiled. They think all you have to do is wait and the birds will come to you." So goes a saying of downstate Illinois birders—and to some degree, they're right. One of the most urbanized environments in America boasts fabulous birding in spring and fall, when migrants throng lakeshore parks offering the only greenery between the concrete sprawl of the city and the watery expanse of Lake Michigan.

● Migration in Chicago's lakeshore parks

● Varied breeders in Shawnee National Forest

Information section p. 270

**10** The most famous bit of vegetation in Chicago is the Magic Hedge at **Montrose Point** (*E from Lake Shore Dr. on Montrose Ave., then SE on Harbor Dr.*), a strip of small trees and shrubs atop a grassy slope between Harbor Drive and the water. Especially after a cold front in fall or inclement weather in spring, this spot can have an overwhelming number of both species and individuals. It's futile to try to list the possibilities, so many of the birds of eastern North America have shown up here (along with a surprising number from the West). Cuckoos, flycatchers, vireos, thrushes, warblers, tanagers, and sparrows are, of course, present in varying numbers, and the list of vagrants seen in the area is long and diverse, from Reddish Egret to Groove-billed Ani to Kirtland's Warbler. Be sure to check the harbor, nearby beaches, and the lake itself for loons, grebes, waterfowl, shorebirds, and gulls.

A few blocks south, the **Lincoln Park Bird Sanctuary** (*Irving Park Rd. E from Lake Shore Dr.*) offers similar birding. South of the Loop, the **Paul Douglas Nature Sanctuary,** also known as **Wooded Isle,** at **Jackson Park** (*across Clarence Darrow Bridge opposite the Museum of Science and Industry*) is another birders' favorite. Watch for the introduced Monk Parakeet, which builds its bulky nest on power poles. Watch, too, for Peregrine Falcon here and elsewhere in Chicago. Reintroduced, this magnificent predator has successfully nested in several spots around town, happily feeding on Rock Doves (the common city pigeon).

**11** North of the city, stretching 7 miles along the Lake Michigan shore almost to Wisconsin, **Illinois Beach State Park** (*Wadsworth Rd. E from Ill. 137*) has long attracted birders to its varied habitats of beach, marsh, grassland, and woods. All these can be found on the trails leading south from the visitor center toward Dead River, where songbirds appear in good numbers in migration. Illinois Beach is also known as a fine spot to watch fall raptor flights. From September through October, Sharp-shinned, Cooper's, Broad-winged, and Red-tailed Hawks; Merlin; Peregrine Falcon; and others may be seen. Days with west winds are best for hawk-watching, since birds traveling south are pushed eastward to the lakeshore and then follow it as they continue their journey.

From fall through spring, **Waukegan Harbor** (*Grand Ave. E from Ill. 137*) is a popular spot to search for loons, waterfowl, and gulls. The beach just to the north often has a good number of shorebirds in migration.

**12** Southwest of Chicago, **Goose Lake Prairie State Natural Area** (*take the Pine Bluff Rd. exit off I-55 and drive W 8 miles*) is an excellent place to find marsh and grassland birds. It's probably the state's best spot to find Henslow's Sparrow, which sings its unimpressive little *si-lick* song in spring and summer. To see one, you may need to walk the trails some distance from the visitor center—try the far end of the **Marsh Loop.**

Among the other nesting birds here: Pied-billed Grebe; Northern Harrier (not every year, but common in winter); King and Virginia Rails; Sora; Field, Savannah, Grasshopper, Song, and Swamp Sparrows; and Bobolink. Rails are always elusive and not easily found. You may have better luck seeing them on exposed mudflats when marshes begin to dry up in late summer. Short-eared Owl is a winter visitor to the grasslands here, appearing at dusk to quarter the fields in search of rodents.

**13** **Chautauqua National Wildlife Refuge,** along the Illinois River about 35 miles southwest of Peoria, is a favorite site to observe waterfowl from fall through spring. As many as 400,000 geese and ducks have been counted on the refuge at the peak of fall migration, along with the usual "camp follower" Bald Eagles, preying on the sick and wounded. Swans, both native Tundra and Trumpeter from reintroduced populations, appear on occasion. Birding on the refuge is dependent on water levels, and in recent years flooding has been a continual problem. Higher dikes, completed in a major construction project, will allow better water control, including management of the south pool of Lake Chautauqua for "moist soils" habitat. Fall shorebirding can be excellent here, and in the future should be much more consistent. Higher water levels will be maintained in the lake's north pool to attract diving ducks.

Snowy Owl with American Crows at Chicago's lakefront

**14** On the southeast side of Springfield, **Lake Springfield** offers an excellent variety of wintering waterbirds. Discharge from a power plant creates an area of open water even in midwinter, and loons (occasional Red-

Carlyle Lake, southern Illinois

throated or Pacific), grebes (the state's second record of Clark's Grebe came here), and dabbling and diving ducks are often numerous. One winter, Harlequin Duck and all three scoters were present, and jaegers have appeared in late fall. Much of the lakeshore is private property, but boat ramps and parks provide birding access. One favorite lookout is **Lincoln Memorial Garden** off East Lake Shore Drive on the southeast part of the lake. Woods and prairies here afford a diversion when waterbirding is slow.

**15** Located in the middle of farm country that Illinois naturalists (semi-)jokingly call "the corn and soybean desert," south of Vandalia, **Carlyle Lake** is a regional hot spot for loons, grebes, herons, egrets, waterfowl, gulls, and terns. Late September may bring a Sabine's Gull, and winter may see rarities such as Thayer's, Lesser Black-backed (becoming fairly regular here), or Glaucous, though Bonaparte's, Ring-billed, and Herring are the common species. Bald Eagles winter here, and some remain to nest; Ospreys appear in migration. **Eldon Hazlet** and **South Shore State Parks** provide viewpoints in the southern section of the lake, and other recreation areas are scattered around this 26,000-acre reservoir. The **Carlyle Lake Wildlife Management Area** at the lake's upper end hosts large concentrations of waterfowl, especially Snow Geese in February and March (hunting can restrict birding here in fall and winter). This area also provides good shorebirding in late summer and fall.

Look for winter finches in conifers in any of the lake's parks and recreation areas, and if luck is on your side, you might run across a Long-eared or Northern Saw-whet Owl perched in a pine or cedar. Winter drives through the surrounding agricultural lands may turn up Northern Harrier, Rough-legged Hawk, or Horned Lark.

**16** **Shawnee National Forest** occupies a highland area where the Ozarks cross the Mississippi River into southern Illinois. Two spots within the forest are especially favored by local birders. To reach the first, start in the small town of Pomona on Ill. 127 and head north, following signs to Pomona Natural Bridge. The forest has specifically designated some 2,000 acres in the vicinity as a nongame bird management area. Trails beginning here lead through forest where you may find Mississippi Kite; Fish Crow; Yellow-throated, Pine, Prairie (occasional), Cerulean, Prothonotary, Worm-eating, and Hooded (occasional) Warblers; Northern Parula; American Redstart; and Summer and Scarlet Tanagers, among many other nesting species. Stands of hardwoods, pine, cane, and shrubs create a varied landscape that makes the Pomona area one of the region's best in spring and fall migration.

The second birding spot within the forest is the **LaRue Pine Hills/Oakwood Bottoms Research Natural Area** in extreme northwestern Union County, which encompasses outstanding biological diversity in a small area, with swamp and limestone bluffs side by side. Take County Road 2 east of Ill. 3, following the levee along the Big Muddy River. Where the road meets Forest Road 345, turn right to reach LaRue Swamp. Listen for the scream of Red-shouldered

Scarlet Tanager, one of the most beautiful birds of eastern deciduous woodland

Hawk, a bird seldom seen in Illinois, and the *who-cooks-for-you* call of Barred Owl here. Green Heron, Wood Duck, Red-headed Woodpecker, and Prothonotary Warbler brighten the woods in old oxbows of the Big Muddy.

Nearby, just southeast of the little town of Ware, **Union County Conservation Area** (*off Ill. 3*) is worth a visit any time of year. Waterfowl are abundant from fall through spring (some 75,000 Canada Geese winter here), and both Bald and Golden Eagles may be seen leaving upland roosts to soar over the winter flocks. Pelicans, egrets, and shorebirds can be found seasonally, and Mississippi Kite nests.

For more bottomlands, head southwest of Vienna to **Cache River State Natural Area** south off Ill. 146. Black Vulture occurs in this area year-round. The boardwalk at **Heron Pond** leads through a beautiful bald-cypress-tupelo swamp, or take the trail at **Wildcat Bluff,** which drops to lowland forest from a higher trailhead. In migration this is a terrific spot, and the elevated viewpoint of the upper trail means you can scan treetops without "warbler neck."

# IOWA

**17** Bordering the Missouri River in southwestern Iowa stretches a line of hills formed of the fine, wind-deposited soil called loess. **Waubonsie State Park,** off Iowa 2 southwest of Sidney, sits atop this ridge, offering visitors a beautiful oak-hickory forest crisscrossed by hiking trails, as well as excellent birding in spring and summer. Wild Turkeys are common, and Broad-winged Hawks give their high whistling call as they soar over the woods. Barred Owl, Whip-poor-will, Ovenbird, Louisiana Waterthrush, Kentucky Warbler, and Summer and Scarlet Tanagers (Waubonsie is one of the best spots in Iowa for the former) nest here. Northern Parula is consistently seen in spring migration, and Black-and-white Warbler, a scarce breeder in the state, has nested here.

Northern Bobwhite, Chuck-will's-widow, Western Kingbird, and Blue Grosbeak are other specialties of this region of Iowa. To hear Chuck-will's-widow in spring and summer, go west from the state park on Iowa 2 to County Road L44. Drive north and take the first gravel road to the east, where you can hear the birds at dusk and dawn.

**18** One of Iowa's finest birding spots lies only a few minutes east of Waubonsie. Take Iowa 2 east to US 275, then continue east on County Road J46 to Riverton. There, take County Road L68 north 2 miles to the headquarters of the **Riverton Wildlife Area,** a 2,721-acre expanse of marsh, open water, and fields that seasonally attracts waders, waterfowl, and shorebirds. Snow Geese numbers here can reach more than 200,000 in late fall, creating what one naturalist has called "the greatest wildlife spectacle in Iowa." Careful observers can usually pick out a few Ross's Geese in these Snow flocks. Bald Eagles perch in tall cottonwoods

● Waterbirds at Lake Red Rock and Saylorville Lake
● Excellent wetlands in the Resthaven area

---

Information section p. 270

Lake Red Rock,
southeast of
Des Moines

and soar overhead, while thousands of Gadwall, Mallard, Northern Pintail, Blue-winged and Green-winged Teals, and other dabbling ducks rest and feed.

Mid-May is the peak of shorebird migration at Riverton, when (if water conditions are right) perhaps 20 species may appear on mudflats. In late summer, waders including occasional Snowy Egret, Little Blue Heron, and Black-crowned and Yellow-crowned Night-Herons can be seen, and Buff-breasted Sandpiper can appear in numbers. Nesting birds at Riverton include Least Bittern, Barred Owl, Willow Flycatcher, Horned Lark, Tree Swallow, Sedge Wren, Prothonotary Warbler, Grasshopper Sparrow, and both Eastern and Western Meadowlarks. A road, part paved and part gravel, runs around the perimeter of the area, and adventurous birders can walk dikes out into the marshes. This is a hunting area, so access can be limited in waterfowl season.

 Southeast of Des Moines, sprawling **Lake Red Rock** hosts loons, grebes, and waterfowl in migration, and

Bald Eagles in winter. The long list of rare or uncommon gulls that have been seen on the lake or along tailwaters below the dam includes Laughing, Mew, California, Thayer's, Iceland, Lesser Black-backed, Glaucous, Great Black-backed, Sabine's, Ross's, Ivory, and Black-legged Kittiwake. Check the river below the dam for Bald Eagle, waterfowl, and terns as well. County Road S71, northeast of Knoxville, leads to **Whitebreast Recreation Area,** a good spot to scan the lake for waterbirds. Northern Saw-whet Owl has been found roosting in cedars here in winter. Long-eared Owl sometimes winters in pines along the road to Red Rock Marina.

Ducks on the lake occasionally include Greater Scaup, Oldsquaw, and all three scoters. Hooded, Common, and Red-breasted Mergansers can number in the hundreds at times. An observation area on Iowa 316 south of Runnells overlooks a part of the lake that may have American White Pelican, waders, ducks, or shorebirds, depending on water levels. Stop by the Corps of Engineers visitor center on County Road T15 for lake maps.

Just north of Des Moines, **Saylorville Lake** offers similar birding. Maps are available at the visitor center on NW 78th Avenue, off NW Bearer Drive. Pacific Loon has been seen here; there are numerous records of both Red-necked and Western Grebes, and Parasitic Jaeger has been seen several times from late September to November.

### Gull-Watching

The dams that have turned the upper Mississippi River into a commercial waterway also make for excellent gull-watching from fall through spring, when flocks of Ring-billed (shown here) and Herring Gulls may be joined by rarities from Lesser Black-backed to Glaucous. The similarity of many species, along with the various plumages of immatures (gulls take two to four years to attain adult appearance), make gull identification daunting for beginners—and the process is complicated by occasional hybrids between species. Spending time at places with lots of gulls, such as Dam No. 15 at Davenport, Iowa, and becoming familiar with the common species are the first steps toward sorting out this challenging group.

**20** Birders visit **Lacey-Keosauqua State Park** in southeastern Iowa, just south of the town of Keosauqua, for several species seldom found elsewhere in the state, as well as a good assortment of more common birds that frequent the woodland alongside the Des Moines River.

Breeding species include Turkey Vulture; Wild Turkey; Acadian Flycatcher (rare elsewhere in Iowa); White-eyed Vireo; Carolina Wren (at the northern edge of its range, and susceptible to severe winters); Northern Mockingbird (occasional, and also affected by bad winters); Northern Parula; Yellow-throated, Cerulean, and Kentucky Warblers; Yellow-breasted Chat; and Summer and Scarlet Tanagers. To reach an area where Henslow's Sparrow has nested in recent years, leave the park by the south entrance, turn west at a four-way stop, and continue 1.4 miles to a field on the left. In open areas near the park you may also see Northern Bobwhite, Bell's Vireo, Grasshopper Sparrow, Dickcissel, and Orchard Oriole.

Another favorite southeastern spot is the **Croton Unit** of **Shimek State Forest** reached by leaving Iowa 394 at the small community of Argyle and driving west from the town's only intersection. After 2 miles, turn right at a road fork, continuing west past the forest boundary sign, watching for a small parking lot just before a bridge. Trails lead into woodland and open areas where you may find Acadian Flycatcher; White-eyed Vireo; Carolina Wren; Wood Thrush; Blue-winged, Prairie (very rare), Cerulean, Worm-eating (a very rare breeder in Iowa), Kentucky, and Hooded Warblers; and Northern Parula, among other birds. There are no facilities here and trails are unmarked, so take care as you explore.

Tundra Swans
in flight

**21** **Cone Marsh Wildlife Area** is a favorite birding site southeast of Iowa City. From Iowa 70 in Conesville, take First Street west and continue 3.4 miles, turning north and driving 0.5 mile to a gravel road on the east that leads to a parking area. (On the way you'll pass a private marsh that can be birded from the road.) Depending on water levels and season, all sorts of waders and waterbirds may be present as you walk the dike eastward, from American and Least Bitterns, King and Virginia Rails, and Sora skulking in the thick vegetation to Sedge and Marsh Wrens and Yellow-headed Blackbird. American Woodcocks perform

their courtship-display flight in early spring, and Prothonotary Warblers sing from marsh-side trees. White-eyed
Vireo has nested here at least once. Good numbers of waterfowl are present in migration, although hunting may inter-
fere with birding in fall. By continuing north and turning
east and south you can circle by private marshland where
there's often good roadside birding. Smith's Longspur has
been seen in area fields from late March through April.

Paint Creek Unit,
Yellow River
State Forest,
northeastern Iowa

**22** The spring "drumming" of Ruffed Grouse (actually
produced by rapid wingbeats) thrills birders walking
trails through the scenic wooded valleys of **Yellow River
State Forest** in northeastern Iowa, southwest of Harpers
Ferry. The grouse is a specialty of this part of the state, as
is Pileated Woodpecker, which might be seen or its loud
calling heard. Red-shouldered Hawk, largely confined to

the eastern part of the state, nests here, as do Veery; Blue-winged, Cerulean, Kentucky, and Hooded Warblers; Oven-bird; and Louisiana Waterthrush. Yellow-bellied Sapsucker, Acadian Flycatcher, and Brown Creeper have nested in Allamakee County, and all might be seen in summer.

Spring migration of warblers and other neotropical birds peaks in early May along the Mississippi River migration corridor at **Effigy Mounds National Monument,** 3 miles north of Marquette on Iowa 76. Fall raptor migration begins in mid-September and continues through October. Winter is the best time to see large numbers of Bald Eagles that feed near the open water of the Mississippi. If you're visiting this area in fall or winter, stop by the visitor center of the **Upper Mississippi River National Wildlife and Fish Refuge** on Business US 18 just north of McGregor. Here you can get advice on seeing waterfowl and Bald Eagles (including hundreds of Tundra Swans in November) on the Mississippi River, above Dam No. 9 near Ferryville, Wisconsin.

**23** In the prairie pothole region of Dickinson, Palo Alto, and Clay Counties in northwestern Iowa, you'll find a birdy landscape of ponds and marshes often referred to as the Ruthven area, named for the town at its center. Several species of ducks and Forster's and Black Terns nest in this region, and large numbers of Franklin's Gulls pass through in fall.

Begin your exploration at **Lost Island Nature Center,** on Lost Island Lake north of Ruthven. From US 18 in Ruthven, take County Road N18 north, turning east on 320th Street to the center. Here you can get local advice and search wetlands where Pied-billed Grebe, American and Least Bitterns, Virginia Rail, Sora, Marsh Wren, and Yellow-headed Blackbird nest. A wide variety of species from American White Pelican to shorebirds to sparrows (including Le Conte's and Nelson's Sharp-tailed) can appear in migration. For more excellent birding opportunities in similar habitat, return to County Road N18 and drive north a mile to **Deweys Pasture Wildlife Area,** where Marsh Wrens stutter, Swamp Sparrows trill, Bobolinks perform their effervescent song flight, and the world can seem a pretty lively place on a spring morning.

# MINNESOTA

**24** Minnesota's most famous birding drive is Cook County Road 12, better known as the **Gunflint Trail.** Winding north for 63 miles from the Lake Superior shore at Grand Marais toward (but not into) Canada, the paved route gains elevation and passes through boreal forest of spruce, fir, pine, and white cedar, with hardwoods, boggy places, and cutover areas intermixed. It's worth driving any time of year—though in winter, of course, travelers should be prepared for spells of snow and intense cold.

At the top of the most wanted list here are Spruce Grouse, Boreal Owl (very rarely seen, but sometimes heard calling in spring), and Black-backed Woodpecker (check burned areas). The list of other possibilities is long and enticing: Northern Goshawk; Ruffed Grouse; Great Gray and Northern Saw-whet Owls; Three-toed Woodpecker (very rare); Yellow-bellied and Alder Flycatchers; Gray Jay; Boreal Chickadee; up to 18 species of warblers including Cape May, Bay-breasted, Mourning, and Canada; and Rusty Blackbird nest here. Winter finches such as Pine Grosbeak, Red and White-winged Crossbills, and Common and Hoary

- Northern specialties on the Gunflint Trail
- Great fall hawk-watching in Duluth
- Greater Prairie-Chickens dancing in western grasslands

---

Information section p. 271

Common Loons with young

Poplar Lake, along the Gunflint Trail, northeastern Minnesota

Redpolls can be found from fall into spring. (Bohemian Waxwing is another sought-after winter visitor to northern Minnesota, though it's most often seen in towns, where fruiting trees and shrubs provide food, and is seldom encountered in backcountry areas like the Gunflint.)

Forest Road 152 (Lima Mountain Road), which branches west from the trail about 20 miles along, is an excellent side road to check for many boreal species. If you're visiting the area for nesting birds, remember that spring comes late to the North Woods, so June and early July are best for many species. Remember, too, that mosquitoes and other insects can make a summer visit a trial for the unprepared.

**25** Just 40 miles northwest of Duluth is another of Minnesota's most famous birding sites, an area of conifer peatland, pasture, and open countryside known as the **Sax-Zim Bog** (*NW from Duluth on US 53 to Cty. Rd. 52, turn W and continue about 7 miles to Cty. Rd. 7*). Drive back roads around the intersection of County Roads 52 and 7 (*try Cty. Rds. 202, 203, and 208*), stopping often to look and listen for nesting species including Sharp-tailed Grouse; Upland Sandpiper; Great Gray Owl; Black-backed Woodpecker; Gray Jay; Boreal Chickadee; Golden-winged, Cape May,

and Connecticut Warblers; and Le Conte's Sparrow. In winter, Sax-Zim is one of the state's best spots to search for Northern Hawk and Great Gray Owls. Other winter possibilities include Northern Goshawk, Snowy Owl, Northern Shrike, and Pine Grosbeak.

**26** Five miles south of McGregor off Minn. 65, **Rice Lake National Wildlife Refuge** is excellent for geese and ducks in migration (as many as 100,000 Ring-necked Ducks may gather in fall to feed on the wild rice for which the refuge was named). Its mixed conifer-hardwood forest, bogs, and grasslands attract a good variety of birds. Common Loon, Bald Eagle, Northern Harrier, Sharp-tailed Grouse, Black Tern, Short-eared Owl, Common Raven, and Le Conte's Sparrow are a few of the species you may see as you drive the refuge roads from spring through fall.

Among the most sought-after birds in North America, the secretive Yellow Rail spends its time in marshes and wet fields, where it gives an unbirdy call that sounds like two small stones being tapped together. This elusive species has made **McGregor Marsh State Natural Area** a popular Minnesota destination, although American Bittern, Sedge and Marsh Wrens, and Nelson's Sharp-tailed Sparrow are among the other species that can repay a breeding-season visit here. An old railroad line *(off Minn. 65 S of McGregor)* converted to a hiking trail provides access, although many birders listen from roads bordering the marsh. Yellow Rails can be heard (mostly at night) fairly easily, but they're very difficult to actually see. Before tramping off into the marsh, bear in mind that "heard" birds count just as much on your life list as "seen" ones.

Bohemian Waxwing, an irregular visitor to the upper Midwest

**27** Northeast of Thief River Falls in the state's northwestern corner, **Agassiz National Wildlife Refuge** comprises 61,500 acres of open water, marsh, forest, and grassland, as well as a fine assortment of birds attracted by the diversity of habitat. A few examples: a colony of more than 20,000 Franklin's Gulls (possibly the largest in the United States), another of hundreds of Black-crowned Night-Herons, thousands of nesting ducks (Mallard and Blue-winged Teals are the most common, but at least 14 others breed), and five species of nesting grebes (Pied-billed, Red-necked, and Eared are seen often; Horned and Western are scarce).

Other notable breeders include American and Least Bitterns (Agassiz may be the best place in the state to see the former), Bald Eagle, Yellow and Virginia Rails, Sora, Sandhill Crane, Forster's and Black Terns, Black-billed Magpie, Sedge and Marsh Wrens, and an assortment of sparrows including Nelson's Sharp-tailed. In fall, as many as 2,000 Sandhill Cranes gather here in migration. Many of these species can be seen from Marshall County Road 7, which crosses the refuge, and from a 4-mile auto tour route. Don't neglect the western and northern boundary roads, which often provide excellent viewing.

**28** Northeast of Moorhead, east of the small town of Felton, **Felton Prairie** is an area of public and private land where several hundred acres of natural prairie have escaped the plow. Public land exists in disjunct tracts, so first-time visitors might do well to stop at nearby Buffalo River State Park, east of Glyndon, for maps and advice. Two prairie areas can be accessed by following County Road 108 east from Minn. 9, south of Felton.

The *old muldoon* call of the Greater Prairie-Chicken is a springtime feature here, along with the various buzzy songs of Clay-colored, Vesper, Savannah, Grasshopper, and Le Conte's Sparrows. There's a chance of seeing Swainson's Hawk and Loggerhead Shrike, the latter a scarce species in Minnesota. Northern Harrier, Upland Sandpiper, Marbled Godwit, and Bobolink breed here. For the state's best spot to see Chestnut-collared Longspur, turn east off Minn. 9 on County Road 26, go 3 miles, and turn north on a "minimum maintenance" road through private land. After a half mile or so, begin watching for longspurs in the grassland.

**29 Rothsay Wildlife Management Area,** just west of Rothsay, can seem a magical place in spring, with American Bitterns giving their pumping call, Greater Prairie-Chickens booming, Soras whinnying, Marbled Godwits *kerwhit*-ing, Common Snipes in display flight, Bobolinks in exuberant song, and Yellow-headed Blackbirds shouting their odd creaks and screeches. Most birding is done from roads through private land around the wildlife management area. One popular route: From County Road 52 in Rothsay, take Third Avenue (*Cty. Rd. 26*) west for 4 miles, turn north for 2 miles, then west again for 2 miles to County Road 15. Turn north for 3 miles, east 1 mile, and north 2 miles to County Road 30. Drive east 1 mile back to County Road 52. The

---

### Duluth's Raptor Road

The city of Duluth, Minnesota, sits at the extreme western end of Lake Superior—a location of more than simple geographic interest. Thousands of hawks migrating south in fall, reluctant to cross the broad expanse of water before them, turn southwest and follow the shore, which becomes a virtual raptor superhighway. Duluth's renowned **Hawk Ridge Nature Reserve** (*Minn. 61 E to 43rd Ave. E, then N to Glenwood St., W to Skyline Pkwy., and N to the reserve. 218-724-0261*) provides a chance to see literally thousands of hawks on good days (when winds blow from the north or west). Here beginners will often find experienced birders who can provide tips on identifying the more than two dozen species that regularly pass by from late August through November, and a naturalist is present every day, weather permitting, in September and October. A special Hawk Weekend is held the second weekend after Labor Day and can serve as a great introduction to the joys of hawk-watching.

Beaver Creek Valley State Park, in Minnesota's south-eastern corner

route sounds more complicated than it is, and the rewards can be great. Sandhill Crane and Short-eared Owl are found in migration and Smith's Longspur sometimes appears in mid-October.

**30** Located on the South Dakota border near Ortonville, **Big Stone National Wildlife Refuge** lies in the broad Minnesota River Valley, offering a diversity of habitats from reservoir to marsh to prairie. Western Grebe, American White Pelican, American and Least Bitterns, Great and Snowy (rare) Egrets, and Swainson's Hawk breed in the refuge or nearby, along with a variety of rails, shorebirds, gulls, and terns. Along the 5-mile **Prairie Drive** loop you may see waders, ducks (13 species nest here), Ring-necked Pheasant, Upland Sandpiper, Marbled Godwit, or Sedge Wren. After driving the auto route, check the viewpoints where US 75 crosses the east end of the refuge. Then return west to Big Stone County Road 19 and turn south, where it soon becomes Lac Qui Parle County Road 15. Where County Road 40 goes west, drive east along a gravel road to a gate and walk in, checking wetlands for waders and marsh birds.

**31** The beauty of **Beaver Creek Valley State Park** would make a visit here worthwhile even if the birds weren't so special. Set within a wooded, steep-sided valley just west of Caledonia, in Minnesota's southeastern corner, the park hosts several southern species seldom seen elsewhere in the state, among them Wild Turkey, Acadian Flycatcher, Tufted Titmouse, Cerulean Warbler, and Louisiana Waterthrush. Among the other birds found here are Ruffed Grouse, Least Flycatcher, Blue-gray Gnatcatcher, Wood Thrush, Blue-winged Warbler, and Scarlet Tanager.

Canada Geese at Big Stone National Wildlife Refuge

**32** Birders in the Minneapolis-St. Paul metropolis enjoy the **Minnesota Valley National Wildlife Refuge,** which stretches along 34 miles of the Minnesota River just above its confluence with the Mississippi. Smack in the middle of suburbia, near the Twin Cities airport and the gargantuan Mall of America, the refuge preserves lake, marsh, bottomland forest, oak savanna, and even bits of prairie, with a corresponding variety of birdlife. Hiking trails and observation points are scattered through the refuge tracts, themselves scattered amid private land. Stop first at the refuge visitor center (*take 34th Ave. S exit from I-494, turn E on 80th St.*) for maps and advice about areas including **Black Dog Preserve,** where warm water from a power plant attracts waterfowl and gulls in winter, and **Louisville Swamp,** where more than 13 miles of trails wind through woods, marsh, and prairie.

# WISCONSIN

- Excellent water-birding at Horicon Marsh
- Northern breeders in Nicolet National Forest

Information section p. 271

**33** The Mississippi River and its tributaries provide pathways for some southern species to range into the northern states, so even in Wisconsin there are places where the *peter-peter-peter* of Tufted Titmouse and the *zweet-zweet-zweet* of Prothonotary Warbler sound through the bottomland woods. One such spot just south of Prairie du Chien is **Wyalusing State Park,** encompassing bluffs, valleys, and lowland where the Mississippi and Wisconsin Rivers meet. This is probably the best place to find Kentucky Warbler in the state, and other noteworthy nesting species include Red-shouldered Hawk; Whip-poor-will; Acadian Flycatcher; Bell's Vireo; Winter Wren (unusual this far south in the state); Yellow-throated, Cerulean, and Hooded Warblers; and Louisiana Waterthrush. The area around the boat landing, on a backwater of the Mississippi River, is the park's best all-around birding spot. Look for Cerulean Warbler near the **Wisconsin Ridge campground,** and for Hooded along the **Bluff Trail** below.

**34** Birders know the ancient uplands of the Baraboo Range as a landscape where diverse habitats and varying elevation create niches for a broad array of breeding species. One favorite site is **Devil's Lake State Park,** just south of Baraboo. The list of nesting birds here reflects a mingling of north and south: Turkey Vulture; Ruffed Grouse; Sandhill Crane; Acadian Flycatcher; Brown Creeper; Black-throated Green, Blackburnian, Cerulean, Kentucky, Mourning, Hooded, and Canada Warblers; and Louisiana Waterthrush. Two favorite locations for a good sampling of species are South Shore Road, along the south end of Devil's Lake, and Steinke Basin. Stop by the nature center on North Shore Road for a park map and bird list.

Nearby **Baxter's Hollow Preserve** *(from US 12, drive W 1.5 miles on Cty. Rd. C, then N on Stone's Pocket Rd.)* is known for its excellent variety of breeding birds, including Worm-eating Warbler and many of the species listed for Devil's Lake. Birding can be excellent from the road, which follows beautiful Otter Creek upstream. A trail at the end of the paved section allows exploration deeper into the forest, and birders can walk or drive the gravel road that continues north.

Wyalusing State Park, on the Mississippi River, southwestern Wisconsin

**35** One of the most famous birding sites in Wisconsin, **Horicon Marsh** encompasses 32,000 acres of marsh and lake, with small areas of grassland, scrub, and woods adding variety. Part national wildlife refuge and part state

Horicon Marsh,
southwest of
Fond du Lac

wildlife area, Horicon survived drainage schemes early in
this century to gain well-deserved status as a Wetland of
International Importance by the Ramsar Convention, an
international conference that identifies marshes and
swamps of global significance. Just a few highlights from
Horicon's bird list of nearly 267 species: Hundreds of thousands of waterfowl gather in fall migration; the **Fourmile
Island** area hosts the state's largest heronry, with nesting
Great Blue Heron, Great Egret, and Black-crowned Night-
Heron; more than 20 species of shorebirds have been seen
in spring or fall. Breeding birds also include Double-crested
Cormorant; American and Least Bitterns; more than a
dozen species of ducks; Northern Harrier; King (rare) and

HEARTLAND

Virginia Rails; Sora; Common Moorhen; Sandhill Crane; Wilson's Phalarope; Forster's and Black Terns; Sedge and Marsh Wrens; Grasshopper Sparrow; Bobolink; and Yellow-headed Blackbird. American White Pelican has begun summering regularly in the marsh, though nesting hasn't yet been observed.

Before you begin your explorations here, stop at the federal refuge visitor center off County Road Z, north of Mayville, for maps and information. Pull-offs along Wis. 49 at the north end of the marsh are excellent places to scan for waders and shorebirds (not to mention huge numbers of Canada Geese) in spring and fall. Watch, too, for Trumpeter Swan, released here as part of Wisconsin's reintroduction program. In the northwestern part of the refuge, a road south of Wis. 49 leads to the 3.2-mile **"TernPike"** auto tour route, and to several miles of hiking trails including the handicapped-accessible **Egret Trail** through a marsh, where you may spot a bittern of either species or, if you're lucky, a rail. Take Old Marsh Road (*open seasonally to hikers and bikers*) west from County Road Z for more good marsh viewing. The **Bud Cook Hiking Trails** off Point Road lead through grassland where you may find nesting Northern Harrier, American Kestrel, Sandhill Crane, or Bobolink. The state Department of Natural Resources field office, just north of the town of Horicon on Wis. 28, offers good views of a broad stretch of the marsh. A hiking trail leads through woodland, scrub, and wetlands. In winter, surrounding farmland may have flocks of Horned Lark, Lapland Longspur, and Snow Bunting.

### Greater Prairie-Chicken

The spring courtship display of the Greater Prairie-Chicken ranks among the most thrilling natural spectacles in North America. As many as a dozen or more males gather at traditional "dancing" grounds called leks, where they give their deep booming calls, inflate their orange neck sacs, raise their horns, and charge each other, all the while posturing and promenading in an attempt to woo a watching female. At some leks, wildlife officials erect blinds to allow close observation. In order not to disturb the prairie-chickens, watchers usually must enter a blind well before dawn and remain until the birds stop displaying, which may be several hours later.

**36** From fall through spring, birders visit the Lake Michigan shore, from the Milwaukee lakefront parks to the harbor at Two Rivers, for migrant and wintering land birds and waterbirds. Among the best sites along this productive stretch is **North Point Park** at Sheboygan, which typifies many of the birding possibilities. Here off North Point Drive a bit of land sticks out into the lake, providing a vantage point to watch for loons, ducks (including occasional Harlequin Duck, Oldsquaw, and scoters), jaegers (rare), gulls, and terns. On the rocky point, and along the mile of beach to the south, shorebirds (including occasional wintering Purple Sandpiper) can be common in migration. The woodland on the bluff above North Point attracts migrant songbirds and can be a good hawk-watching location in fall.

**Sheboygan Harbor** at the east end of Pennsylvania Avenue may have thousands of resting ducks, especially when Lake Michigan is rough. Check the breakwaters here in winter for Snowy Owl. Peregrine Falcon nests on the local power plant, on the lakefront 2.5 miles south.

**37** Covering some 30,000 acres and located midway between Sheboygan and Fond du Lac, the **Northern Unit** of **Kettle Moraine State Forest** has long been a favorite of birders. Obtain a map of the forest at the Ice Age Visitor Center, west of Dundee on Wis. 67. Three of the best spots are within a few miles. One is the southernmost black-spruce-tamarack bog in the state, **Spruce Lake Bog,** where nesting species include Nashville and Canada Warblers and White-throated Sparrow. The restored prairie at **Jersey Flats** hosts such grassland species as Grasshopper and Henslow's Sparrows, Dickcissel, and Bobolink, while **Haskell Noyes Memorial Forest** is good for woodland species including Acadian Flycatcher and Cerulean and Hooded Warblers.

**38** Just northeast of the town of Grantsburg, **Crex Meadows Wildlife Area** constitutes one of the finest birding sites in the Midwest. Much of the 30,000-acre area is composed of brush-prairie, a habitat threatened elsewhere by fire suppression but maintained here through management practices. Marshes and other wetlands attract flocks of waterfowl as well as an excellent variety of shorebirds. Two of the area's most sought-after nesting species, Yellow Rail and Nelson's Sharp-tailed Sparrow, are difficult to find.

Try listening for them at dawn and dusk. Chances are better for Common Loon; Red-necked Grebe; American and Least Bitterns; Osprey; Bald Eagle; Northern Harrier; Ruffed Grouse; Virginia Rail; Sora; Sandhill Crane (gathering by the thousands in fall); Upland Sandpiper; Wilson's Phalarope; Black Tern; Short-eared Owl; Horned Lark; Sedge and Marsh Wrens; Clay-colored, Vesper, Savannah, Le Conte's, and Swamp Sparrows; and Yellow-headed Blackbird. Sharp-tailed Grouse has seen impressive population gains with habitat management and is common in places. Blinds for observing their "dancing" courtship displays are erected in April (reservations are needed for viewing), but grouse may be seen throughout the year.

Northern Unit of Kettle Moraine State Forest, near Dundee

A network of roads provides access to keep any birder busy for days, and the visitor center (*Cty. Rd. D*) offers maps, a bird list, and advice. Don't neglect the nonmeadow parts of Crex, since mixed deciduous-coniferous woodlands and scrub host nesting birds including Red-headed Woodpecker; Alder and Least Flycatchers; Yellow-throated and Warbling Vireos; Golden-winged, Chestnut-sided, Pine, and Black-and-white Warblers; Scarlet Tanager; and Indigo Bunting.

**39** The vast and sometimes lonely expanse of forest and bog that is the **Nicolet National Forest** is home to some of Wisconsin's most exciting birds, and there are many miles of roads for intrepid explorers to drive, as well as trails and recreation areas to search. One area favored by birders is the region between Eagle River and Argonne. Begin your journey by taking Wis. 55 north from Argonne, turning west after 15 miles onto Forest Road 2182, which bisects the **Headwaters Wilderness.** Stop wherever you like on both roads, looking and listening for Ruffed Grouse; Black-backed Woodpecker; Olive-sided and Yellow-bellied Flycatchers; Blue-headed Vireo; Gray Jay; Common Raven; Boreal Chickadee; Hermit Thrush; Nashville, Magnolia, Black-throated Green, Blackburnian, Palm, Black-and-white, Mourning, and Canada Warblers; Northern Parula; Ovenbird; Lincoln's Sparrow; Red and White-winged Crossbills; and Evening Grosbeak. In winter, look for Bohemian Waxwing and Pine Grosbeak.

Dedicated or lucky birders might find a Northern Goshawk, Spruce Grouse, or Connecticut Warbler, but these species are hard to find. Those who are willing to hike into the interior of the Headwaters Wilderness might find the grouse and the warbler in pines at the edges of bogs. A bit farther south, the trail at **Shelp Lake** can be good for Black-backed Woodpecker, Olive-sided and Yellow-bellied Flycatchers, and Blackburnian Warbler, among many of the previously listed species. The yodeling call of Common Loon sounds across lakes in the forest, while overhead Ospreys soar and occasionally give their sharp whistles.

East of Eagle River, just south of Wis. 70, the **Anvil Lake Trail System** is a convenient series of loops that makes for good hiking and birding. Forest Road 2178 loops north and west from near here, skirting the edge of the **Blackjack Springs Wilderness.** Be advised that the squat jack pines north of this wilderness sometimes reward searchers with a Connecticut Warbler, and this is another area where Spruce Grouse might appear. Recently Kirtland's Warbler, that endangered specialty of neighboring Michigan, has been found annually in jack pines near the Nicolet National Forest. Local birders hope it's only a matter of time until the species nests here.

# Heartland
## Information

**?** Visitor Center/Information    **$** Fee Charged    **🍴** Food

**🚻** Rest Rooms    **🚶** Nature Trails    **🚗** Driving Tours    **♿** Wheelchair Accessible

*Be advised that facilities may be seasonal and limited. We suggest calling or writing ahead for specific information. Note that addresses may be for administrative offices; see text or call for directions to sites.*

## Rare Bird Alerts

Missouri:
Statewide *573-445-9115*
St. Louis *314-935-8432*
Kansas City *913-342-2473*

Illinois:
Central *217-785-1083*
Northwestern
   *815-965-3095*
Chicago *847-265-2118*

Iowa:
Statewide *319-338-9881*

Minnesota:
Statewide *612-780-8890*
Duluth *218-525-5952*

Wisconsin:
Statewide *414-352-3857*
Madison *608-255-2476*

## MISSOURI

### Table Rock State Park
*(Page 237)*
5272 Mo. 165
Branson, MO 65616
*417-334-4704*

🍴 🚻 🚶

### Prairie State Park
*(Page 237)*
128 NW 150th Lane
Liberal, MO 64762
*417-843-6711*

? 🚻 🚶 ♿

### Taberville Prairie Conservation Area and Schell-Osage Conservation Area *(Page 238)*
722 Highway 54 East
El Dorado Springs,
   MO 64744
*417-876-5226*

🚻

### Squaw Creek National Wildlife Refuge
*(Page 239)*
P.O. Box 158
Mound City, MO 64470
*660-442-3187*

? 🚻 🚶 🚗

### Swan Lake National Wildlife Refuge
*(Page 240)*
Rural Route 1, Box 29A
Sumner, MO 64681
*660-856-3323*

### Eagle Bluffs Conservation Area
*(Page 240)*
6700 West Route K
Columbia, MO 65203
*573-445-3882*

🚻 🚶 🚗 ♿

### Shaw Arboretum of the Missouri Botanical Garden *(Page 240)*
P.O. Box 38
Gray Summit, MO 63039
*314-451-3512*

? $ 🚻 🚶 🚗 ♿

### Riverlands Environmental Demonstration Area
*(Page 241)*
301 Riverlands Way
West Alton, MO 63386
*314-899-2600* or
   *888-899-2602*
bird hotline: *888-899-2650*

? 🚻 🚶 🚗 ♿

### Mingo National Wildlife Refuge *(Page 242)*
24279 Mo. 51
Puxioco, MO 63960
*573-222-3589*

? $ 🚻 🚶 🚗 ♿

# ILLINOIS

## Chicago Park District, Lakefront Region
*(Page 243)*
7059 South Shore Drive
Chicago, IL 60649
*312-747-2474*

🚶♿

*Contact for Montrose Point, Lincoln Park Bird Sanctuary, and Jackson Park*

## Illinois Beach State Park *(Page 244)*
300 Lakefront
Zion, IL 60099
*847-662-4811*

❓🍴🚻🚶♿

## Goose Lake Prairie State Natural Area
*(Page 244)*
5010 North Jugtown Road
Morris, IL 60450
*815-942-2899*

❓🚻🚶

## Chautauqua National Wildlife Refuge
*(Page 245)*
19031 East County
   Road 2105 N
Havana, IL 62644
*309-535-2290*

🚻🚶〰️♿

*One of the Illinois River National Wildlife and Fish Refuges*

## Lincoln Memorial Garden *(Page 246)*
2301 East Lake Drive
Springfield, IL 62707
*217-529-1111*

❓🚻🚶♿

*Nature center closed Mon.*

## Eldon Hazlet and South Shore State Parks
*(Page 246)*
20100 Hazlet Park Road
Carlyle, IL 62231
*618-594-3015*

❓🍴🚻🚶♿

## Carlyle Lake Wildlife Management Area
*(Page 246)*
Rural Route 2, Box 233
Vandalia, IL 62471
*618-594-5253*

❓🍴🚻🚶〰️♿

## Shawnee National Forest *(Page 247)*
50 Highway 145 South
Harrisburg, IL 62946
*618-253-7114 or
   800-699-6637*

❓🚻♿

## Union County Conservation Area
*(Page 248)*
2755 Refuge Road
Jonesboro, IL 62952
*618-833-5175*

## Cache River State Natural Area *(Page 248)*
930 Sunflower Lane
Belknap, IL 62908
*618-634-9678*

🚻🚶♿

# IOWA

## Waubonsie State Park
*(Page 249)*
Rural Route 2, Box 66
Hamburg, IA 51640
*712-382-2786*

🚻🚶♿

## Riverton Wildlife Area
*(Page 249)*
2321 330th Avenue
Riverton, IA 51650
*712-374-2510*

## Lake Red Rock
*(Page 250)*
Army Corps of Engineers
1105 Highway T-15
Knoxville, IA 50138
*515-828-7522*

❓🚻🚶♿

## Saylorville Lake
*(Page 251)*
5600 NW 78th Avenue
Johnston, IA 50131
*515-964-0672*

❓🚻🚶♿

## Lacey-Keosauqua State Park *(Page 251)*
P.O. Box 398
Keosauqua, IA 52565
*319-293-3502*

🚻🚶

## Shimek State Forest
*(Page 252)*
Rural Route 1, Box 95
Farmington, IA 52626
*319-878-3811*

## Cone Marsh Wildlife Area *(Page 252)*
Iowa Department of
   Natural Resources
109 Trobridge Hall
Iowa City, IA 52242
*319-335-1575*

## Yellow River State Forest *(Page 253)*
729 State Forest Road
Harpers Ferry, IA 52146

❓🚻🚶〰️♿

**Effigy Mounds National Monument** *(Page 254)*
151 Highway 76
Harpers Ferry, IA 52146
*319-873-3491*

**Upper Mississippi River National Wildlife and Fish Refuge** *(Page 254)*
401 Business US 18 N
McGregor, IA 52157
*319-873-3423*

**Lost Island Nature Center** *(Page 254)*
3259 355th Avenue
Ruthven, IA 51358
*712-837-4866*

# MINNESOTA

**Rice Lake National Wildlife Refuge**
*(Page 257)*
Route 2, Box 67
McGregor, MN 55760
*218-768-2402*

**McGregor Marsh State Natural Area** *(Page 257)*
Minnesota Department of
    Natural Resources
500 Lafayette Road
St. Paul, MN 55155
*651-296-2835*

**Agassiz National Wildlife Refuge**
*(Page 258)*
Rural Route 1, Box 74
Middle River, MN 56737
*218-449-4115*

**Felton Prairie** and **Rothsay Wildlife Management Area**
*(Pages 258, 259)*
Minnesota Department of
    Natural Resources
1221 First Avenue East
Fergus Falls, MN 56537
*218-739-7576*

**Big Stone National Wildlife Refuge**
*(Page 260)*
Rural Route 1, Box 25
Odessa, MN 56276
*320-273-2191*

**Beaver Creek Valley State Park** *(Page 261)*
Route 2, Box 57
Caledonia, MN 55921
*507-724-2107*

**Minnesota Valley National Wildlife Refuge**
*(Page 261)*
3815 East 80th Street
Bloomington, MN 55425
*612-854-5900*

# WISCONSIN

**Wyalusing State Park**
*(Page 262)*
13081 State Park Lane
Bagley, WI 53801
*608-996-2261*

**Devil's Lake State Park**
*(Page 262)*
S5975 Park Road
Baraboo, WI 53913
*608-356-8301*

**Baxter's Hollow Preserve** *(Page 263)*
The Nature Conservancy
107 Walnut Street
Baraboo, WI 53913
*608-356-5300*

**Horicon National Wildlife Refuge** *(Page 263)*
W4279 Headquarters Road
Mayville, WI 53050
*920-387-2658 or*
    *920-387-7860*

**North Point Park**
*(Page 266)*
2026 New Jersey Avenue
Sheboygan, WI 53081
*920-459-3444*

**Kettle Moraine State Forest, Northern Unit**
*(Page 266)*
N1765 County Highway G
Campbellsport, WI 53010
*920-533-8322*

**Crex Meadows Wildlife Area** *(Page 266)*
P.O. Box 367
Grantsburg, WI 54840
*715-463-2896*

**Nicolet National Forest**
*(Page 268)*
68 South Stevens Street
Rhinelander, WI 54501
*715-362-1300*

North-Central
States

The Great Lakes wrap around the top of this part-northern, part-eastern, part-midwestern section of the country, acting as both a passageway and a barrier for birds. They're a path mostly for waterbirds, of course—even those usually thought of as seabirds, which find familiar territory on the broad expanses of these "inland seas." As a result, diligent birders can at times turn up such anomalies as King Eider in Ohio or Parasitic Jaeger in Indiana.

The lakes are a barrier, too—a fact that birders put to good use in spring migration. Northbound land birds arrive at the lakes, look out over seemingly endless stretches of water offering no food, no place to rest, and often decide to take a break before continuing. As a result, impressive numbers of birds can pile up along shorelines, especially at isolated patches of trees such as Indiana's famous Migrant

*Preceding pages:* Michigan's endangered Kirtland's Warbler *Above:* Blackburnian Warbler *Right:* Birding at Ballard Wildlife Management Area in Kentucky

NORTH-CENTRAL STATES

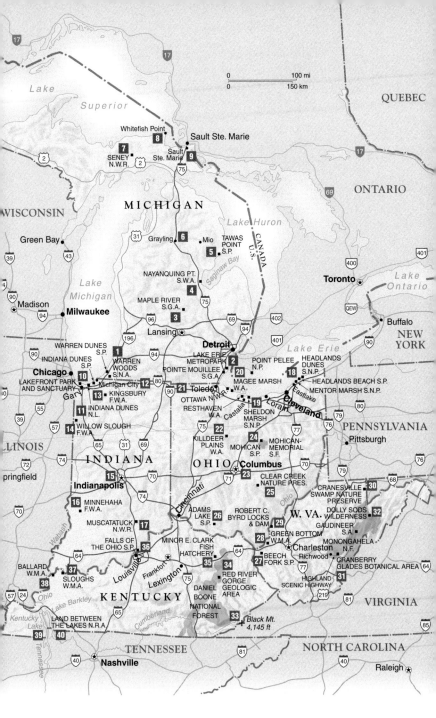

Lake **Superior**

Whitefish Point

**8**

**7**
SENEY
N.W.R.

Sault Ste. Marie

Sault
Ste.
Marie

**9**

QUEBEC

ONTARIO

75

**MICHIGAN**

*Lake Huron*

Green Bay

WISCONSIN

31

Grayling

**6**

Mio

TAWAS
POINT
S.P.

**5**

CANADA
U.S.

400

401

Toronto

*Lake Ontario*

NAYANQUING PT.
S.W.A.

*Saginaw Bay*

**4**

MAPLE RIVER
S.G.A.

*Lake Michigan*

Madison

Milwaukee

96

75

69

402

494

**3**

Lansing

QEW

Buffalo

Detroit

401

*Lake Erie*

**NEW YORK**

Chicago

WARREN DUNES
S.P.

**1**

WARREN
WOODS
S.N.A.

LAKE ERIE
METROPARK

**2**

POINT PELEE
N.P.

HEADLANDS
DUNES
S.N.P.

**18**

INDIANA DUNES
S.P.

POINTE MOUILLEE
S.G.A.

**20**

MAGEE MARSH
W.A.

HEADLANDS BEACH S.P.

MENTOR MARSH S.N.P.

LAKEFRONT PARK
AND SANCTUARY

**10**

Michigan City

**12**

**13**

KINGSBURY
F.W.A.

Gary

80

90

**21**

Toledo

OTTAWA N.W.R.

RESTHAVEN
W.A.

Castalia

Eastlake

Lorain

Cleveland

**19**

SHELDON
MARSH
S.N.P.

79

80

**11**

INDIANA DUNES
N.L.

**14**

WILLOW SLOUGH
F.W.A.

75

**22**

KILLDEER
PLAINS
W.A.

**24**

MOHICAN
S.P.

MOHICAN-
MEMORIAL
S.F.

77

**PENNSYLVANIA**

Pittsburgh

76

76

57

65

31

69

**INDIANA**

**OHIO**

Columbus

**23**

70

71

CLEAR CREEK
NATURE PRES.

79

CRANESVILLE
SWAMP NATURE
PRESERVE

**30**

68

springfield

72

74

**15**

Indianapolis

70

74

Cincinnati

**25**

*Ohio*

**W. VA.**

DOLLY SODS
WILDERNESS

**32**

70

**16**

MINNEHAHA
F.W.A.

ADAMS
LAKE
S.P.

**26**

ROBERT C.
BYRD LOCKS
& DAM

**29**

GAUDINEER
S.A.

MUSCATATUCK
N.W.R.

**17**

GREEN BOTTOM
W.M.A.

**28**

MONONGAHELA
N.F.

BALLARD
W.M.A.

FALLS OF
THE OHIO S.P.

**36**

MINOR E. CLARK
FISH
HATCHERY

64

**35**

**34**

BEECH
FORK S.P.

**27**

Charleston

Richwood

CRANBERRY
GLADES BOTANICAL AREA

64

*Wabash*

64

Louisville

Frankfort

Lexington

75

RED RIVER
GORGE
GEOLOGIC
AREA

77

HIGHLAND
SCENIC
HIGHWAY

**31**

**37**

SLOUGHS
W.M.A.

DANIEL
BOONE

NATIONAL
FOREST

**33**

Black Mt.
4,145 ft

219

81

**VIRGINIA**

85

**38**

57

24

*Ohio*

*Kentucky
Lake*

*Lake Barkley*

LAND BETWEEN
THE LAKES N.R.A.

65

**KENTUCKY**

*Cumberland*

**39**

**40**

*Tennessee*

**TENNESSEE**

81

**NORTH CAROLINA**

40

Nashville

40

Raleigh

0    100 mi
0    150 km

17

17

17

2

2

39

43

4

90

94

55

90

39

INOIS

LINOIS

69

81

Trap, in Hammond, or Ohio's equally famous Crane Creek boardwalk, east of Toledo. In places like these, on any day from mid-April through May one is likely to find birders scanning the trees in anticipation of a "fallout" day when 20 or more species of warblers may be found in just a few hours. Beginning birders do well to visit such popular sites, since there's always a veteran around willing to share his or her knowledge, and more birds may be seen in one place in a single morning than in days of solitary wandering. Local Audubon chapters and bird clubs hold regular field trips to productive spots year-round. Beginners are always welcome, especially if they identify themselves as such and ask for help in seeing and learning about new birds. In addition, many parks and wildlife areas hold spring warbler walks, "owl prowls," hawk-watches, and similar programs, all of which can be great ways to get acquainted with the species found in an area. State parks and nature centers can usually provide contact names if a local birding group isn't listed in the telephone directory.

**Special Birds of the North-Central States**

*Spruce Grouse*

Spruce Grouse
Sharp-tailed
  Grouse
Yellow Rail
Sandhill Crane
Upland Sandpiper
Common Tern
Snowy Owl
Great Gray Owl
Black-backed
  Woodpecker
Gray Jay
Bohemian
  Waxwing
Kirtland's Warbler
Henslow's Sparrow
Le Conte's
  Sparrow
Pine Grosbeak
Red Crossbill
White-winged
  Crossbill
Common Redpoll
Hoary Redpoll

This region's birds are as varied as its geography, from Ohio River bottomland in Kentucky to Indiana beaches to the boreal forests of Michigan's Upper Peninsula. For city birding, Indianapolis has its Eagle Creek Park, Columbus its Green Lawn Cemetery and Arboretum, Louisville its Falls of the Ohio. For solitude, travel to Kentucky's expansive Land Between the Lakes, walk the trails at Michigan's Warren Woods State Natural Area, or explore the highlands of West Virginia, where great birding is set in one of the most beautiful landscapes of the eastern United States.

This chapter begins in Michigan and moves south through Indiana, Ohio, and West Virginia before finishing in Kentucky. ■

# MICHIGAN

**1** In the extreme southwestern corner of Michigan, just a few miles from the Indiana state line, **Warren Woods State Natural Area** attracts birders looking for southern species seldom seen elsewhere in the state. In addition, it's great for migrant songbirds in spring. To reach it from I-94, exit to the north on South Lakeside Road and drive a half mile to West Warren Woods Road. Turn east; the entrance is a bit more than 2 miles ahead. Here you can explore trails through beech-maple forest (the largest undisturbed tract in the state) near the Galien River for Red-headed (population varies from year to year) and Pileated Woodpeckers and Carolina Wren (hard to find after bad winters). In breeding season, look for Acadian Flycatcher; Yellow-throated, Cerulean, Black-and-white, and Hooded Warblers; Louisiana Waterthrush; and Scarlet Tanager.

**Warren Dunes State Park** (*S of Bridgman, take Red Arrow Hwy. exit off I-94, then drive S*) stretches along 2.5 miles of Lake Michigan shoreline, with scenic sand dunes rising as high as 240 feet above the water. Some of the park's best birding is found in its northern section, on the trail system north of Floral Lane. The short **Golden Rod** and longer **Yellow Birch Loops** pass through varied habitats including marshy areas and old fields, excellent in spring migration (look for the elusive Connecticut Warbler in late May). Nesting birds include Black-throated Green, Hooded, and Canada Warblers, and occasionally Worm-eating Warbler. In addition, Prairie Warbler has nested along the **Blue Jay Trail.** Spring or fall days with east winds can be productive for migrant raptors here. Local birders sometimes set up a hawk-watching site at the Floral Lane parking lot (or on the nearby boardwalk trail), or you can climb one of the dunes for a high viewpoint. From fall

- ● Wetland species at Pointe Mouillee
- ● Migration at Tawas Point and Whitefish Point
- ● Tours to see Kirt-land's Warbler
- ● Winter around Sault Ste. Marie

Information section p. 309

Wetlands at Maple River State Game Area, north of St. Johns

through spring, scan Lake Michigan from the beach area in the southern part of the park for loons, ducks, gulls, terns, occasional jaegers, and other waterbirds.

**2** Two areas on the Lake Erie shore south of Detroit rate among the state's most popular birding sites. **Lake Erie Metropark** *(from the suburb of Gibraltar, drive S for 2 miles on W. Jefferson Ave.)* is known for its excellent fall hawk migration on days with north or northwest winds. Tens of thousands of Broad-winged Hawks may pass through in the second half of September, along with other raptors including Osprey, Bald Eagle, Sharp-shinned and Cooper's Hawks, American Kestrel, Merlin, and Peregrine Falcon. Long known as a prime waterfowl migration site, the lake and marsh attract thousands of geese and ducks and a wintering population of Tundra Swans.

Continue south on Jefferson Avenue to Campau Road and turn east to the headquarters of **Pointe Mouillee State Game Area,** a 4,000-acre expanse of natural wetlands and diked marshes at the mouth of the Huron River. Obtain maps and advice here, then return to Jefferson Avenue and

278

drive south—Jefferson becomes U.S. Turnpike—a short distance to Sigler Road; turn east to reach a prime marsh area. Walk the dikes here (many birders use bicycles to cover more ground) and look for waders, waterfowl, rails, shorebirds, gulls, and terns. American and Least Bitterns, Great Egret, Black-crowned and Yellow-crowned Night-Herons, and the state's best variety of shorebirds are found here seasonally. Drive south on U.S. Turnpike a mile to Labo Road; turn east and then take Roberts Road south to its end, where the south dike leads to a spit of land (locally called the Banana) extending into Lake Erie. Check the waters here for wintering scoters, Oldsquaw, Common Goldeneye, and many other waterfowl, and for occasional wintering Snowy Owls.

### Point Pelee

The most famous birding spot near Detroit is outside the United States: About 50 miles southeast, Ontario's **Point Pelee National Park** lies on a finger of land jutting out nearly 10 miles into Lake Erie. In spring, north-bound migrants, weary from their overwater crossing, home in on this relatively tiny area by the thousands. A visit here from mid-April into early June can bring close views of a breathtaking number of birds, as songbirds rest and feed before resuming their migration. Birders flock here, too, so word is usually spread quickly of any rarities that arrive. Enjoy the spectacle, but take care as you observe not to put more stress on birds that often are already tired to the point of exhaustion.

**3** North of St. Johns along US 27, **Maple River State Game Area** covers 9,000 acres of varied wetlands, fields, and woods. A parking lot on the east side of US 27, north of the Maple River, provides access to dikes. Look for waders including American and Least Bitterns, Great Blue Heron, Great Egret, and for shorebirds in spring and fall. Common Moorhen breeds among the marsh vegetation, and Prothonotary Warbler nests along the Maple River, especially west of US 27. Osprey and Bald Eagle pass through in migration. A hacking program is attempting to reestablish Osprey here, while Bald Eagle has attempted to nest in recent years. Continue north a half mile to Ranger Road, turn east and go less than a mile to Baldwin Road. Follow this south to Taft Road and an observation tower where large numbers of waterfowl are present fall through spring. King Rail has nested in this area. Drive east a mile to Crapo Road, then north to Ranger Road, where Northern Harrier and Short-eared Owl winter, and Northern Shrike is a winter possibility.

**4** Many areas along the shore of Saginaw Bay offer excellent birding, among them **Nayanquing Point State Wildlife Area** (*N from Bay City on Mich. 13, then E on Kitchen Rd. 3 miles past Linwood turnoff*). Migrant waterfowl are abundant here, and several species of dabbling ducks remain in summer to nest. Among other breeding species are American and Least Bitterns, Ring-necked Pheasant, King (scarce) and Virginia Rails, Common Moorhen, Forster's and Black Terns, Willow Flycatcher, Sedge and Marsh Wrens, and Yellow-headed Blackbird. Many rarities have appeared here over the years, from Tricolored Heron and Cinnamon Teal to Ruff and Laughing Gull. Stop at the area office on Tower Beach Road for advice. Dikes around some marshes can be walked, but much of the area south of Kitchen Road is closed to entry without permission. Continue east on Kitchen Road to a south turn and an observation tower good for scanning fields and the bay.

### Kirtland's Warbler

One of our rarest birds, Kirtland's Warbler nests only in areas of jack pine less than 15 feet tall. The species' range is almost entirely restricted to north-central Michigan, where biologists work to improve their habitat and control Brown-headed Cowbirds, which lay their eggs in the warblers' nests, harming breeding success. After falling to only 167 territorial males in the late 1980s, the population has steadily increased and in 1998 numbered 805 singing males. (See p. 281 for information on tours to observe this very special endangered species.)

**5** About 45 miles north of Nayanquing Point, **Tawas Point State Park** sits on a sandy spit stretching into Lake Huron, creating a sheltered bay on the west side. Tawas Point is best known for spring and fall songbird migration—flycatchers, vireos, thrushes, warblers, and others can throng trees and shrubs here, especially after a cold front in spring—and for migrant waterbirds, including loons, grebes, ducks, shorebirds, and gulls. Drive to the southernmost parking lot and walk the **Sandy Hook Nature Trail,** checking the beach for migrant shorebirds (including rare Piping Plover), gulls, and terns. In spring, warblers and other migrants can be found in low shrubs where they're easily seen. In fall, watch for Merlin or Peregrine Falcon zooming along the shore. In spring or fall, scan the waters of the lake and bay for Common Loon (Red-throated is possible in fall), grebes, Greater and Lesser Scaups, scoters, Oldsquaw (sometimes thousands

pass the point daily in April), and Red-breasted Merganser. Tawas Point is also famed for rarities too numerous to list, but including such oddities as Wilson's Plover, Say's Phoebe, and Black-throated Gray Warbler.

Seney National Wildlife Refuge in Michigan's Upper Peninsula

**6** Michigan's most famous bird is undoubtedly the Kirtland's Warbler, an endangered species slowly recovering in population thanks to protection and intensive habitat management (see sidebar p. 280). The heart of the bird's range is the north-central part of Michigan's **Lower Peninsula;** it's very rarely seen on migration to and from its winter home in the Bahamas. The warbler is strictly protected, and the best way to see it is on tours conducted by the U.S. Fish and Wildlife Service *(517-351-2555)* from **Grayling** and by the U.S. Forest Service *(517-826-3252)* from **Mio.** Tours are usually offered from mid-May to the first week of July; call for days and times. Though singing males are almost always heard, the chance of actually seeing one is about 80 percent—less on cloudy or rainy days.

**7** Michigan's Upper Peninsula is known for its remoteness, solitude, natural beauty, and for some excellent birding sites. One of the best is **Seney National Wildlife**

Gyrfalcon at Sault Ste. Marie's power plant, Michigan's Upper Peninsula

**Refuge,** covering 95,212 acres of coniferous and hardwood forests, marshes, bogs, meadows, and lakes. The lengthy list of species that have nested here includes Common Loon; American and Least (rare) Bitterns; Hooded and Common Mergansers; Osprey; Bald Eagle; Northern Harrier; Spruce and Sharp-tailed Grouse; Yellow and Virginia Rails; Sora; Sandhill Crane; Common and Black Terns; Black-backed Woodpecker; Olive-sided Flycatcher; Nashville, Chestnut-sided, Magnolia, Cape May, Black-throated Blue, Blackburnian, Pine, Palm, Mourning, and Canada Warblers; and Vesper and Le Conte's Sparrows. In addition, Trumpeter Swan has been successfully reintroduced at Seney.

The refuge visitor center, south of Seney and just west of Mich. 77, can provide bird lists and advice; a nature trail winds around a nearby wetland. The 7-mile **Marshland Wildlife Drive** makes a fine diversity of habitat available to anyone, and many more miles of trails are open for walking or biking. The refuge's most famous nesting bird is probably the Yellow Rail, but as always this species is secretive and very difficult to see. The usual encounter is simply hearing its tapping-pebbles call, most often given at night.

**8** Set at the tip of a Lake Superior peninsula 10 miles north of Paradise, **Whitefish Point** and **Whitefish Point Bird Observatory** compose one of the legendary locations of American migration-watching. Tens of thousands of birds pass over, pass by, or stop here in spring and fall. In addition, boreal species such as Spruce Grouse, Gray Jay, Boreal Chickadee, and Pine and Evening Grosbeaks are often found. Loons (mostly Common but with good numbers of Red-throated), grebes (including thousands of Red-necked in fall), ducks, shorebirds, gulls, and terns fly past Whitefish Point. All three species of jaegers have been found, with the best chance to see these predatory gull-like birds in September.

Among the thousands of raptors seen in spring, Sharp-shinned and Broad-winged Hawks are most common; other hawks, eagles, and falcons seen here include rare but regular Northern Goshawk, Golden Eagle, Merlin, and Peregrine Falcon. Whitefish Point is also known for owls: Snowy, Great Gray, Long-eared, Boreal (very rare), and Northern Saw-whet are all possible.

**9** Though it's not something to be undertaken lightly, a winter visit to **Sault Ste. Marie** (*Visitor's Bureau 906-632-3301 or 800-647-2858*) has long been a favorite birding expedition for Michiganders. If you decide to make this trip, be prepared for occasional severe weather. Drive through the open country south of town, between Mich. 129 and Riverside Drive, to look for Rough-legged Hawk, Sharp-tailed Grouse, Snowy Owl, Northern Shrike, Snow Bunting, and Common Redpoll (with perhaps a few Hoary Redpolls intermixed). Some winters find Northern Hawk Owl, Great Gray Owl, or even Boreal Owl appearing in the "Soo" area.

Gyrfalcon, that rare and majestic raptor, has been seen in winter regularly on the large electric power plant on Portage Avenue near the canal locks; also check the nearby railroad bridge over the **St. Mary's River.** Quite often parts of the river remain open when most water in the area is frozen; look for Harlequin Duck, Oldsquaw, Common Goldeneye, Common Merganser, Bald Eagle, and Glaucous Gull. Bohemian Waxwing is often found in residential areas where there are ornamental trees with fruit.

# INDIANA

**10** The United States boasts many "migrant traps"—sites that in spring or fall attract birds in outstanding diversity or number, or both—but one spot on Indiana's Lake Michigan shoreline at Hammond has become known as the **Migrant Trap** for its concentrations of flycatchers, vireos, thrushes, warblers, sparrows, and other birds. Officially called **Lakefront Park and Sanctuary,** it's located less than a mile from the Illinois state line, north of US 12/20/41 (Indianapolis Boulevard). Park in the large lot west of the Hammond Marina; the sanctuary is adjacent. This small patch of trees and scrub can be thronged with birds in spring (mid-April through May is best) and fall, from the expected eastern songbirds to occasional surprises like herons, rails, and owls. Good birding isn't guaranteed even at peak migration times, but the Migrant Trap is always worth a look in spring and fall on the chance that you'll visit on a truly extraordinary day.

Red-eyed Vireo

**11** A rewarding amount of birding opportunity is crowded along the 40 miles of Lake Michigan shore between Chicago and Michigan. Loons, grebes, waterfowl, shorebirds, and gulls frequent the lake and beaches. In spring, hawks moving north cruise the shoreline, reluctant to fly across the expanse of water before them, and wetlands attract dabbling ducks and wading birds. Luckily, a substantial part of this crowded area is preserved within the **Indiana Dunes National Lakeshore** and **Indiana Dunes State Park.** As their names imply, the predominant landscape here is sand dunes, built as winds carry beach sand inland, forming towering dunes one grain at a time. Forests form in protected places, and low areas between dunes often have swampy or marshy spots, creating notable diversity of habitat.

Lake Michigan, Indiana Dunes National Lakeshore

In Gary, follow Lake Street north from US 12. On your left is the national lakeshore's **Paul H. Douglas Center for Environmental Education,** with trails through oak savanna and along dune ponds. The woods here can be full of birds in migration. At the end of the street, the parking lot at **Marquette Park** makes a good viewpoint for scanning the lake from fall through spring for waterfowl and gulls. Jaegers, though rare, are seen here with some regularity in fall. Return to US 12 and drive east 2.3 miles to County Line Road and follow it north to the entrance road to West Beach. Check **Long Lake** on the south side of the road for waterfowl and waders. Trails beginning at the visitor center wind through dunes and along Long Lake.

Nine miles east, Indiana Dunes State Park offers extensive trails through fine woodlands where breeding birds include Red-shouldered Hawk (rare), Acadian Flycatcher, Yellow-throated Vireo, Cerulean and Hooded Warblers,

American Redstart, and Ovenbird. Check the beach here (as anywhere along the lake) for shorebirds, especially in late summer and fall, and for migrant Peregrine Falcon in September and October. At nearby **Porter Beach** (*N end of Waverly Rd.*), local birders hold hawk-watches in spring.

Take East State Park Road north from US 12 to Kemil Beach and drive east on Lakefront Drive for more lake and shoreline viewing. Beverly Drive, which parallels Lakefront Drive inland through the community of Beverly Shores, passes through wetlands where Virginia Rail and Sora can be heard calling in spring. At the eastern end of the national lakeshore, the high dune called **Mount Baldy** makes an excellent lookout for spring hawk migration, as raptors follow the shoreline east and north (days with south winds are best). Watch also for flocks of Sandhill Crane passing overhead in early spring. Mount Baldy itself is migrating about 4 feet a year, as winds slowly change its position.

**12** At the corner of Pine Street and US 12 in Michigan City, drive north to **Washington Park** and the **Michigan City Harbor,** the top waterbird-watching spot on the Indiana lakeshore. In spring, Washington Park can be a bit of a migrant trap itself, but the main focus here is on waterfowl, shorebirds, gulls, and terns from fall through spring. Many rarities have appeared in the harbor, on beaches, or on the breakwaters over the years, including King Eider, Harlequin Duck, many unusual gulls, and Snowy Owl. Look for the rare Purple Sandpiper on rock jetties in winter and gulls and ducks in open water near the electric power plant.

**13** Southeast of La Porte, **Kingsbury Fish and Wildlife Area** (*from Kingsbury drive E for 4 miles on Cty. Rd. 500S to Stillwell Rd., then S to Hupp Rd.*) is one of the state's top inland shorebirding sites. From Hupp Road, drive south on River Road and watch for a marsh on the east. Depending on the water level, the mudflats exposed here attract all the regularly occurring migrant shorebirds as well as scarcer species such as White-rumped (regular in spring), Baird's, and Stilt Sandpipers and Long-billed Dowitcher. This marsh, a remnant of the once extensive Great Kankakee

Marsh, also hosts waterfowl from spring through fall and waders in the warmer months. American White Pelican, Bald Eagle, and Sandhill Crane are seen occasionally, and Reddish Egret and White-faced Ibis are among the rarities that have appeared. In recent winters Kingsbury has been a good spot for Merlin, and Rough-legged Hawk sometimes appears over open fields.

**14** **Willow Slough Fish and Wildlife Area,** beside the Illinois state line about 45 miles south of Gary, is known for fine marsh and grassland habitats and a good assortment of nesting birds. Least Bittern and Common Moorhen have nested in the marsh on the north side of J.C. Murphey Lake, and Virginia Rail and Sora can be heard calling in spring; King Rail may nest as well. American Bittern stops here in migration, and even the elusive Yellow Rail has been found by determined searchers. (If the road is closed you may need to walk to this area.) Elsewhere, Chestnut-sided Warbler, Lark and Henslow's Sparrows, and Blue Grosbeak breed. Tundra Swan is fairly regular in migration, along with good numbers of dabbling ducks, and by walking through grassy spots you may flush up a Le Conte's or Nelson's Sharp-tailed Sparrow in migration.

**Great Blue Heron**

The Great Blue Heron is probably our best known wading bird, a familiar sight on lakes, marshes, and riverbanks as it quietly stalks fish, frogs, snakes, and even rodents and birds. The Great Blue winters in good numbers farther north than any of its heron and egret relatives, enduring cold weather around the Great Lakes and into Canada. Some people call this species "blue crane," but despite their long legs cranes are in an entirely different order, related to rails and coots.

**15** Indianapolis residents don't need to go far for excellent birding: **Eagle Creek Park** (*exit at 71st Street from I-465 or I-65*), one of the largest municipal parks in America at more than 5,000 acres, makes a superb destination near at hand in the northwestern part of the city. Eagle Creek is excellent for spring songbird migration, with 30 species of warblers possible on a good day in the beautiful deciduous woods. Begin south of the nature center (*map and trail information available*) at an overlook above **Eagle Creek Reservoir;** also walk the trails circling the lake. Nesting birds are a mix of southern birds such as

Willow Slough Fish and Wildlife Area, south of Gary

Yellow-throated and Worm-eating Warblers with species more typical of the north-central states.

The reservoir can be good for waterbirds. Parts are deep enough for Common Loon (both Red-throated and Pacific have also been found here), while the shallower north end attracts dabbling ducks. With low water levels, this area can also have migrant shorebirds and waders. Look in migration for Double-crested Cormorant, Osprey, and Bald Eagle.

**16** Just east of Sullivan, **Minnehaha Fish and Wildlife Area** encompasses reclaimed strip mines now covered in extensive grasslands. In winter Northern Harrier and Short-eared Owl fly low, looking for rodents, and an occasional Rough-legged Hawk hovers in the wind. Le Conte's Sparrow is a rare winter resident, while nesting birds include Great Blue Heron (several heronries are located in the area); Loggerhead Shrike; Bell's Vireo; Lark, Grasshopper, and Henslow's Sparrows; Blue Grosbeak; and Dickcissel. American Bittern and Common Snipe are possible breeders. The entrance to the area is north off Ind. 54, and county roads provide easy access throughout.

**17** Migrant and wintering waterfowl are the focus at **Muscatatuck National Wildlife Refuge,** located on US 50 just east of I-65 in Seymour. As many as 15,000 geese and ducks may be present in spring and fall migration; the common species include Canada Goose, Wood Duck, American Black Duck, Mallard, Blue-winged Teal, Gadwall, and Ring-necked Duck, but Tundra Swan and Greater White-fronted and Snow Geese appear occasionally. Refuge roads pass wetlands where not only waterfowl but waders (Least Bittern and Green Heron have nested) and rails can be seen seasonally. Osprey and Sandhill Crane may pause at Muscatatuck in migration.

Diverse habitats mean nesting birds include such woodland species as Red-shouldered Hawk; Great Horned and Barred Owls; Red-headed Woodpecker; Wood Thrush; and Yellow-throated, Prothonotary, and Kentucky Warblers; and such scrub or open-country birds as Northern Bobwhite; Willow Flycatcher; White-eyed Vireo; Eastern Bluebird; Blue-winged Warbler; Indigo Bunting; Grasshopper and Henslow's Sparrows; and Dickcissel. In early spring, American Woodcock performs its courtship flight at dusk.

# OHIO

● Spring migration
  at Crane Creek
● Winter birding at
  Killdeer Plains
  Wildlife Area
––––––––––––––––
Information
section p. 310

**18** Several adjoining sites on Lake Erie just east of Cleveland provide fine birding opportunities year-round. From Ohio 2 between Mentor and Painesville, take Ohio 44 north to **Headlands Beach State Park** and continue to the extreme eastern parking area. From here, walk northeast to **Headlands Dunes State Nature Preserve,** a remnant beach dune ecosystem that can be excellent for spring songbird migration. Spring can also bring good hawk-watching, as raptors follow the lakeshore rather than cross the water on their northward flight; Merlin is fairly regular in spring and fall. Walking through the dunes may scare up a migrant Common Snipe, American Woodcock, or Grasshopper or Le Conte's Sparrow. In late fall and winter, look for Northern Saw-whet Owl (rare) roosting in shrubs, and Lapland Longspur and Snow Bunting along the beach.

Check the beach for migrant shorebirds and gulls and the offshore waters for diving ducks. From fall through spring, continue east to the breakwater for a view of **Fairport Harbor,** where loons, grebes, ducks, and gulls congregate. This has traditionally been a good spot for rarities, from King Eider to all three jaegers to Little, Mew, and Glaucous Gulls. In late fall, scan the breakwater for the rare Purple Sandpiper. **Shipman Pond** (*via Headlands Rd.*) on the state park's southwestern boundary is worth a look for waders and waterfowl.

Then continue west on Headlands Road to **Zimmerman Trail,** part of **Mentor Marsh State Nature Preserve.** This area protects more than 600 acres of marsh (the largest reed-grass marsh in Ohio and a national natural landmark), with beech-maple and oak-hickory woodland around the edges. The trail, which follows an old bank of the Grand River, provides access to wetlands where you may find nesting

Pied-billed Grebe, Wood Duck, Virginia Rail, Sora, Common Moorhen, Red-headed Woodpecker, and Prothonotary Warbler, and in migration American and Least Bitterns (both rare but regular; Least may breed in the area) or Black-crowned Night-Heron. Mentor can also host a fine diversity of migrant songbirds in spring, with more than 250 species documented in recent years. The visitor center is on Corduroy Road, just to the southwest.

Six miles west, warm water from a power plant in **Eastlake** attracts large numbers of gulls and flocks of waterfowl in winter. To reach it, take Erie Road north from Ohio 283 to Lake Erie. Ring-billed and Herring are the common gull species, but a great number of rarities have been found. Check winter flocks of Bonaparte's Gull for the rare Little Gull, seen here with some regularity. On the western side of Cleveland, another power plant just north of US 6 on the lakeshore at **Avon Lake** provides similarly fine gull-watching in winter.

The harbor at the western Cleveland suburb of **Lorain** is noted for hosting rare shorebirds in spring and fall. (Remember that for shorebirds, "fall" starts in July.) From US 6 just east of the Black River, take Arizona Avenue

Headlands Dunes State Nature Preserve, on Lake Erie northeast of Cleveland north and walk out to the breakwater, checking the flats to the east for loons, occasional scoters, Oldsquaw, and flocks of Red-breasted Merganser from fall through spring. Purple Sandpiper and Snowy Owl have been found here in winter.

**19** Take US 6 and Ohio 2 west from Huron, continuing on US 6 where the highways diverge. In less than a mile you'll reach **Sheldon Marsh State Nature Preserve,**

Magee Marsh
Wildlife Area, east
of Toledo

where varied wetlands from cattail marsh and swamp to mudflats and Lake Erie barrier beach attract waders, waterfowl, and shorebirds. From the parking lot, follow the old road north to the beach, where fall and winter may bring thousands of ducks. In spring, vireos, warblers, thrushes, and other migrant songbirds are abundant in woodlands. An observation deck allows scanning of a marsh where in breeding season you may find Great Blue and Green Herons, Great Egret, Wood Duck, Sora, Common Moorhen, Prothonotary Warbler, Common Yellowthroat, or Swamp Sparrow.

Just north of Castalia off Ohio 269, **Resthaven Wildlife Area** is worth a visit for its habitats of woods, lake, and the largest tract of prairie remaining in the state. Bald Eagle nests nearby, and winter can bring flocks of ducks to wetlands, especially when rough weather pushes waterfowl inland from Lake Erie. Check grassy and scrubby areas for sparrows in migration and for nesting birds including Ring-necked Pheasant, American Woodcock, Yellow Warbler, and Indigo Bunting. Bell's Vireo has been seen in the area in summer. In Castalia itself, **Castalia Pond** (*E of Ohio 269, S of Ohio 101*) is noted for amazing concentrations of wintering ducks, sometimes numbering in the thousands. Look for all sorts of dabbling ducks (Eurasian Wigeon has appeared on occasion) and divers including Red-head, Ring-necked Duck, Lesser Scaup, Bufflehead, Hooded Merganser, and Ruddy Duck.

Spring at Crane Creek's famed boardwalk, near Lake Erie east of Toledo

**20** The most famous birding site in Ohio is really two sites, side by side on Lake Erie. Located about 15 miles east of Toledo on Ohio 2, they are collectively called **Crane Creek** by local birders. First is **Magee Marsh Wildlife Area,** renowned as a spring "migrant trap" where phenomenal numbers of songbirds pause on northbound migration before flying over Lake Erie. A boardwalk through a patch of woods near the beach (*park at adjoining Crane Creek State Park*) is immensely popular from mid-April through May, when cuckoos, flycatchers, vireos, thrushes, warblers (more than 30 species have been seen), tanagers, and other songbirds rest and feed in the trees. To spread out human visitation a bit, a second trail has been built near the **Sportsmen's Migratory Bird Center,** where there's an observation tower good for watching hawks in spring.

Bald Eagle nests at Magee Marsh, and Trumpeter Swan has been reintroduced here. Tundra Swan is one of many species of waterfowl common in migration. The road to the beach passes through marshland where nesting birds may include Pied-billed Grebe, Black-crowned Night-Heron, American and Least Bitterns, American Black and Wood

Ducks, Hooded Merganser, King and Virginia Rails, Sora, Common Tern, Sedge and Marsh Wrens, Yellow Warbler, and occasionally Yellow-headed Blackbird. Waders can be common from spring through fall, as are shorebirds in migration. Look for Northern Harrier and Short-eared Owl in winter. Except for Sundays, Magee Marsh is closed during the fall hunting season, although the bird center remains open year-round.

Next door, **Ottawa National Wildlife Refuge Complex** offers more birding opportunities, with miles of trails through wetlands, scrubby areas, and woods. Tens of thousands of waterfowl gather on the refuge in late fall, including Snow and Canada Geese, Tundra Swan, and 18 or more species of ducks. Depending on water levels in "moist soils" areas, shorebirding can be excellent in spring and fall migration.

**21** Toledo's **Oak Openings Preserve Metropark** is one of the region's most popular birding locations. Here the oak barrens habitat of open woodland, prairie, and wet meadows is overlaid on sandy soil left from an ancient glacial lake. From I-80, take Ohio 2 west 2.8 miles, then turn south on Girdham Road. After about 1.5 miles, check the sand dunes for nesting Lark Sparrow, a very rare breeder in Ohio (about 20 pairs nest in the park). Be sure to keep disturbance of the birds to a minimum; you can see them without leaving paths. Continue south to Reed Road and drive east on Oak Openings Parkway about 0.6 mile to the Mallard Lake area, where a number of trails fan out through varied habitats. The **Red Trail** heads north to the dunes, while the **Silver Trail** goes south to wet areas around Swan Creek. Some of the breeding birds of the park include Barred Owl; White-eyed, Blue-headed, Yellow-throated, and Red-eyed Vireos; Eastern Bluebird; Chestnut-sided, Cerulean, Kentucky, and Hooded Warblers; American Redstart; and Summer and Scarlet Tanagers.

For more good woodland habitat, go north on Ohio 295 to US 20 (West Central Avenue) in Berkey, then east about 2.5 miles to **Secor Metropark,** where the Nature Discovery Center offers information and maps. Blue Grosbeak has been seen at the feeders here during migration. **Irwin Prairie,** on Bancroft Street just to the south, has a 2-mile

boardwalk trail through wet prairie and swamp, often flooded in spring, where you may find nesting rails, Sedge and Marsh Wrens, and Blue-winged Warbler.

Canada Goose brood at Ottawa National Wildlife Refuge Complex, east of Toledo

**22** Located about 10 miles northwest of Marion, **Killdeer Plains Wildlife Area** ranks with Ohio's favorite birding spots, known for wintering owls and hawks, migrant shorebirds and waterfowl, and for nesting Bald Eagles. Much of the area is flat, open cropland, with about a third of the 8,627 acres in woods, second growth, and wetlands, including more than 800 acres of marsh and more than 125 small ponds. (The 3,750-acre waterfowl area is closed to the public except by special permit.) In winter, look for Northern Harrier, Rough-legged Hawk, American Kestrel, and Short-eared Owl in open places, along with flocks of Horned Lark, American Pipit, Lapland Longspur, and Snow Bunting. Check pine groves along County Road 71 for roosting Long-eared and Northern Saw-whet Owls.

Nesting birds at Killdeer Plains include Pied-billed

Grebe; American Bittern; Great Blue Heron; Ring-necked Pheasant; Red-headed Woodpecker; Vesper, Lark, Savannah, and Grasshopper Sparrows; and Bobolink. In fall, huge numbers of Tree, Northern Rough-winged, Bank, and Barn Swallows feed over wetlands, and American Woodcock is common. Canada Goose and dabbling duck numbers can build to 40,000 or more. Depending on water level, shorebirding can be productive in migration; fall may bring White-rumped, Baird's, and Buff-breasted Sandpipers along with more-common species such as Black-bellied and Semipalmated Plovers; Greater and Lesser Yellowlegs; and Solitary, Semipalmated, Least, and Pectoral Sandpipers.

**Short-eared Owl**

Though owls are often thought of as forest birds, the Short-eared Owl prefers open grassland for nesting and wintering. At dusk they fly low over the ground like huge moths, searching for mice and other rodents, or an occasional small bird. While mostly nocturnal, they're sometimes seen in daylight sitting on the ground. Look for them in prairies and fields such as those at **Killdeer Plains Wildlife Area** (see p. 295) in Ohio and **Minnehaha Fish and Wildlife Area** (see p. 288) in Indiana.

**23** Birders in Columbus consider **Green Lawn Cemetery and Arboretum** one of the state's finest sites for spring migration. (*From I-71, exit W on Greenlawn Ave.*) Birders are welcome at this venerable institution, where a special Audubon Society kiosk shows bird lists and notes on recent sightings. In addition to the expected flycatchers, vireos, thrushes, and warblers, many rarities have appeared, including Mississippi Kite, Western Kingbird, and Kirtland's Warbler. Northern Saw-whet Owl is sometimes found in early spring roosting in conifers, and Cooper's Hawk, Yellow-billed Cuckoo, Great Horned Owl, and Great Crested Flycatcher nest among the fine old trees.

**24** Southeast of Mansfield, **Mohican State Park** and **Mohican-Memorial State Forest** center on the beautiful gorge through which the Clear Fork of the Mohican River flows. Up to 300 feet deep, the gorge shelters stands of white pine and hemlock where northern warblers—Magnolia, Blackburnian, and Canada Warblers, and Northern Waterthrush—have nested, along with Brown Creeper and Winter Wren. Blue-winged, Yellow, Chestnut-sided,

Cerulean, and Worm-eating Warblers; Northern Parula; American Redstart; and Ovenbird are among more than 20 warblers that nest in the area, creating perhaps the greatest diversity of this group in the state.

**25** A diverse collection of nesting warblers is also the main attraction in the **Clear Creek Valley.** To reach it, take US 33 south of Lancaster about 7 miles and turn west on Clear Creek Road (County Road 116). Here a pretty, tree-lined stream flows through a gorge beneath sandstone bluffs. Part of the valley is protected as the **Clear Creek Nature Preserve,** and a few trails lead up from the road into the woods here. Bird along the road and in the forest for nesting birds including Black Vulture (here at the northern edge of its range in Ohio), Red-shouldered and Broad-winged Hawks; Yellow-throated Vireo; Cedar Waxwing; Blue-winged, Yellow, Black-throated Green, Yellow-throated, Prairie, Cerulean, Black-and-white, Worm-eating, and Kentucky Warblers; American Redstart; Ovenbird; Louisiana Waterthrush; and Summer and Scarlet Tanagers, among many others. Magnolia and Canada Warblers have nested in the valley at times.

**26** Ohio birders travel to Adams County to look for a few southern species: specifically Chuck-will's-widow, Blue Grosbeak, and Summer Tanager. A walk around the lake at **Adams Lake State Park** near West Union can turn up nesting Warbling Vireo; Blue-winged, Pine, and Prairie Warblers; American Redstart; Summer Tanager; and both Orchard and Baltimore Orioles.

Follow Ohio 125 east about 8 miles from West Union to Waggoner Riffle Road and turn south along Ohio Brush Creek. After about 2.5 miles, Beasley Fork Road on the west leads to a bridge where Chuck-will's-widow calls after dark. Check scrubby areas anywhere along the creek for Blue Grosbeak. In a bit more than 2 miles, take Abner Hollow Road to the northeast and park at the old cemetery. This area is good for a variety of warblers including Yellow-throated, Cerulean, Worm-eating, and Hooded. Keep an eye out anywhere in this vicinity for Black Vulture, Red-shouldered Hawk, Ruffed Grouse, and Wild Turkey.

# WEST VIRGINIA

**27** There's some fine birding to be enjoyed amid the beautiful mountains, peaceful valleys, and wild rivers of West Virginia, a state that, though small, nonetheless spans the Appalachian Mountains from the Ohio River in the west to the Potomac Valley in the east. Diverse landscapes produce a pleasing variety of birding opportunities. Spring and fall migrations are rewarding times to visit **Beech Fork State Park,** where wooded hills border a reservoir just minutes south of Huntington. A walk through the campground or along a park trail here in May will produce a good list of songbirds—perhaps an excellent one, depending on the vagaries of weather and other factors affecting migration. Cliff Swallow nests in the campground area, and from the forest in spring you may hear the "drumming" of male Ruffed Grouse. Other breeding birds include Cooper's and Red-shouldered Hawks; American Woodcock; Black-billed and Yellow-billed Cuckoos; Eastern Screech-, Great Horned, and Barred Owls; Whip-poor-will; Blue-winged, Pine, Prairie, Worm-eating, Kentucky, and Hooded Warblers; and American Redstart.

**28** With several access points on W. Va. 2, about 3 miles south of Glenwood, **Green Bottom Wildlife Management Area** offers excellent birding year-round. Least Bittern, Virginia Rail, and Common Moorhen nest in the marshes here. Sora is found commonly in migration and has nested, and King Rail has summered in the area. In addition, American Bittern is seen in migration, and in late summer waders feed in wetlands: Great Blue and Green Herons and Great Egret are most common, with occasional sightings of Snowy and Cattle Egrets and both Black-crowned and Yellow-crowned Night-Herons. Little Blue

Heron is regular in late summer or fall. In winter, Northern Harrier and an occasional Short-eared Owl hunt over the marshes, and Mute and Tundra swans have appeared in the flocks of wintering waterfowl.

When low water levels expose mudflats, Green Bottom attracts migratory shorebirds; the state's only recorded Black-necked Stilt was found here. Nesting birds of the area include Willow Flycatcher, Warbling Vireo, Tree Swallow,

Baltimore Oriole, a brightly colored relative of the blackbirds

Prothonotary Warbler, Blue Grosbeak (one of the few places in the state for this species), and both Orchard and Baltimore Orioles.

**29** A few minutes upstream on the Ohio River, **Robert C. Byrd Locks and Dam** (*2 miles N of Apple Grove on W. Va. 2*) ranks with the state's favorite birding locations. Check grassy and scrubby areas along the entrance road for nesting Willow Flycatcher, Savannah and Grasshopper Sparrows, Blue Grosbeak, and Dickcissel. In fall, American Golden-Plover and Upland and Buff-breasted Sandpipers may stop to rest, and even Snow Bunting has been found here in winter, when Short-eared Owl sometimes quarters the fields at dusk. Cross the locks to an island and walk north to scan another island just upstream for geese and shorebirds, which in spring may include Willet and Marbled Godwit. Along the river, look for migratory and wintering waterfowl, gulls, and terns; the state's only two records of Ross's Goose occurred here.

**30** Just south of the small town of Cranesville, near the Maryland state line, the Nature Conservancy's 1,200-acre **Cranesville Swamp Nature Preserve** protects a peat bog with acidic, nutrient-poor soil where few trees can grow. Among them, though, is the southernmost tamarack forest in the country and a notably diverse association of other plants typical of more northern regions. To reach the swamp from Terra Alta, take County Road 47 north about 7 miles and turn right on County Road 49. Drive a bit more than a mile and turn left; the preserve will be on your right. Intersecting trails traverse part of the preserve, leading to a boardwalk into a wetland. Nesting birds are the attraction here: Look for Sora (in migration, and a possible breeder); Northern Saw-whet Owl (a rare breeder); Alder and Willow Flycatchers; White-eyed, Blue-headed, and Red-eyed Vireos; Veery; Wood Thrush; Golden-winged, Nashville, Chestnut-sided, Magnolia, and Black-throated Green Warblers; American Redstart; Northern Waterthrush; Scarlet Tanager; Eastern Towhee; and Savannah, Song, and Swamp Sparrows.

**31** Fine birding lures travelers to the rugged Allegheny Mountains of eastern West Virginia, where remarkable scenery adds to the enjoyment of a visit. One favorite, and quite accessible, site to see some of the distinctive high-country birds is **Cranberry Glades Botanical Area,** southwest of Marlinton, in the 900,000-acre **Monongahela National Forest.** Stop at the Cranberry Mountain Nature Center at the junction of W. Va. 39/55 and W. Va. 150 (Highland Scenic Byway) for information and maps, then continue a mile north on Forest Road 102 to a parking lot. Here at an elevation of about 3,400 feet, a half-mile boardwalk trail passes through low shrubland with scattered trees and across two "glades," or peat bogs. In summer, look here for Yellow-bellied (rare) and Alder Flycatchers; Blue-headed Vireo; Common Raven; Black-capped Chickadee; Red-breasted Nuthatch; Winter Wren; Veery; Swainson's and Hermit Thrushes; Magnolia, Black-throated Blue, Blackburnian, Mourning, and Canada Warblers; and Northern Waterthrush. Purple Finch and Red Crossbill may also be present at times.

The national forest's **Highland Scenic Highway** follows

W. Va. 39/55 and W. Va. 150 for 43 miles from Richwood to US 219, offering more birding opportunities. Many of the same birds listed for Cranberry Glades can be seen in summer from overlooks and trails along this marvelous route, which climbs to over 4,500 feet. Look for Mourning Warbler in regrowing logged areas, and listen for Northern Saw-whet Owl after dark in spring.

Cranberry Glades Botanical Area, part of the Monongahela National Forest, southwest of Marlinton

About 40 miles north, in the central part of the national forest, **Gaudineer Knob** and nearby **Gaudineer Scenic Area** comprise another good birding destination. From Huttonsville, take US 250 southeast about 17 miles; turn north on Forest Road 27. In about a mile, drive to the summit of the 4,445-foot knob, and look for Red-breasted Nuthatch, Winter Wren, Golden-crowned Kinglet, several species of warbler including Chestnut-sided, Magnolia, and Yellow-rumped, and Dark-eyed Junco. Continue north on Forest Road 27 a short distance to the scenic area, 140 acres that include a parcel of virgin red spruce forest, left uncut decades ago through a surveyor's error. Four species of thrushes—Veery, Swainson's, Hermit, and Wood—nest in spruce woods in this general area, along with the species listed for Cranberry Glades.

High-elevation vegetation at Dolly Sods, south of Thomas

**32** The **Dolly Sods** region of the northern part of Monongahela National Forest is known to birders for two reasons. Near the **Red Creek Campground,** members of a local bird club have conducted a birdbanding operation each fall since 1961. From mid-August into early October, banders catch birds in mist nets, record statistical information, attach leg bands, and then release them. Among the most commonly captured species are Golden-crowned Kinglet; Tennessee, Cape May, Black-throated Blue, Black-throated Green, Blackburnian, Bay-breasted, and Blackpoll Warblers; and Dark-eyed Junco. Visitors are welcome to observe the banding process—a great chance to see close-up many species usually observed flitting through foliage in the treetops. To reach the site from W. Va. 32, 12 miles south of Thomas, drive east on Forest Road 19 for about 10 miles, then north about 5 miles on Forest Road 75.

Only a short distance north on Forest Road 75, the overlook at **Bear Rocks** has become a regular fall hawk-watching site. While not recording the numbers or variety of some more famous spots, Bear Rocks provides good viewing on days with northeast winds.

# KENTUCKY

**33** Spectacular scenery draws travelers to southeastern Kentucky's rugged Cumberland Mountains, where highways afford views of hills rolling to the horizon. These same highlands attract nesting birds rare or unknown elsewhere in the state. Big **Black Mountain,** near the Virginia state line, has been a favorite site to find many of these species in breeding season. From Lynch, go east on Ky. 160 about 6 miles and turn south onto a small paved road just before the state line. Some of the area's uncommon to rare nesting songbirds can be seen during the ascent on Ky. 160, while others are found along the side road to the 4,145-foot summit, Kentucky's highest point. Watch for Ruffed Grouse and Common Raven (both resident, but rarely seen except by chance); Black-billed Cuckoo (rare); Blue-headed Vireo; Veery; Golden-winged (uncommon), Chestnut-sided, Black-throated Blue, Blackburnian (rare), and Canada Warblers; Dark-eyed Junco; and Rose-breasted Grosbeak. In some years, Least Flycatcher sings from the scrubby woodland edges. The entire summit area is privately owned, but strolling around the gravel roads has long been acceptable.

**34** Interesting breeders are also the attraction at **Red River Gorge Geologic Area** in the **Daniel Boone National Forest.** To reach one excellent spot, drive east 18 miles from Stanton on the Bert T. Combs Mountain Parkway to the Rogers exit and follow Ky. 15 west to Ky. 715 north; shortly after recrossing the parkway, turn east on Rock Bridge Road (Forest Road 24) and drive 3 miles to the Rock Bridge picnic area. Walk the **Rock Bridge Trail,** which loops down to Swift Camp Creek, and then hike as much of the 6.7-mile **Swift Camp Creek Trail** (not a loop) as you want. In spring and summer, watch for Ruffed Grouse,

- ● Waterbirds at the Falls of the Ohio
- ● Wintering Bald Eagles, gulls, and waterfowl at Land Between the Lakes

---

Information section p. 311

Blue-headed Vireo, and warblers including Northern Parula, Black-throated Green (in hemlocks), Yellow-throated and Pine (on the ridges), Black-and-white, Worm-eating, Ovenbird, Louisiana Waterthrush, and Hooded. Two special breeding birds of this beautiful area are Red-breasted Nuthatch, which has nested near Rock Bridge, and Swainson's Warbler, regularly found along Swift Camp Creek, especially in the thick patches of rhododendron.

**35** A short distance to the north, the **Minor E. Clark Fish Hatchery** has a reputation for attracting over the years waterbirds and some outstanding rarities; the total list for the area is more than 250 species. (*From jct. of US 60 and Ky. 801 W of Morehead, drive 1.5 miles S on Ky. 801.*) The more than one hundred ponds at the hatchery can host waders, waterfowl, shorebirds, gulls, or terns depending on the season. Osprey may stop to fish in migration, and Bald Eagles are regularly seen in the trees along the adjacent **Licking River,** especially from November through March. Several species of waders and up to ten species of shorebirds are commonly observed from August to October. Some waterbirds are present during spring migration, but as all of the basins are full at that time, shorebirds may be scarce. Among the unusual sightings here have been Tundra Swan, Wood Stork, Oldsquaw, Surf, and Black Scoters, Marbled Godwit, and American Avocet. A dam just upstream forms 8,270-acre **Cave Run Lake;** check overlooks here and at several points farther along Ky. 801 from fall through spring for loons, grebes, waterfowl, and Bald Eagle.

**36** Though the best access is across the Ohio River in Indiana, Louisville birders consider the **Falls of the Ohio** their home turf. From I-65 take the Jeffersonville exit on the Indiana side of the river and follow signs to the **Falls of the Ohio State Park** visitor center. Birding here depends on water level: When the river is low, shallow pools in the exposed rocks (containing masses of 400-million-year-old fossils from a Devonian period seabed) can attract waders and shorebirds. Activity is best in late summer and fall, but spring can be good if the river is not high. Along with more common shorebirds, look for Baird's and Buff-breasted

Red River Gorge
Geologic Area,
east-central Kentucky

Sandpipers (August through September) and Dunlin (October). Gulls sometimes gather in numbers from November through March, and among the common Ring-billed and Herring have been such rarities as Laughing, Franklin's, Black-headed, Iceland, and Great Black-backed. Peregrine Falcon has begun nesting on a nearby bridge, and occasionally one of these powerful raptors scatters the birds at the falls on a hunting flight.

**37** Although closed from mid-October to mid-March, the **Sauerheber Unit** of **Sloughs Wildlife Management Area** offers fine birding the rest of the year. Located in the bottomlands of the Ohio River, the area hosts thousands of wintering geese and ducks, some of which can be seen from observation platforms along Ky. 268 northwest of Geneva, a small town on Ky. 136 west of Henderson.

These platforms and roadside birding allow limited waterfowl viewing even when the area is closed. Sloughs Wildlife Management Area can be a good place in migration to see American and Least Bitterns, rails (Sora is common here at times, Virginia and King sporadic), shorebirds, Sedge and Marsh Wrens, and for locally uncommon sparrows such as Le Conte's and Nelson's Sharp-tailed (mostly early October). A pair of Bald Eagles nest, and the area is home to a colony of Great Blue Herons. Eastern songbirds are well represented in woods during migration.

Nesting Bald Eagles, Ballard Wildlife Management Area, west of Paducah

**38** Farther down the Ohio, near its confluence with the Mississippi, **Ballard Wildlife Management Area** (*off Ky. 473, W of Bandana*) is also good for waders and waterfowl—though, like Sloughs, it's closed from mid-October to mid-March. Small numbers of Ross's Geese regularly winter with large flocks of Snow Geese; birds can sometimes be found feeding in private land near the management area. Mississippi Kite breeds and is often seen soaring over wooded tracts, and two pairs of Bald Eagles typically nest here. Waders including Great and Snowy Egrets and Little Blue Heron feed in wetlands in summer. Spring migration can be excellent here in varied habitats of bottomland hardwoods, wetlands, croplands, and fields.

**39** Tennessee Valley Authority and U.S. Army Corps of Engineers dams on the Tennessee and Cumberland Rivers have created two huge adjacent and parallel reservoirs, **Kentucky Lake** and **Lake Barkley,** as well as one of the region's finest sites for wintering waterfowl and gulls. Easily accessible just south of I-24, Kentucky and Barkley Dams and lakes have rewarded birders with a long list of rarities, as well as amazing numbers of common waterbirds. Thousands of Bonaparte's, Ring-billed, and Herring gulls sometimes gather in fall and winter below the dams (*observation points are located below both dams: Kentucky on US 62/641 and Barkley S for 2 miles on Barkley Dam Rd.*) or on the lakes. Visitor centers at the dams provide maps of the area and both lakes offer many access points and recreation areas from which to scan for waterbirds (best from November through March), including Common Loon, Pied-billed and Horned Grebes, Double-crested Cormorant, Great Blue Heron, waterfowl, and gulls. November through March are the best months to view waterbirds.

Both Osprey and Bald Eagle nest around the lakes, and

the state resort parks of **Kentucky Dam Village** (502-362-4271), **Kenlake** (502-474-2211), and **Lake Barkley** (502-924-1131) offer special programs and tours in winter to see some of the many eagles that winter here.

Barkley Dam and Lake Barkley, western Kentucky

**40** The strip of land between the two lakes makes up a national recreation area called, logically enough, **Land Between the Lakes National Recreation Area:** 170,000 acres of mostly forested terrain open to hiking, biking, camping, picnicking, hunting, fishing, and, of course, birding. Stop at the North Welcome Station, south of Grand Rivers, to pick up a map before continuing south along the main north-south road, called the Trace.

Begin your visit at the **Land Between the Lakes Nature Station** (*Silver Trail Rd. E off the Trace; station usually closed in winter*). Check feeders here, and ask about guided walks and special wildlife events such as canoe trips, nocturnal "owl prowls," and winter Bald Eagle viewing excursions. Then walk trails to **Hematite Lake** or **Honker Bay** for a

Land Between the Lakes National Recreation Area, west Kentucky

diversity of forest and wetland habitats, keeping an eye out for breeding Cerulean Warbler in large trees.

Land Between the Lakes is an excellent destination for migrant songbirds in spring and fall, and a good variety of warblers nest here including Blue-winged and Prairie (old fields), Northern Parula, Yellow-throated and Pine (pine plantings), American Redstart, Prothonotary, Worm-eating, Ovenbird, and Louisiana Waterthrush. You might want to make a special effort to find the beautiful Kentucky Warbler, the state's namesake, which sings its repeating *churry churry churry* song from wetter woods throughout the area.

# North-Central States
## Information

**?** Visitor Center/Information    **⑤** Fee Charged    **🍴** Food

**🚻** Rest Rooms    **🥾** Nature Trails    **🚗** Driving Tours    **♿** Wheelchair Accessible

*Be advised that facilities may be seasonal and limited. We suggest calling or writing ahead for specific information. Note that addresses may be for administrative offices; see text or call for directions to sites.*

## Rare Bird Alerts

Michigan:
Statewide *616-471-4919*
Detroit *248-477-1360*
Sault Ste. Marie
   *705-256-2790*

Indiana:
Statewide *317-259-0911*

Ohio:
Northwest *419-877-9640*
Southwest *937-277-6446*
Cleveland *216-526-2473*
Central *614-221-9736*
Youngstown *330-742-6661*

West Virginia:
Statewide *304-736-3086*
Northern *304-284-8217*

Kentucky:
Statewide *502-894-9538*

## MICHIGAN

**Warren Dunes State Park** *(Page 277)*
12032 Red Arrow Highway
Sawyer, MI 49125
*616-426-4013*

⑤ 🍴 🚻 🥾 ♿

**Lake Erie Metropark**
*(Page 278)*
32481 West Jefferson
   Avenue
Brownstown, MI 48173
*734-379-5020*

? ⑤ 🍴 🥾 ♿

**Pointe Mouillee State Game Area** *(Page 278)*
37205 Mouillee Road
Rockwood, MI 48173
*734-379-9692*

? 🍴

*Access restricted in hunting season*

**Point Pelee National Park** *(Page 279)*
Rural Route 1
Leamington, Ontario
   Canada N8H 3V4
*519-322-2365*

? ⑤ 🍴 🚻 🥾 ♿

**Maple River State Game Area** *(Page 279)*
c/o Rose Lake Wildlife
   Field Office
8562 East Stoll Road
East Lansing, MI 48823
*517-373-9358*

🥾 ♿

*Area open to public hunting*

**Nayanquing Point State Wildlife Area** *(Page 280)*
1570 Tower Beach Road
Pinconning, MI 48650
*517-697-5101*

**Tawas Point State Park** *(Page 280)*
686 Tawas Beach Road
East Tawas, MI 48730
*517-362-5041*

⑤ 🍴 🥾 ♿

**Seney National Wildlife Refuge** *(Page 282)*
HCR 2, Box 1
Seney, MI 49883
*906-586-9851*

? 🍴 🥾 🚗 ♿

*Visitor center and wildlife drive open mid-May– mid-Oct.*

**Whitefish Point Bird Observatory** *(Page 283)*
16914 North Whitefish
   Point Road
Paradise, MI 49768
*906-492-3596*

? 🍴 🥾 ♿

*Visitor center open mid-April–mid-Oct.*

## INDIANA

**Lakefront Park and Sanctuary** *(Page 284)*
5825 Sohl Avenue
Hammond, IN 46320
*219-853-6378*

🥾 ♿

*Known as the Migrant Trap*

**Indiana Dunes National Lakeshore** *(Page 284)*
1100 North Mineral
 Springs Road
Porter, IN 46304
*219-926-7561*

**Indiana Dunes State Park** *(Page 284)*
1600 North 25 East
Chesterton, IN 46304
*219-926-1952*

**Kingsbury Fish and Wildlife Area** *(Page 286)*
5344 South Hupp Road
La Porte, IN 46350
*219-393-3612*

**Willow Slough Fish and Wildlife Area** *(Page 287)*
2042 South 500 West
Morocco, IN 47963
*219-285-2704*

**Eagle Creek Park**
*(Page 287)*
7840 West 56th Street
Indianapolis, IN 46254
*317-327-7110*

**Minnehaha Fish and Wildlife Area** *(Page 288)*
2411 East Street, Ind. 54
Sullivan, IN 47882
*812-268-5640*

**Muscatatuck National Wildlife Refuge**
*(Page 289)*
12985 East US 50
Seymour, IN 47424
*812-522-4352*

# OHIO

**Headlands Beach State Park** *(Page 290)*
9601 Headlands Road
Mentor, OH 44060
*216-881-8141*

**Mentor Marsh State Nature Preserve**
*(Page 290)*
5185 Corduroy Road
Mentor, OH 44060
*440-257-0777*

*Nature center open April–Oct. Sat.–Sun., or by appt. Call for program schedule.*

**Sheldon Marsh State Nature Preserve**
*(Page 292)*
2715 Cleveland Road West
Huron, OH 44839
*419-433-4919*

**Resthaven Wildlife Area**
*(Page 292)*
P.O. Box 155
Castalia, OH 44824
*419-684-5049*

**Magee Marsh Wildlife Area** *(Page 293)*
13229 West Ohio 2
Oak Harbor, OH 43449
*419-898-0960*

*Known as Crane Creek. Limited access in fall hunting season, mid-Oct.–Nov.*

**Ottawa National Wildlife Refuge Complex**
*(Page 294)*
1400 West State Route 2
Oak Harbor, OH 43449
*419-898-0014*

**Oak Openings Preserve Metropark** *(Page 294)*
4139 Girdham Road
Swanton, OH 43558
*419-826-6463*

**Secor Metropark**
*(Page 294)*
1000 West Central Avenue
Berkey, OH 43504
*419-829-6866*

*Nature Discovery Center open Wed.–Sun.*

**Killdeer Plains Wildlife Area** *(Page 295)*
19100 County Road 115
Harpster, OH 43326
*740-496-2254*

*Waterfowl area closed to the public except by special permit*

**Mohican State Park**
*(Page 296)*
3116 Ohio 3
Loudonville, OH 44842
*419-994-4290*

🚻🚶

**Mohican-Memorial State Forest** *(Page 296)*
3060 County Road 939
Perrysville, OH 44864
*419-938-6222*

🚻

**Adams Lake State Park**
*(Page 297)*
14633 Ohio 4
West Union, OH 45693
*937-544-3927*

🚻🚶♿

*A satellite of Shawnee State Park, 20 miles E, which has full facilities*

# WEST VIRGINIA

**Beech Fork State Park** *(Page 298)*
5601 Long Branch Road
Barboursville, WV 25504
*304-522-0303*

❓🍴🚻🚶♿

**Green Bottom Wildlife Management Area** *(Page 298)*
Rural Route 1, Box 484
Point Pleasant, WV 25550
*304-675-0871*

🚶♿

**Cranesville Swamp Nature Preserve**
*(Page 300)*
c/o The Nature
   Conservancy
P.O. Box 3754
Charleston, WV 25337
*304-345-4350*

🚶〰️

**Monongahela National Forest** *(Page 300)*
200 Sycamore Street
Elkins, WV 26241
*304-636-1800*

❓🚻♿

*Encompasses Cranberry Glades, Gaudineer, and Dolly Sods areas*

# KENTUCKY

**Red River Gorge Geologic Area** *(Page 303)*
Daniel Boone National
   Forest
705 West College Avenue
Stanton, KY 40380
*606-663-2852*

❓🚻🚶〰️

**Minor E. Clark Fish Hatchery** *(Page 304)*
120 Fish Hatchery Road
Morehead, KY 40351
*606-784-6872*

❓🚻♿

**Falls of the Ohio State Park** *(Page 304)*
201 West Riverside Drive
Clarksville, IN
*812-280-9970*

❓💲🚻🚶♿

*Access via I-65, in Indiana*

**Sauerheber Unit of Sloughs Wildlife Management Area**
*(Page 305)*
9956 Ky. 268
Corydon, KY 42406
*502-827-2673*

♿

*Closed mid-Oct.–mid-March, but elevated observation areas along Ky. 268 open year-round*

**Ballard Wildlife Management Area**
*(Page 306)*
864 Wildlife Lodge Road
La Center, KY 42056
*502-224-2244*

❓〰️

*Closed mid-Oct.–mid-March*

**Lake Barkley** *(Page 306)*
U.S. Army Corps of
   Engineers
Barkley Dam Road
   (US 62 West)
Grand Rivers, KY 42045
*502-362-4236*

❓🚻🚶〰️♿

**Kentucky Lake Visitor Center** *(Page 306)*
2261 US 62
Gilbertsville, KY 42044
*502-362-4128 or*
   *800-467-7145*

❓🚻〰️♿

**Land Between the Lakes National Recreation Area**
*(Page 307)*
100 Van Morgan Drive
Golden Pond, KY 42211
*502-924-2000 or*
   *800-525-7077*

❓💲🚻🚶〰️♿

# Regional Birding Guides

## New England

*A Birder's Guide to Maine*, Elizabeth Pierson, Jan Erik Pierson, and Peter D. Vickery (Down East Books, 1996). Detailed descriptions of sites, divided into seven geographic regions.

*A Birder's Guide to New Hampshire*, Alan Delorey (American Birding Association, 1996). Twenty-one top birding areas, from coastal islands to the Connecticut Lakes.

*A Birder's Guide to Eastern Massachusetts* (Bird Observer, American Birding Association, 1994). Twenty-three top areas, west to Quabbin Reservoir.

*Birding Cape Cod* (Cape Cod Bird Club and Massachusetts Audubon Society, 1990). Detailed coverage of the area from Bourne and Falmouth outward.

*Bird Walks in Rhode Island*, Adam J. Fry (Backcountry Publications, 1992). Twenty-two of the state's best locations.

*Connecticut Birding Guide*, Buzz Devine and Dwight G. Smith (Thomson-Shore, 1996). A very detailed guide to the state, divided into seven geographic regions.

*Bird Finding in New England*, Richard K. Walton (David R. Godine, 1988). A selection of the best birding spots in each of the six states.

## Mid-Atlantic

*Where to Find Birds in New York State: The Top 500 Sites*, Susan Roney Drennan (Syracuse University Press, 1981). Despite its age, still contains lots of good information.

*City Cemeteries to Boreal Bogs: Where to Go Birding in Central New York*, Dorothy W. Crumb and James Throckmorton (eds.) (Onondaga Audubon Society, 1996). Sites mostly in the Syracuse-Utica area.

*A Guide to Bird Finding in New Jersey*, William J. Boyle, Jr. (Rutgers University Press, 1986). A very complete and detailed guide to the state.

*Birder's Guide to Pennsylvania*, Paula Ford (Gulf Publishing, 1995). Covers more than 180 sites throughout the state.

*Finding Birds in the National Capital Area*, Claudia Wilds (Smithsonian Institution Press, 1992). Including areas from the North Carolina Outer Banks to western Virginia to Maryland and Delaware.

## South Atlantic

*A Birder's Guide to Virginia*, David W. Johnston (compiler) (American Birding Association, 1997). More than 70 major birding areas statewide.

*Birds of the Blue Ridge Mountains*, Marcus B. Simpson, Jr. (University of North Carolina Press, 1992). Covers sites from northern Georgia to southern Pennsylvania.

*Finding Birds in the National Capital Area*, Claudia Wilds (Smithsonian Institution Press, 1992). Including areas from the North Carolina Outer Banks to western Virginia to Maryland and Delaware.

*A Birder's Guide to Coastal North Carolina*, John O. Fussell III (University of North Carolina Press, 1994). An extremely comprehensive guide to the eastern part of the state.

*Finding Birds in South Carolina*, Robin M. Carter (University of South Carolina Press, 1993). More than 200 sites, arranged by county.

*A Birder's Guide to Georgia*, Joel R. Hitt and Kenneth Turner Blackshaw (eds.) (Georgia Ornithological Society, 1996). Statewide coverage with sites described by local birders.

## Florida

A *Birder's Guide to Florida*, Bill Pranty (American Birding Association, 1996). The best site guide to the state, with charts listing seasonal abundance and advice for finding state specialties.

## South-Central States

A *Birder's Guide to Alabama,* John Porter (ed.) (University of Alabama Press, 1999). Statewide coverage with maps and charts.

*Birder's Guide to Alabama and Mississippi*, Ray Vaughn (Gulf Publishing, 1994). Covers more than 100 areas in the two states.

A *Birder's Guide to Arkansas*, Mel White (American Birding Association, 1995). Fifty-nine of the state's top birding sites, arranged by region.

## Eastern Texas

A *Birder's Guide to the Texas Coast*, Harold R. Holt (American Birding Association, 1993). A must for birders visiting the coast, this standard reference covers sites along the entire coast, plus a few in the lower Rio Grande Valley. It includes a chart showing seasonal distribution.

A *Birder's Guide to the Rio Grande Valley*, Harold R. Holt (American Birding Association, 1992). Similar in format to the above guide, this book includes sites from the Gulf of Mexico to El Paso.

A *Birder's Guide to Texas*, Edward A. Kutac (Gulf Publishing, 1989). More than 150 sites covering the entire state.

*Birding Texas*, Roland H.Waver and Mark A. Elwonger (Falcon Press, 1998). More than 200 birding locations around the state.

## Heartland

A *Birder's Guide to Minnesota*, Kim R. Eckert (Williams Publications, Inc., 1994). An amazingly detailed guide to birding sites in all the state's counties.

*Traveler's Guide to Wildlife in Minnesota*, Carrol L. Henderson et al. (Minnesota Department of Natural Resources, 1997). Covers all wildlife, but includes much information about birds.

*Wisconsin's Favorite Bird Haunts*, Daryl D. Tessen (ed.) (Wisconsin Society for Ornithology, 1989). Includes 120 birding sites throughout the state.

A *Guide to the Birding Areas of Missouri*, Kay Palmer (ed.) (Audubon Society of Missouri, 1993). Birding sites organized by region.

A *Guide to Bird Finding in Kansas and Western Missouri*, John L. Zimmerman and Sebastian T. Patti (University Press of Kansas, 1988). Covers Missouri sites east to Sedalia and Springfield.

*Birds of the St. Louis Area* (Webster Groves Nature Study Society, 1998). Covers 120 locations within 50 miles of St. Louis.

## North-Central States

*Bird Finding Guide to Michigan*, C.T. Black and C. Roy Smith (compilers) (Michigan Audubon Society, 1994). Descriptions of 131 sites written by local birders.

*Birding in Ohio*, Tom Thompson (Indiana University Press, 1994). More than 300 sites organized by three divisions of the state.

*Birds of the Indiana Dunes*, Kenneth J. Brock (Indiana University Press, 1997). Descriptions of sites along the Lake Michigan shore and notes on more than 350 species recorded here.

# Index

# Illustrations Credits

All the bird paintings are from the *National Geographic Society Field Guide to the Birds of North America, Third Edition* © 1999, reprinted with permission of the National Geographic Society.

Cover, Phillip Singer; 1, Erwin & Peggy Bauer/Bruce Coleman, Inc.; 2-3, Wendell Metzen/Bruce Coleman, Inc.; 4, Art Wolfe/Tony Stone Images; 4-5, Fred Hirschmann; 9, Johann Schumacher Design; 10-11, Medford Taylor/NGS Image Collection; 12, P. La Tourrette/VIREO.

### New England
14-15, Jerry & Marcy Monkman; 16, Johann Schumacher Design; 20, Tom Payne; 22, Dwight Kuhn; 23, Johann Schumacher Design; 25, Carr Clifton/ Minden Pictures; 27, Jerry & Marcy Monkman; 28, Jerry & Marcy Monkman; 30, Bill Silliker, Jr.; 34-35, Susan Cole Kelly; 37, Barrett & MacKay Photo; 41, Susan Cole Kelly; 42-43, Barrett & MacKay Photo; 44, Susan Cole Kelly; 45, David Witbeck/ The Picture Cube; 46, Bates Littlehales; 48, Susan Cole Kelly; 49, Tim Fitzharris/Minden Pictures; 51, Susan Cole Kelly.

### Mid-Atlantic
56-57, Arthur Morris/VIREO; 58, Johann Schumacher Design; 62, Al Messerschmidt/Folio, Inc.; 65, Sonja Bullaty & Angelo Lomeo; 66-67, Arthur Morris/Birds As Art; 67, T. Vezo/VIREO; 68, John Heidecker; 70, Arthur Morris/Birds As Art; 71, Irene Hinke-Sacilotto; 73, Johann Schumacher Design; 74, Johann Schumacher Design; 77, Steven Holt/Aigrette Photography; 78-79, A. & E. Morris/Birds As Art; 81, Michael P. Gadomski/ Bruce Coleman, Inc.; 83, A. & E. Morris/VIREO; 84, Irene Hinke-Sacilotto; 87, Tom Payne; 88, Heather R. Davidson; 90-91, Rob & Ann Simpson.

### South Atlantic
96-97, Starke Jett/Folio, Inc.; 98, Jane Faircloth/Transparencies, Inc.; 101, Rob & Ann Simpson; 102, Skip Brown/Folio, Inc.; 103, Layne Kennedy; 105, Medford Taylor/NGS Image Collection; 106, Frederic B. Siskind; 107, Tom Till; 109, Tom Payne; 111, Les Saucier/Transparencies, Inc.; 112-113, Mike Booher/Transparencies, Inc.; 115, Kelly Culpepper/Transparencies, Inc.; 116, Richard A. Cooke, III; 118, James P. Blair; 119, Raymond Gehman/NGS Image Collection; 120, Kelly Culpepper/Transparencies, Inc.; 123, Tim Thompson; 124, Tom Till; 126-127, Andre Jenny/Unicorn Stock Photos; 129, Byron Jorjorian; 130, Terry Donnelly/Tony Stone Images; 131, Jeff Foott/Bruce Coleman, Inc.; 132, Billy E. Barnes/Transparencies, Inc.

### Florida
136-137, Rick Poley; 140, W. Perry Conway; 142-143, Randy Wells/Tony Stone Images; 145, Rick Poley; 146, Tony Arruza/Bruce Coleman, Inc.; 147, Laura Riley/Bruce Coleman, Inc.; 149, Larry Ulrich/Tony Stone Images; 150, Janis E. Burger/Bruce Coleman, Inc.; 151, A. & E. Morris/VIREO; 153, Jim Brandenburg/Minden Pictures; 154, Heather R. Davidson; 156, Bates Littlehales; 159, John Shaw/Bruce Coleman, Inc.

### South-Central States
162-163, Joel Sartore; 164, Rick Poley; 167, Richard A. Cooke, III; 168-169, Bruce Clarke/Transparencies, Inc.; 170, Gary Meszaros/Bruce Coleman, Inc.; 171, Byron Jorjorian; 173, Byron Jorjorian; 176, Willard Clay; 177, Tom Ulrich/ Tony Stone Images; 178, Mike Clemmer; 180, Robert P. Falls, Sr.; 183, Tim Thompson; 184, Rob & Ann Simpson/Visuals Unlimited; 185, U.S. Fish & Wildlife Service, Felsenthal N.W.R.; 187, John Elk, III/Bruce Coleman, Inc.; 188, Terry Donnelly/Tony Stone

Images; 190, Cliff Beittel; 193, C.C. Lockwood/Bruce Coleman, Inc.; 195, John Cancalosi; 196, A. & E. Morris/VIREO.

### Eastern Texas
200-201, W. Perry Conway; 204, Jeff Foott/Bruce Coleman, Inc.; 206, James P. Blair; 209, Kathy Adams Clark/KAC Productions; 210-211, Kathy Adams Clark/ KAC Productions; 213, Raymond Gehman; 214, Steven C. Wilson/ Entheos; 216, Patricia Caulfield; 217, Joel Sartore; 218, Doug Wechsler/VIREO; 220, Richard Day/Daybreak Imagery; 221, Tom Bean/Tony Stone Images; 222, Gary Kramer; 223, John Cancalosi; 225, Bates Littlehales; 226, Rick Poley.

### Heartland
232-233, Richard Hamilton Smith; 234, Richard Hamilton Smith; 238-239, Fredrick Sears; 240, Joseph S. Klune/ColePhoto; 241, Ruth Hoyt/Close to Nature; 245, Rob Curtis/The Early Birder; 246-247, Richard Hamilton Smith; 248, Tom Edwards/Visuals Unlimited; 250, Clint Farlinger; 252, Jim Brandenburg/ Minden Pictures; 253, Clint Farlinger; 255, Steve Gettle/ENP Images; 256-257, Steve Solum/Bruce Coleman, Inc.; 258, Cathy & Gordon Illg; 260, Clint Farlinger; 261, Richard Hamilton Smith; 263, Terry Donnelly/Tony Stone Images; 264, Wayne Nelson/ Earth Images; 267, Tom Bean.

### North-Central States
272-273, Scot Stewart/Nature's Images; 274, Gene Boaz; 278, David Stimac; 281, Ed Simpson/Tony Stone Images; 282, David Stimac; 284, Johann Schumacher Design; 285, David Muench/Tony Stone Images; 288-289, Cathlyn Melloan/Tony Stone Images; 291, Carl A. Stimac/The Image Finders; 292, Kent & Donna Dannen; 293, A. & E. Morris/Birds As Art; 295, Kent & Donna Dannen; 299, John Heidecker; 301, Thomas R. Fletcher; 302, Carr Clifton/Minden Pictures; 305, Gene Boaz; 306, Gene Boaz; 307, Gene Boaz; 308, Emory Kristof.

# Credits

# About the Author

Copyright © 1999 National
Geographic Society

*Published by*
THE NATIONAL
GEOGRAPHIC SOCIETY

John M. Fahey, Jr.
*President and
Chief Executive Officer*

Gilbert M. Grosvenor
*Chairman of the Board*

Nina D. Hoffman
*Senior Vice President*

William R. Gray
*Vice President and Director,
Book Division*

David Griffin
*Design Director*

Elizabeth L. Newhouse
*Director of Travel Publishing*

Barbara A. Noe
*Assistant Editor*

Caroline Hickey
*Senior Researcher*

Carl Mehler
*Director of Maps*

*Staff for this Book*

Mary Luders
*Project Editor*

Joan Wolbier
*Art Director*

Marilyn Mofford Gibbons
*Illustrations Editor*

Paul Lehman
*Chief Consultant*

Paulette L. Claus
Lise Sajewski
*Editorial Consultants*

Jenifer Blakemore,
Anna Gallegos, Sean M.
Groom, Deavours Hall,
Mary E. Jennings
*Editorial Researchers*

Anne K. McCain
*Indexer*

Keith R. Moore,
Jehan Aziz, Sven M.
Dolling, Thomas L. Gray,
Sean M. Groom
*Map Research and
Production*

Meredith C. Wilcox
*Illustrations Assistant*

Richard S. Wain
*Production Project Manager*

Mel White's earliest birding
memory is of a Western Tanager
he saw on a family vacation to
Arizona when he was six years
old. Four decades later, he still
recalls this meeting of boy and
bird when he considers the
pleasures of travel—the delight
in the new, whether expected or
un-, and the transforming
moment when a vision that
existed only in the imagination
is replaced by the real thing
in binoculars.

An Arkansas native and a
former newspaper reporter and
magazine editor, Mel White is
now a free-lance writer specializing in travel and nature.
A contributing editor for
*National Geographic Traveler*, he
writes frequently for other
National Geographic Society
publications and is author of the
American Birding Association's
*A Birder's Guide to Arkansas* and
a volume of the *Smithsonian
Guide to Natural America* series.
His assignments have taken
him from New Zealand to
Amazonia to the Swiss Alps—
and he usually manages to find
time for birdwatching no matter
where he goes.

Composition for this book by the
National Geographic Society Book
Division. Printed and bound by R.R.
Donnelley & Sons, Willard, Ohio.
Color separations by North American
Color, Portage, MI. Covers printed by
Miken Inc., Cheektowaga, New York.

**Library of Congress Cataloging-in-Publication Data**

White Mel, 1950-
    National Geographic guide to birdwatching sites : Eastern U.S. /
by Mel White.
        p.    cm.
    Includes index.
    ISBN 0-7922-7374-5
    1. Bird watching—East (U.S.)—Guidebooks.   2. Birding sites—East
(U.S.)—Guidebooks.   3. East (U.S.)—Guidebooks.   2. Birding sites—East
II. Title: Birdwatching sites.
    QL683.E27W48   1999
598'.07'23474—dc21                                          98-53023
                                                                CIP

Society's website at http://www.nationalgeographic.com